Matthew Scialabba & Melissa Pellegrino

The Italian Farmer's Table

AUTHENTIC RECIPES AND LOCAL LORE
FROM NORTHERN ITALY

ThreeForks

AN IMPRINT OF GLOBE PEQUOT PRESS
GUILFORD, CONNECTICUT
HELENA, MONTANA

To Mom, who taught me that the recipe for success is to follow your heart.
This book is just as much a part of you; may your memory
live on through these pages. —MP

ThreeForks is a registered trademark of Morris Book Publishing, LLC.

Photos by Melissa Pellegrino and Matthew Scialabba

Project editor: Jessica Haberman
Text design: Sheryl P. Kober
Layout artist: Nancy Freeborn
Maps: M. A. Dubé © Morris Book Publishing, LLC

Library of Congress Cataloging-in-Publication Data
Scialabba, Matthew.
  Italian farmer's table : authentic recipes and local lore from northern Italy / Matthew Scialabba and Melissa Pellegrino.
    p. cm.
  ISBN 978-0-7627-5264-5
  1. Cookery, Italian—Northern style. 2. Farms—Recreational use—Italy. I. Pellegrino, Melissa. II. Title.
  TX723.2.N65S34 2009
  641.5945'1—dc22
                                                                                                            2009018501

Printed in China
10 9 8 7 6 5 4 3

CONTENTS

ACKNOWLEDGMENTS

Tra il dire e il fare c'è di mezzo il mare.
"Between saying and doing lies half the ocean."

We first heard this Italian proverb while living in Rome together, and at the time we thought very little of it except that it had a nice poetic ring to it. Seven years later, this expression has been the foundation for our perseverance on this project, which led us to Italy to pursue our dream of writing this cookbook. We extend our deepest gratitude to everyone who believed in us and our project along the way.

This book would not have been possible without the generosity and enthusiasm of each farm. A heartfelt thanks to everyone at La Giara, Giandriale, Terre Bianche, Tra Sole e Vigne, La Traversina, Ca' Villa, La Quercia Rossa, La Miniera, La Capuccina, Les Ecureuils, Maison Rosset, Plan de la Tour, Cascina Caremma, La Ribunta', Casa Clelia, Macesina, Baite di Pra, Casa al Campo, Glinzhof, Perusini, La Subida, Casale Cjanor, I Comelli, Rechsteiner, Le Vescovane, Corte Verze, Le Occare, Cavazzone, Fattoria Paradiso, and Ca' d'Alfieri. We were welcomed into these people's lives and kitchens to learn all that they had to share.

To our moms: Barb and Karen, for all of your support and assistance in the kitchen.

To our fathers: Fran and Jim, for always providing the wine and hearty appetites.

To our brothers and sisters: Bryan, Chris, Jeff, Lindsey, and Steph.

To Japhy, who is always hungry.

To Jonathan Teller-Elsberg, for being the first to believe.

To Brian Buckley, who has always been there for advice.

To Moe and Tastebuds, mere words are not enough to thank you for everything you have done.

To Jim and Deb Cianciolo, for your passion for good food and wine.

To Antonio, for always giving us a home in Italy.

To Bishop's, Forte's Market, and Star Fish Market, for your superior products in a small town like Guilford, Connecticut.

To Heather and Scott, for giving us a chance and keeping it local.

To Jess Haberman and everyone at GPP, for making this look so good.

INTRODUCTION

AGRITURISMI

Small family farms are the face and backbone of rural Italy. Their picturesque stone farmhouses and manicured fields create a beautiful landscape whose bounty represents the soul of regional Italian cuisine. The agriturismi system was developed by the Italian government in 1985 to help preserve these farms throughout the country. Allowing farm owners to open their doors to overnight guests and provide them with meals helps these small farms supplement their incomes and continue living off the land. Strict laws mandate that a certain percentage of the food served be grown on the property, with all other ingredients sourced from nearby farms. Sustainability and dedication to a farm-fresh cuisine created by the seasons are the two most common threads linking these farms. A meal at an agriturismo speaks volumes more than mere satiation, for there is a story behind every ingredient used in a finished and plated dish. Are the vegetables grown outdoors in nutrient-rich soil or beneath the glow of artificial heat? Are they cultivated in verdant green pastures or in a windowless shed? Knowing and controlling these circumstances are fundamental principles of the agriturismi philosophy. The food agriturismi serve is the final result of their commitment and dedication to working their land. The tomatoes started as seeds dried from last year's harvest, the summer-milk cheese from cattle fed fresh flowers and herbs, the olive oil's vibrant green color from barely pressed organic olives: All of these factors, revealing the underlying superiority and goodness of farm-fresh ingredients, show why it is so beneficial to cook with locally grown products. In addition to agriculture, many agriturismi have taken sustainability a step further by going off the grid, producing their own energy with fuel sources cultivated from their surroundings. It is a proactive approach toward a viable and economical alternative to traditional living, utilizing local resources for a low-impact, earth-friendly lifestyle. Today, the agriturismi movement is booming, as thousands of abandoned farms across the country have undergone an agrarian revolution. Beautiful old farmhouses, once left to crumble and decay, have been restored to splendor and now offer country retreats for tourists seeking rural solace and tranquility in the Italian countryside and a cuisine not readily found in cities and towns.

OUR EXPERIENCES

While on a vacation in southern Tuscany some years ago, we found ourselves driving aimlessly at dusk. Lost, hungry, and without accommodations for the night, we followed a dark and winding road into the countryside with only the rumblings from our stomachs to pierce the silence around us. Suddenly, around a turn, we spotted a magnificent stone farmhouse on a hill, bathed in light and surrounded by tall cypress trees. Farther down the road, we passed a sign that read AGRITURISMO and had a symbol of a bed and a plate, fork, and knife. Was some kind of guardian angel leading us to this oasis in the thick of the black Tuscan night? Pulling into the driveway, we noticed cars with license plates from all over Europe. We approached the large antique wooden door with eager anticipation of what awaited us inside and opened it slowly. Wonderful aromas, laughter, and the joyous sounds of people having a good time engulfed us. A beautiful dining room lay before us, with diners enjoying numerous plates of delicious-looking food at long wooden tables. Immediately we felt warm, welcomed, and very hungry. "I'm sorry, signori, but we are completely full tonight," a voice said from behind us. "Please take our card and reserve the next time you are traveling through." Thus went our first experience with Italian agriturismi.

After graduating from culinary school, we desired a hands-on experience where we could continue our education and share a direct connection with the ingredients we use in the kitchen. Remembering that fateful night in Tuscany, we contacted several agriturismi and spent a year working in the fields and kitchens of farms throughout central Italy. Upon returning to the States, the uniqueness of our experiences began to sink in. The simple daily tasks of walking into the fields to gather vegetables from the garden for the night's meal, venturing into the chicken coop to search for eggs to make fresh pasta, and heading down into the cantina to fill carafes with wine from large wooden barrels, were all replaced with the giant urban supermarkets of home. While the reveries of our Italian farm life eventually waned, the farm philosophies and approaches toward cooking had planted a seed about the importance of knowing where our food comes from. As we soon discovered, a movement to support local farms was underway in America, signaled by the sudden surge in popularity of farmers' markets. We realized we could rekindle our Italian agriturismi days and cook using fresh native ingredients, and by conversing with the growers, we could share a connection with the land through the food we were eating. Our year at the farms revealed our passion for local and organic products in conversations with others, and tales of our travels helped sparked interest in the Italian countryside lifestyle. As two chefs, we thought that a cookbook would be the perfect way to bring these farms to life.

THE BOOK

Choosing to focus solely on the north of Italy for its varied and diverse cuisine, we thoroughly researched the many agriturismi through Italy's eight most northern regions and chose thirty that we felt best represented the agriturismi of the north. For four months we traveled from farm to farm, greeted with open arms and embraced with warm and generous Italian hospitality, as well as unbridled enthusiasm for our book. From the end of summer, into the heart of fall, and extending into the early days of winter, we toured northern Italy, gaining an immense appreciation for the natural beauty of a land whose varied landscape of rugged mountains, vast plains, verdant valleys, pristine lakes, and immense coastlines is packed with culinary delights. Spending four nights at each farm provided ample opportunity to become involved in daily farm activities, and throughout the four months we were exposed to all facets of agricultural life. Our immersion went deep into the belly of the Italian countryside. We worked the grape harvest, getting sticky cutting the ripe bunches, and visited cantinas, becoming extremely jealous of a three-thousand-bottle wine cellar. Traveling high up into the mountains, we visited happy alpine dairy cows, spent a day helping make goat cheese from freshly pumped milk, and indulged in intensely rich just-churned butter. We walked unending fields of corn, manicured rows of organic vegetable gardens, vast flooded rice plains, and groves of knotty olive trees. We plucked apples in the crisp fall air and gained an understanding of the richness of the Italian soil. Witnessing the beauty of the birth of a baby lamb and the raw violence of a pig slaughter taught us that not all meat comes in a tidy cellophane package, and a labor-intensive day of grinding, stuffing, and tying salami showed us the thriftiness of rural Italy through the consumption of nearly every part of the swine. We donned bee suits to inspect a queen bee and learned about the importance of pollination on a farm. Walking deep into the woods, we found where to find the free-range black pigs, whose succulent meat comes from their acorn-rich diet, and a truffle hunt led by a pack of four-legged truffle hunters unearthed the knotty spore, to the joyous shrill of their owner. We also listened to the racket of a thousand geese, smelled the pungent odor of ripening kiwis, ate juicy figs straight from the tree, made jam with fresh summer berries, were invited on a snowy mountain hunt for wild deer, and sat among casks of one-hundred-year-old aging balsamic vinegar, but best of all, we were encouraged to come into the kitchen and roll up our sleeves, to work, and learn, and become intertwined with the pulse of agriturismo life. In the following pages we pass this along to you. We hope our writing and recipes inspire you to cook with ingredients from your local farms and get to know a little about where your food comes from. Maybe we will even convince some of you to travel to the source—to have your own culinary adventures and to experience firsthand the wonders and charms of this vital segment of Italian food culture.

Salute e Buon Appetito!!!

BASIC RECIPES

Basic Pasta Dough
PASTA FRESCA ALL'UOVO

3¼–3½ cups (400–420g)
   all-purpose flour

4 large eggs, room temperature

Make a well with the flour and add the eggs to the center. With a fork, lightly beat the eggs and gradually pull some of the flour into the egg mixture. Mix the flour and eggs together until well combined. Knead the dough until it becomes smooth and elastic.

Cover the dough with a towel and let rest for 20 minutes.

Cut the dough into 6 pieces and cover with a towel. Pass one section at a time through a pasta machine. Alternatively, you may choose to roll the dough out by hand, a significantly more difficult method. Start on the widest setting and pass the dough through. Begin lowering the pasta machine setting down one notch at a time, and pass the dough through once on each setting, finishing on the last (thinnest) setting.

Lay the dough on a flat surface sprinkled lightly with flour and let the dough dry slightly. It should still be a little tacky and pliable, or it will not cut properly.

Cut the dough into desired shapes (tagliatelle, taglierini, spaghetti) or use the sheets to make stuffed pastas (ravioli, cappelletti).

SERVES 4

Potato Gnocchi
GNOCCHI DI PATATE

Place the potatoes whole in a saucepan and cover with cold water. Bring to a boil over medium heat, salt liberally, and cook at a gentle simmer until the potatoes are extremely tender, 35 to 40 minutes. Drain the potatoes and peel while they are still warm. Pass through a ricer onto a clean work surface.

Sprinkle the flour evenly over the potatoes and form into a well. Crack the egg into the well and gently beat with a fork. Gradually incorporate the egg into the flour mixture. Knead the dough until smooth.

Cut the dough into 4 even pieces. Roll each piece out into a 1-inch-thick rope, then cut each rope with a pastry cutter or knife into ¼-inch pieces. Place the gnocchi on sheet pans lightly dusted with flour, cover, and refrigerate until ready to use.

SERVES 6

2 pounds (900 g) russet potatoes

Salt as needed

2⅓ cups (300 g) all-purpose flour

1 egg

Crepes
CRESPELLE

Place the flour, water, eggs, and salt in a blender and pulse until a smooth batter is formed. Heat an 8-inch nonstick skillet over medium-high heat, brush the skillet with a little melted butter, and ladle enough batter into the skillet to coat the bottom. Make the coating as thin as possible. Cook the crepe until it begins to dry and set, about 1 minute, then use a spatula to flip the crepe over and cook it another 30 seconds to 1 minute. Remove the crepe from the pan and lay it flat on a dish. Continue cooking the crepes in this manner until the batter is finished.

YIELDS 16 CREPES

1 cup (125 g) all-purpose flour

1 cup (8 fl. oz. / 240 ml) water or milk

3 large eggs

Pinch of salt

1 tablespoon (½ oz. / 15 g) unsalted butter, melted

Polenta
POLENTA

1 quart (32 fl. oz. / 960 ml) water

1 cup (170 g) stone-ground cornmeal

Pinch of kosher salt

2 tablespoons (1 oz. / 30 g) unsalted butter

¼ cup grated Parmigiano Reggiano

Bring the water to a boil in a heavy-bottomed casserole pan over medium-high heat and add the salt. Pouring it in a steady stream, gradually whisk in the cornmeal, making sure there are no lumps. Reduce the heat to low and stir continuously with a wooden spoon until the polenta starts to pull away from the sides of the pan and is smooth and creamy, 40 to 45 minutes. Stir in the butter and grated Parmigiano Reggiano.

SERVES 4

Béchamel
BESCIAMELLA

4 tablespoons (2 oz. / 60 g) unsalted butter

4 tablespoons (40 g) all-purpose flour

3 cups (24 fl. oz. / 720 ml) whole milk

Pinch of freshly grated nutmeg

Freshly ground white pepper

Pinch of kosher salt

Melt the butter in a 3-quart sauté pan over medium heat. Add the flour and cook 2 minutes, until the mixture is a golden brown.

Meanwhile, warm the milk in a 2-quart saucepan over medium-low heat. Whisk the milk into the butter mixture a ladleful at a time and bring the mixture up to a simmer. Cook until the sauce has thickened. Add the nutmeg, white pepper, and salt.

YIELDS 3½ CUPS

Savory Pie Crust
PASTA FROLLA SALATA

2¼ cups (280 g) all-purpose flour

Pinch of table salt

16 tablespoons (8 oz. / 226 g) European-style unsalted butter, cold and cut into pieces

⅓ cup (3 fl. oz. / 80 ml) ice water

In the bowl of an electric mixer fitted with the paddle attachment, combine the flour, salt, and butter and mix at low speed until the dough forms coarse crumbs the size of hazelnuts. Gradually add the water in a steady stream, mixing until the dough just comes together. Turn the dough out onto a sheet of plastic wrap, flatten into a disc, and refrigerate for at least 1 hour.

YIELDS 2 9-INCH PIE CRUSTS

Sweet Pastry Crust
PASTA FROLLA

In the bowl of an electric mixer fitted with the paddle attachment, cream together the butter and sugar until light and fluffy, 2 to 3 minutes. Add the egg and beat another 45 seconds. Lower the speed and add the flour, salt, lemon zest, and vanilla and mix until a dough forms.

Turn the dough out onto a work surface lightly dusted with flour and knead the dough until smooth. Flatten the dough into a round disc and wrap in plastic wrap. Refrigerate the dough at least 2 hours.

YIELDS 1 12-INCH CRUST

8 tablespoons (4 oz. / 115 g) unsalted butter, at room temperature
$\frac{1}{3}$ cup (90 g) superfine sugar (castor sugar)
1 egg
1 $\frac{2}{3}$ cups (215 g) all-purpose flour
Pinch of table salt
1 tablespoon lemon zest
1 teaspoon vanilla

Chicken Broth
BRODO DI POLLO

Place all ingredients in a large 8-quart stockpot and add water to cover. Bring the contents of the pot up to a slow boil. Reduce heat and simmer gently for 2 to 3 hours, skimming any scum from the surface.

Strain the broth into a clean bowl and refrigerate until needed. Remove any hardened fat that rises to the top. The broth can remain in the refrigerator for up to 5 days or be frozen.

YIELDS ABOUT 3½ QUARTS

6 pounds (2$\frac{3}{4}$ kg) chicken parts
2 yellow onions, cut into large dice
2 stalks celery, cut into large dice
2 carrots, peeled and cut into large dice
2 bay leaves
4 sprigs flat-leaf parsley
3 sprigs thyme

Vegetable Broth

BRODO DI VERDURE

1 roughly chopped yellow onion

2 cleaned and sliced leeks

2 roughly chopped stalks celery

2 peeled and roughly chopped
   carrots

8 ounces (225 g) sliced mushrooms

1 potato, peeled and cut into
   large dice

1 bay leaf

1 sprig flat-leaf parsley

1 sprig thyme

1 teaspoon black peppercorns

Place all ingredients in a large 6-quart stockpot and add water to cover. Slowly bring the contents of the pot up to a boil, reduce heat, and simmer 1 to 2 hours.

Strain the broth into a clean bowl and keep in the refrigerator for up to 5 days or freeze.

Note: Other vegetables, such as turnips, parsnips, asparagus, and red onion, can be included in the broth. Steer clear of overly strong vegetables such as cauliflower, cabbage, broccoli, and beets.

YIELDS ABOUT 2 QUARTS

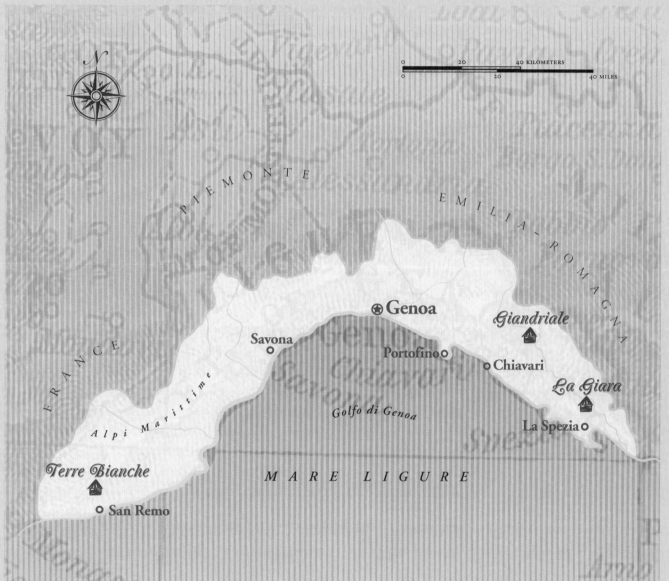

Part One: LIGURIA

0   20   40 KILOMETERS
0   20   40 MILES

PIEMONTE

EMILIA-ROMAGNA

FRANCE

★ Genoa

Giandriale

Savona

Portofino ○

○ Chiavari

La Giara

Alpi Marittime

La Spezia ○

Golfo di Genoa

Terre Bianche

MARE LIGURE

○ San Remo

The "Mediterranean diet" epitomizes good healthy living, with connotations of sun-kissed lands, shimmering blue oceans, and lush terrain ripe with olive groves, vineyards, and gardens. Nowhere is this more typified than in the narrow ribbon of land known as Liguria. Bordering the four powerhouse food regions of Tuscany, Piemonte, Emilia-Romagna, and Provence, France, Liguria borrows little from its neighbors' cuisine, as Ligurians prefer to cook with their own native ingredients grown on their own soil. While Ligurians do eat copious amounts of their ubiquitous pesto and lap up the region's renowned extra-virgin olive oil, they have a greatly varied cuisine that relies heavily on the land. Though Liguria is most often visited for its many picturesque coastal fishing villages and affluent harbors filled with the sleek yachts of Europe's jet-setting elite, its agriturismi offer a glimpse into the rural hinterland of the region. High above the sea, the Maritime Alps are an entirely different Liguria, a world removed from the glitter, glamour, and congestion of the coast. Dizzying narrow roads head up into the mountains, passing sleepy hamlets and dense vegetation where fig trees burst with giant purple and green fruit, enticing passersby to stop and indulge in their sweetness. Deep within these mountains exists a different Liguria, with a cuisine forged from a shorter growing season and heavily dependent on root vegetables, potatoes, and Brus, an incredibly strong fermented ricotta-type cheese. Porcini mushrooms proliferate in the rich dense forests at lower elevations, and on into fall months their sublime, earthy flavor dominates menus.

Away from the mountains and closer to the Ligurian Sea, a sunny climate and warm Mediterranean air provide a long and fruitful growing season for herbs and vegetables that represent the true core of the Ligurian diet. Whether bursting with flavor from just-picked herbs or incorporating myriad vegetables simply dressed, slow-cooked for fresh pasta sauces, or pureed and used as stuffing, the land's bounty is omnipresent in all Ligurian dishes. Salty sea air rendered bread baking impractical, leading to the creation of spongy focaccia that requires little more than a drizzle of olive oil and a sprinkling of salt. Often imitated with dismal results in bakeries throughout the world, true focaccia shows the Ligurian kitchen's ability to transform a few simple ingredients into pure perfection. Although one is never very far from the sea in Liguria, very little seafood makes its way inland. Anchovies, however, whether fresh or preserved, play a formidable role in Ligurian cuisine and are served stuffed with herb filling, fried whole with sea salt and lemon, or stewed with tomatoes into a meltingly briny pasta sauce. Because most agrarian land is devoted to vegetable gardens and fruit trees, the Ligurian meat course is mostly poultry and rabbit. While chickens are more commonly raised for their eggs (used to make fresh Ligurian pasta), rabbits are reared for their incredibly succulent meat and eaten in great abundance. Liguria represents a resourceful population whose cuisine was born from a gentle climate and what their land gave them, creating a healthy diet that embodies the Mediterranean spirit.

CHAPTER 1
❧ LA GIARA ❧

La Giara's urban location in the town of Beverino is close to the Ligurian Sea and the Cinque Terre. Terraces of grapevines and olive trees built into the surrounding hills cascade like giant steps down to the small stone farmhouse, while coniferous tree–covered mountain ranges loom in the distance. Rita Pascotto, the farm's proud owner, embraces guests with glowing enthusiasm, immediately making them feel welcomed and at home.

Eating at La Giara is Italian home cooking at its best, with three generations of women working together in the kitchen. Rita, her mother, Silva, and her daughter, Michela, prepare tasty Ligurian dishes that have been handed down through the family for generations. Absorbed in Rita's blood since childhood, these recipes are rich in history and lineage and trace a family's close connection to their land and to the Tyrrhenian Sea. Today, the all-women kitchen bustles, with fresh pastas handmade by Silva, desserts baked by Michela, and Rita serving as the backbone and main cook. Menus change daily, following the bounty of Rita's garden and the availability of local fish. Fresh anchovies are a house specialty, and their distinct oily flavor tastes best in the family's signature recipe, stuffed and fried. An imposing brick fireplace and grill gets plenty of use and sets the stage for second courses of various meats grilled over hardwood. Testaroli, a type of local flatbread, are baked in terra-cotta plates fired over

Vermentino grapes ready for harvest

hot coals and eaten with an assortment of cured meats and cheeses. Charismatic Rita enlivens her small dining room, greeting diners with a genuine concern for their enjoyment of her cooking. It is evident that she takes extreme joy in knowing that her family's hard work has brought her diners pleasure and a full belly. This warm reception allows guests of La Giara a unique opportunity to enter the home of an Italian family and feel welcomed, embraced, and fed like a true Italian.

Sardine Sauce over Linguine
LINGUINE CON LE SARDE

Fresh sardines are not always readily available, but they can be specially ordered from your local fishmonger. It's well worth the effort, because the stronger flavor of the preserved anchovies melds nicely with the sweet flavor of the fresh sardines, giving depth to the sauce and making it difficult to stop eating.

½ pound (225 g) fresh sardines

2 peeled cloves of garlic

½ cup flat-leaf parsley, plus more
   for garnish

½ red onion, cut into small dice

2 tablespoons (1 fl. oz. / 30 ml)
   olive oil

1 teaspoon crushed red pepper
   flakes

6 fillets preserved anchovies
   in oil, drained

1 pound (450 g) quartered cherry
   tomatoes

1 pound (450 g) linguine

Kosher salt and freshly ground black
   pepper to taste

Clean the sardines by removing their heads and splitting open the bellies, removing the intestines and spines with your fingers or with a small paring knife. Finally, remove the small fin on the back (skin side) of the fish. Rinse the sardines and then cut into 1-inch pieces.

Bring 6 quarts of salted water to a boil.

Mince together the garlic and parsley and set aside in a small bowl. In a 10- to 12-inch sauté pan over medium heat, sauté the red onion in the olive oil until tender, about 7 minutes. Add the garlic and parsley to the pan, along with the red pepper flakes and anchovy fillets, and continue to cook another 5 minutes, being careful not to burn the garlic.

Add the cherry tomatoes and a pinch of salt to the sauté pan and cook the sauce for another 5 minutes. Add the fresh sardines and another 5 minutes or until the sardines are cooked through.

Meanwhile, drop the pasta into the boiling water and cook until al dente. Reserve ⅓ cup of the pasta water, and then drain well in a colander. Add the pasta to the sauté pan, along with the reserved water, and toss it together with the sauce to coat. Season to taste with salt and pepper. Garnish with fresh parsley and serve immediately.

SERVES 6

Grandma Silva's daily ritual

Taglierini with summer vegetable sauce

Taglierini with Vegetable Sauce
TAGLIERINI CON SUGO DI VERDURE

Radicchio often has a strong and bitter flavor. In this recipe the bitterness is tamed by soaking it in cold water prior to cooking and by pairing it with sweet and juicy vegetables. The quality of the vegetables used is of extreme importance, since they are the highlight of the dish.

Cut the zucchini into quarters, and then into ¼-inch slices. Mince together the garlic and parsley.

Shred the radicchio and soak shreds in cold water for 15 minutes to remove the bitterness. Drain and shake out excess water.

Bring about 6 quarts of salted water to a boil. In a 10- to 12-inch sauté pan, combine olive oil, leek, and red pepper flakes and cook over medium heat until the leeks are tender but not browned. Add the zucchini and the garlic and parsley, and cook for about 10 minutes. Add the tomatoes and cook for an additional 5 minutes. Add the radicchio to the sauce, season to taste with salt and pepper, and continue cooking for 10 minutes.

Meanwhile, drop the pasta in the boiling water and cook 2 to 3 minutes for fresh pasta or follow cooking instructions for boxed pasta. Drain pasta and immediately toss with vegetable sauce. Serve with freshly grated Parmigiano Reggiano.

SERVES 4

1 medium-size zucchini (courgette)

2 peeled cloves of garlic

¼ cup flat-leaf parsley

1 head radicchio

2 tablespoons (1 fl. oz. / 30 ml) extra-virgin olive oil

1 leek, cleaned and cut into ¼-inch slices

1 teaspoon crushed red pepper flakes

1 pound (450 g) mixed tomatoes, cut into bite-size pieces

Kosher salt and freshly ground black pepper

1 pound (450 g) homemade taglierini pasta (or substitute boxed spaghetti)

¼ cup grated Parmigiano Reggiano

Stuffed Sardines
SARDE RIPIENE

12 fresh sardines (about 1 pound /
 900 g)

¼ cup flat-leaf parsley

1 peeled clove of garlic

4 ounces (115 g) finely chopped
 mortadella

2 large eggs

½ cup grated Parmigiano Reggiano

Kosher salt and freshly ground black
 pepper

1 cup (125 g) plain bread crumbs

2 tablespoons (1 fl. oz. / 30 ml)
 whole milk

½ cup (4 fl. oz. / 120 ml) canola oil,
 for frying

Lemon wedges, for garnish

At La Giara, Rita uses fresh anchovies, a Ligurian staple hard to come by in the United States. For this recipe, we have substituted fresh sardines, which taste just as delightful with this scrumptious filling.

Clean the sardines by removing their heads and splitting open the bellies, removing the intestines and spines with your fingers or with a small paring knife. Finally, remove the small fin on the back (skin side) of the fish.

Prepare the filling by mincing the parsley together with the garlic. Place in a medium-size bowl and add the mortadella, the eggs, and the Parmigiano Reggiano, and season to taste with salt and pepper. Dampen ½ cup of the bread crumbs with the milk, and then add to the bowl, mixing well to fully combine all of the ingredients.

Fried stuffed sardines

Lay the sardines flat on a cutting board, skin side down. Stuff the sardines with a tablespoon of the filling, and spread evenly over the fish fillet. Dredge the sardines in the remaining ½ cup of bread crumbs, lightly coating each fish. Place in refrigerator for at least 30 minutes.

Heat the canola oil in a large skillet or cast-iron pan over medium heat. Once the oil is hot, place the sardines, skin side up, in the pan and cook about 2 to 3 minutes per side, ensuring that each side is nicely golden brown. Cook the fish in batches if necessary. Drain on paper towels and serve with fresh lemon wedges.

SERVES 6

Sardine fillets ready for stuffing

TESTAROLI

Testaroli are a traditional La Spezian flatbread and a specialty of La Giara. To make them, an extremely hot fire is stoked using medium-size logs. Terra-cotta plates are placed over the blazing fire and left until they turn a reddish color. Then the plates are removed from the fire, and a pancake-like batter is poured onto the individual plates. As each plate is filled with batter, the plates are stacked upon one another, with the residual heat retained by the terra-cotta cooking the dough. Making testaroli takes an experienced cook, as the plates need to be at the precise temperature that will cook the batter quickly without causing it to stick or burn. Once cooked, the testaroli are knocked out of the plates and are ready to eat. The chewy yet crispy bread-like discs can then be filled with meats, cheeses, or even chocolate Nutella.

Apple Cake
TORTA DI MELE

3 peeled and cored Golden Delicious
  apples

¾ cup (150 g) granulated sugar

1 tablespoon (½ fl. oz. / 15 ml) lemon
  juice

2 teaspoons lemon zest

3 large eggs, separated

11 tablespoons (5½ oz. / 150 g)
  unsalted butter, plus more for the
  pan

1 tablespoon (½ fl. oz. / 15 ml) extra-
  virgin olive oil

1 tablespoon (½ fl. oz. / 15 ml) whole
  milk

1½ cups (200 g) all-purpose flour

Confectioners' sugar (icing sugar),
  for garnish

A breakfast staple at La Giara, this simple cake can also be served with gelato or ice cream to end a meal. The cake gets its volume and moist texture from the whipped egg whites.

Heat the oven to 350°F (180°C), and butter a 9 x 13 x 2-inch cake pan and line with parchment paper.

Cut two of the apples into fine dice and set aside to be used for the cake batter. Cut the third apple into thin slices and place it in a bowl with 1 tablespoon of sugar, the lemon juice, and the lemon zest and let macerate.

Whip the egg whites until they form stiff peaks, being careful not to overbeat.

In a bowl of a double boiler, melt the butter with 1 tablespoon of olive oil.

In a medium-size bowl, whisk together the remaining sugar with the egg yolks until thick and pale yellow. Add the apple pieces, milk, flour, and the butter mixture and stir well with a wooden spoon to incorporate. With a rubber spatula, gently fold the egg whites, in three additions, into the cake batter.

Pour the batter into the prepared pan and then fan the reserved apple slices across the top. Bake until golden brown, about 1 hour or until a toothpick inserted into the center comes out dry.

Cool the apple cake and dust with confectioners' sugar prior to serving.

SERVES 6–8

Rita's Cake
TORTA DI RITA

This cake is Rita's house concoction, which she whips up for breakfast or as a late-afternoon treat. She uses ground amaretti cookies interchangeably with chocolate for two distinct variations of her delicious baked good. The base for this cake does not resemble traditional cake batter; it is crumbly and it comes together as it bakes. The rich and creamy ricotta filling complements the cake's coarse texture.

Heat the oven to 350°F (180°C). Butter a 9 x 13 x 2-inch pan, and line with parchment paper.

In the bowl of an electric mixer fitted with the paddle attachment, combine all of the ingredients for the cake base and mix on low speed until mixture resembles coarse crumbs.

In a medium-size bowl, prepare the filling by mixing together the ricotta, eggs, and sugar with a wooden spoon until fully combined. Gently fold in the chocolate pieces or amaretti cookies.

Spread half of the cake base into the prepared pan. Drop spoonfuls of the ricotta filling evenly over the base. Top with the remaining half of base, and bake for 30 to 40 minutes, until the top of the cake is golden brown.

SERVES 6–8

Cake base

2¾ cups (350 g) all-purpose flour

¾ cup (150 g) granulated sugar

1 large egg

9 tablespoons (4½ oz. / 120 g) unsalted butter, at room temperature, cut into pieces, plus more for the pan

1 teaspoon (7 g) baking soda

1¼ teaspoons (8 g) baking powder

1 teaspoon vanilla

Filling

1½ cups ricotta

2 large eggs

½ cup (100 g) granulated sugar

4 ounces (115 g) bittersweet (60%) chocolate, finely chopped, or ⅓ cup ground amaretti cookies

Just-picked porcini and ovoli mushrooms

CHAPTER 2

GIANDRIALE

Giandriale lies in an oasis of valleys and green mountains and affords its guests a haven of peace, tranquility, and superior eating. A long, tortuous gravel road through dense woods opens to two separate stone farmhouses perched atop a hill, with spectacular views of green mountains in every direction. Giandriale is a true escape into rural Liguria and a far cry from the tourist-laden coastal villages.

The property has a long history, rooted in agriculture, which continues today through the dedication and hard work of husband-and-wife owners Nereo Giani and Lucia Marelli. Before World War II, the farm consisted of seven houses spread out over 150 hectares, with more than seventy people working there and living off its land. After the war, the farm was abandoned when its inhabitants left the country to find work in the cities and emigrate to America. Today, the once-deserted farm thrives as an all-organic agriturismo, with everything on the property grown and raised naturally and humanely.

Dinner is a communal affair served family style, with guests from all over the world sitting down together at one large farm table. Local Ligurian wine flows freely, as does conversation, with talk often centering on what Lucia has prepared for the evening. A self-taught, nonconventional cook, Lucia prepares Ligurian recipes with an unorthodox approach, realizing that her organic ingredients need little manipulation. With such an abundance of beautiful products at her disposal, only simple techniques are needed to bring out their true essence. In the basic, no-frills kitchen, a conventional blender has become Lucia's favorite appliance: she uses it to bring ingredients together, creating deep, rich flavors. Plum tomatoes stuffed with a medley of pureed garden produce and gnocchi tossed with a simple tomato sauce fortified with a pungent pesto exemplify her cooking style. Meals at Giandriale are a testimony to the efforts of Lucia and Nereo, and the compliments they receive are their reward for their passion and devotion. It is no wonder that people return year after year and that reservations are hard to come by during the summer and fall months.

Stuffed Tomatoes
POMODORI RIPIENI

These stuffed tomatoes are labor intensive but definitely worth the effort. Since the filling is hearty and substantial, the tomatoes can be served alone as a first course or appetizer or alongside a simple meal.

10 plum tomatoes

3 tablespoons (1½ fl. oz. / 45 ml) extra-virgin olive oil

½ red onion, cut into medium dice

1 green bell pepper, cut into medium dice

1 small eggplant (aubergine), cut into medium dice

Kosher salt and freshly ground black pepper

1½ cups ricotta

2 large eggs

⅔ cup (100 g) bread crumbs

½ cup grated pecorino cheese

½ cup plus 2 tablespoons grated Parmigiano Reggiano

2 tablespoons chopped flat-leaf parsley

1 tablespoon chopped oregano

2 tablespoons chopped basil

Heat the oven to 375° F (190°C).

Cut the tomatoes in half lengthwise and scoop out the seeds and flesh, reserving ½ cup for the filling. Salt the insides of the tomatoes and turn them over to drain excess water.

Add 2 tablespoons of the olive oil to a medium-size skillet and add the red onion and cook over medium heat until tender, about 5 minutes. Add the green pepper and the eggplant and continue to cook for about 10 minutes, stirring occasionally. Add the reserved tomato flesh with a bit of the juices and sauté for another 5 minutes, or until all the vegetables are tender. Season to taste with salt and pepper and set aside to cool.

Place the ricotta, eggs, ½ cup bread crumbs, the grated pecorino cheese, ½ cup grated Parmigiano Reggiano, herbs, and vegetable mixture in the bowl of a food processor or blender. Puree ingredients until well combined. Season to taste with salt and pepper.

Stuff tomatoes with the filling, using a spoon or a pastry bag without a tip, and place stuffing side up on an oiled baking dish. Sprinkle the tomatoes with the remaining 2 tablespoons grated Parmigiano Reggiano and the remaining bread crumbs and drizzle with the remaining 1 tablespoon olive oil.

Bake for about 30 minutes or until the tomatoes are tender and the filling is golden brown. Can be served immediately or at room temperature. The tomatoes can be made a day in advance and gently reheated.

SERVES 10–12

Stuffed tomatoes

Swiss Chard and Ricotta Tart
TORTA SALATA CON BIETOLE E RICOTTA

2 heads Swiss chard

1 peeled clove of garlic

3 tablespoons (1½ fl. oz. / 45 ml) extra-virgin olive oil, or as needed

3 cups ricotta

5 large eggs, plus 1 egg yolk for egg wash

½ cup (62 g) bread crumbs

½ cup grated Parmigiano Reggiano

1 tablespoon fresh oregano

Kosher salt and freshly ground black pepper

1 recipe savory pie crust (see page x)

Tavarone, a small town below Giandriale, is recognized for its annual August porcini mushroom festival, celebrating the earthy fungus in all its glory. The surrounding forests provide a perfect climate for porcini to thrive and people from all over Italy come to indulge in the prized delicacy.

Savory tarts are a common appetizer at the Ligurian table, and how they are made depends on the cook. Each agriturismo we visited had its own variation on this classic dish; however, the common thread found throughout was the use of Swiss chard for the filling. Spinach, kale, or any other green leafy vegetable can be substituted.

Rinse the Swiss chard in cold water to remove any dirt and then cut both the stems and leaves into ¼-inch ribbons. Heat a 10- to 12-inch skillet over medium-high heat, and add the Swiss chard, a tablespoon of water, and a generous pinch of salt, and cover, cooking until the Swiss chard is wilted, about 5 minutes.

Slice the garlic clove into thin pieces. In a 10- to 12- inch sauté pan, heat 2 tablespoons of olive oil and sauté the garlic until golden brown. Add the Swiss chard to the pan and cook over medium heat for 10 minutes. Let Swiss chard cool.

In the bowl of a food processor, add the ricotta, 5 eggs, 6 tablespoons bread crumbs, 6 tablespoons Parmigiano Reggiano, oregano, Swiss chard, and salt and pepper to taste, and puree until smooth. Taste for seasoning.

Heat the oven to 350°F (180°C). Roll out the dough into a 14-inch circle about ¼ inch thick. Place dough on an oiled baking sheet and add the filling to the center of the dough. Spread the filling, leaving ½ inch uncovered at the edges of the dough. Fold the dough over the filling, leaving the center of the filling exposed. Sprinkle with the remaining 2 tablespoons of grated Parmigiano Reggiano and the remaining 2 tablespoons of bread crumbs and drizzle with a little olive oil.

Brush the crust with the egg yolk and bake in the oven for 35 to 40 minutes, or until the crust is a rich golden brown and the filling has slightly puffed. Let cool and serve warm or at room temperature.

SERVES 8

Roasted Garden Vegetables
INSALATA DI VERDURE AL FORNO

The pureed tomatoes become a sweet, concentrated base for the roasted vegetables. This dish tastes best when eaten at room temperature, which makes it pop with summer flavor.

Heat the oven to 425°F (220°C).

On a sheet pan, mix together the eggplant, green pepper, red onion, basil, parsley, oregano, and garlic with the olive oil and 1 tablespoon of red wine vinegar. Sprinkle mixture with 2 teaspoons salt. Mix in the niçoise olives and bake in the oven for about 20 minutes.

Meanwhile, in a blender, roughly puree the plum tomatoes with the red pepper flakes. Add to the vegetable mixture, sprinkle with the remaining tablespoon of red wine vinegar, and continue to bake for another hour, stirring occasionally, until the vegetables are very tender. Season to taste with salt and pepper. Serve at room temperature.

SERVES 4

1 small eggplant (aubergine), cut into large dice

1 green bell pepper, cut into large dice

1 sliced red onion

1 cup chopped basil

½ cup chopped flat-leaf parsley

2 tablespoons chopped oregano

2 cloves of garlic, peeled and minced

¼ cup (2 fl. oz. / 60 ml) olive oil

2 tablespoons (1 fl. oz. / 30 ml) red wine vinegar

Kosher salt and freshly ground pepper

½ cup pitted niçoise olives

2 pounds (900 g) plum tomatoes, seeds removed and cut into large dice

1 teaspoon crushed red pepper flakes

Pasta Coins with White Sauce
CROXETTI CON SUGO BIANCO

Croxetti are typical pasta of the region, traditionally made with an ornate stamp. The pasta is rolled out into thin sheets, cut into circles, and then pressed between two wooden dowels with an elaborate design, leaving an imprint on the dough. These stamps are custom made, allowing each household to stamp pasta with its family crest. Since croxetti stamps are hard to come by outside of Liguria, we've adapted the recipe below to use either homemade pasta cut into coins without the elaborate designs or boxed fettuccine.

1 recipe basic pasta dough (see page x) or 1 pound (450 g) boxed fettuccine

Kosher salt and freshly ground black pepper

4 tablespoons (2 oz. / 60 g) unsalted butter

1 cup (150 g) pine nuts

2 cloves of garlic, peeled and roughly chopped

¼ cup (2 fl. oz. / 60 ml) extra-virgin olive oil

¼ cup (2 fl. oz. / 60 ml) whole milk

2 tablespoons chopped marjoram

¼ cup grated Parmigiano Reggiano

If using pasta dough, roll it out to the thinnest setting on your pasta maker. Using a small round cookie cutter or a small glass, cut the pasta into silver-dollar-size coins. Place on a sheet pan lightly dusted with flour and set aside until ready to cook.

Bring about 6 quarts of salted water to a boil.

Meanwhile, melt the butter in a small saucepan and set aside to let cool slightly. In a blender, combine the pine nuts, garlic, oil, milk, and marjoram. Blend until smooth. Gradually add the butter to the blender to prevent the mixture from foaming. Season to taste with salt and pepper. (The sauce can be prepared ahead of time; gently reheat it over a water bath before serving.)

Add the pasta to the boiling water and cook until tender, 2 to 3 minutes for fresh pasta or following the directions for boxed pasta. Reserve ¼ cup of the pasta water. Drain pasta well.

Thin the sauce with the reserved pasta water and toss with the drained pasta. Serve immediately with the Parmigiano Reggiano.

SERVES 6

Making Croxetti Pasta

Gnocchi Portofino ready for dinner

Potato Dumplings with Sauce from Portofino
GNOCCHI CON SUGO ALLA PORTOFINO

This dish derives its name from the nearby coastal village of Portofino, on the Ligurian Riviera. A blend of fresh tomatoes with the classic Ligurian pesto creates a light sauce packed with regional flavor. The sauce is a perfect companion for gnocchi, but it is equally tasty with any type of boxed pasta for a quick summertime meal.

Blanch the basil in boiling salted water for about 1 minute. Drain and immediately submerge in ice water. Lay basil on paper towels or a kitchen towel to dry.

In a blender, add the basil, pine nuts, Parmigiano Reggiano, and garlic, and puree to combine. With the blender running, add the olive oil in a steady stream to emulsify the pesto.

Cut the tops off the plum tomatoes and cut in half, discarding the seeds. Place tomatoes in the bowl of a food processor and puree until smooth.

Bring 6 quarts of salted water to a boil.

Meanwhile, heat 1 tablespoon of the olive oil in a 12-inch sauté pan over medium-high heat and add the tomato puree. Cook for about 15 minutes and season with salt and pepper to taste. Add ½ cup of pesto to the tomato sauce and stir until fully incorporated, adjusting seasoning if needed.

Add the gnocchi to the boiling water, and cook until they rise to the surface, 3 to 5 minutes. Drain well in a colander, and then add gnocchi to the pan with the sauce. Toss to coat evenly and serve with grated Parmigiano Reggiano on the side.

SERVES 6

Pesto

3 cups packed basil

2½ tablespoons pine nuts

⅓ cup grated Parmigiano Reggiano, plus more for serving

1 clove of garlic, peeled and roughly chopped

½ cup (4 fl. oz. / 120 ml) extra-virgin olive oil

Tomato sauce

2 pounds (900 g) plum tomatoes

1 tablespoon (½ fl. oz. / 15 ml) extra-virgin olive oil

Kosher salt and freshly ground black pepper

1 recipe potato gnocchi (see page ix)

Lemon Tart
TORTA DI LIMONE

A base of ground almonds add an interesting element to the silky custard that fills this lemon tart. The tangy citrus flavor is mellowed by the sweet pastry crust.

Crust

9 tablespoons (4½ oz. / 120 g) unsalted butter at room temperature, plus extra for the pan

¾ cup (150 g) granulated sugar

2 large egg yolks

1 tablespoon lemon zest

2 cups (250 g) all-purpose flour, plus extra as needed

½ cup (55 g) ground blanched almonds

Lemon cream

8 tablespoons (4 oz. / 115 g) unsalted butter

5 large eggs

1 cup (200 g) granulated sugar

1½ tablespoons lemon zest

1 cup (8 fl. oz. / 240 ml) lemon juice

Make the crust: In an electric mixer fitted with the paddle attachment, cream together the butter and sugar. Add the egg yolks and lemon zest and mix until incorporated. Add the flour and mix until all ingredients are well combined.

Heat the oven to 325°F (170°C). With lightly floured hands, spread the dough into a buttered 12-inch tart pan. Prick the dough all over with the tines of a fork and sprinkle with the almond crumbs. Line the dough with parchment paper and fill with pie weights or dried beans. Bake until the edges are just beginning to turn golden brown, about 15 minutes. Take out of the oven; remove the parchment paper and weights. Cool tart shell completely on a wire rack.

Lemon tart

Prepare the filling: In a small saucepan, melt the butter over medium heat. Remove from heat and let cool slightly.

In a blender, combine the melted butter, eggs, sugar, lemon zest, and lemon juice. Blend until smooth and frothy, about 3 minutes. Pour over the crust and bake in the oven for about 40 minutes, or until the filling is set and the crust is a deep golden brown. Cool completely on a wire rack.

YIELDS 1 12-INCH TART

BEEKEEPING

Long rows of brightly painted boxes teeming with the rhythmic buzz of thousands of honeybees at work are a common sight at farms throughout Italy. Beekeeping is an essential activity for farmers, not only for the bees' production of honey, but for their ability to pollinate the fields, bringing greater productivity to plants and trees. By providing homes for the bees, agriturismo owners ensure themselves bountiful crops to be used in their kitchens, further enhancing their farms' sustainability.

Checking for the queen bee

CHAPTER 3

TERRE BIANCHE

High in the Ligurian Maritime Alps, the Terre Bianche agriturismo sits in a dramatic position atop a hill, with expansive views of the Mediterranean Sea and Corsica's rocky outline on the horizon. The tall rectangular stone farmhouse, with its forest green shutters and burnt orange roof, nestles into a lush landscape of vines, fig trees, and olive groves. The vineyard, recognized as one of the premier wine estates in Liguria, owes its success to the rich "white earth" for which the farm is named. Shell deposits from thousands of years ago, when the ocean covered these high and rugged peaks, have created a chalky soil rich in minerals that grows exceptionally fine native red and white grapes.

Paolo Rondello, the agriturismo's proud owner, returned to his family's vineyard after a career in engineering that took him around the world. With a greater appreciation and fondness for his origins and the surrounding land, he opened the agriturismo, desiring to share his property with others, allowing visitors to spend the night and to indulge in the vineyard's wines, olive oil, and vegetables. A cheerful and gregarious host, Paolo greets his guests for breakfast in the morning and offers up a wealth of historical information about the area and his vineyard, which has been in his family since 1870.

With an incredible panoramic vista of valleys, mountains, and ocean, the agriturismo makes dining an ethereal experience, enhanced by the superb cooking of Terre Bianche's talented young chef, Diego. Born and raised in a nearby village, Diego left Liguria at a young age to attend culinary school in Switzerland. Years later, he found himself in nearby Monte Carlo, honing his cooking skills in the kitchens of five-star hotels and feeding Europe's elite. When he heard about Paolo's desire to open Terre Bianche's restaurant, he jumped at the opportunity to return to his roots. He brought along his French wife, Mariella, to work the front of the house, and she charms diners with her charisma and passion for her husband's cuisine. Today, the couple run the acclaimed restaurant, bringing sophistication and refinement to rural Liguria. Diego's mastery of culinary technique is evident in everything he prepares, yet his respect for traditional recipes dominates his cooking. His repertoire includes classic local dishes such as barbajaii (a puffy, golden fried butternut squash ravioli), an intoxicatingly sweet onion tart, and a slowly braised rabbit whose tender succulence bursts with Ligurian flavor. His dishes maintain a degree of simplicity, allowing individual elements to shine, redolent of the clean and invigorating air surrounding Terre Bianche.

Terre Bianche farmhouse at dusk

Stuffed onions

VERDURE FARCITE

Stuffed vegetables are eaten in abundance throughout the Ligurian summer. While the ingredients may vary slightly from one household to another, these dishes all represent the region's appreciation for the homegrown vegetables that constitute the bulk of Liguria's diet.

Heat the oven to 400°F (200°C).

Bring a 5- to 6-quart pot of salted water to a boil and add the onion. Let the water return to a boil and cook until tender about 3 minutes. Drain the onion and run under cold water to cool. Let dry on a kitchen towel. Separate the larger outer rings and reserve. Chop up the smaller inner rings and save for filling.

Add the zucchini to boiling water and cook until tender, about 3 minutes for baby zucchini and 5 minutes for larger zucchini. It is important not to overcook the zucchini. Drain zucchini and immediately submerge in ice water. Remove zucchini from water and pat dry with a towel. With a spoon, scoop out the seeds and some of the flesh from the zucchini and set aside for the filling. Set the hollowed zucchini aside.

Meanwhile, place the potatoes in a 4-quart pot of salted water and bring up to a boil over high heat. Lower heat to medium low and simmer until tender when pierced with a skewer, about 12 minutes. Drain potatoes and let cool. Pass the potatoes through a ricer into a large bowl. Add the eggs, herbs, nutmeg, chopped onion, reserved zucchini flesh, and Parmigiano Reggiano and mix until well combined. Season with salt and pepper to taste.

Fill the onion rings and each hollowed zucchini half with a generous amount of the filling and place on a sheet pan. Drizzle with olive oil and sprinkle lightly with grated Parmigiano Reggiano. Bake until the tops are golden brown and crispy, about 25 minutes. Remove from the oven and place on a wire rack to cool. Serve warm.

SERVES 8

1 sweet yellow onion, cut in half crosswise

6 baby zucchini (courgettes) cut in half lengthwise, or 3 small zucchini cut in half lengthwise

3 Yukon Gold potatoes, peeled and cut into quarters

2 large eggs

2 tablespoons chopped marjoram

1 tablespoon chopped thyme

1 tablespoon chopped flat-leaf parsley

1 teaspoon freshly grated nutmeg

1 cup grated Parmigiano Reggiano, plus more for sprinkling

Kosher salt and freshly ground black pepper

2 tablespoons (1 fl. oz. / 30 ml) extra-virgin olive oil

Onion Tart
TORTA DI CIPOLLA

This tart is influenced by neighboring France, which is only a stone's throw away from Terre Bianche. The olive oil dough is silky and pliant, making it easy to roll out. Spread the onions thinly over the dough so their pungent flavor will not overpower the subtle crust.

Crust

8 cups (1 kg) all-purpose flour

1¼ cups (10 fl. oz. / 280 ml) water

1 cup (8 fl. oz. / 240 ml) olive oil

1 tablespoon salt

Filling

2 tablespoons (1 fl. oz. / 30 ml) extra-virgin olive oil

6 sweet yellow onions, cut into ¼-inch slices

¼ cup (2 fl. oz. / 60 ml) white wine

Kosher salt and freshly ground pepper

1 tablespoon chopped marjoram

Make the dough: In the bowl of an electric mixer fitted with a dough hook, mix the flour, water, olive oil, and salt on low speed until they come together, 8 to 10 minutes. Turn the dough out onto a floured surface and knead the dough until smooth and elastic, 2 to 3 minutes. Set the dough aside, covered with a kitchen towel.

Prepare the filling: In a 12-inch sauté pan, heat the olive oil over medium-low heat, add the onions to the pan, and cook slowly until onions are very tender and lightly browned, about 20 minutes. Raise the heat to high, and add the wine to the pan, along with 2 teaspoons of salt, ½ teaspoon pepper, and marjoram, and continue to cook until the wine has reduced to dry.

Remove the onions from pan and place in a strainer to drain some of the excess moisture, about 15 minutes.

Heat the oven to 375°F (190°C). Cut the dough in half and roll out each half into a large rectangle ¼ inch thick. Place one half of the dough on a sheet pan. Top with the onions and cover with the second piece of dough. Seal the edges of the dough by crimping them together. With the tines of a fork, poke holes in the top crust and bake in the oven until golden brown, about 35 minutes.

SERVES 12

Alta Via dei Monti Liguri, Liguria's Salt Road

Once known as "the salt road," which led from the ports of Liguria and over the Maritime Alps and into inland Europe, today Alta Via dei Monti Liguri is a maintained hiking trail that runs through the Terre Bianche farm. Merchants would travel the high mountain paths of this legendary trade route, traversing mountain peaks to avoid bandits. Salt, an essential preservative harvested on Ligurian shores, was a highly taxed item. To avoid paying the tax, traders would fill the bottom halves of their sacks with salt and the top halves with anchovies. Tax collectors would see (and smell) the decomposing fish and let the traders continue on without paying any taxes. Upon arriving in Piemonte, the first region after Liguria, traders eventually noticed that the anchovies closest to the salt were preserved beautifully—and a delicious addition to Piemontese cuisine was born.

Fried Butternut Squash Ravioli
BARBAJAII

Each fall, in the villages surrounding Terre Bianche, an annual festival, or sagra, is held in celebration of barbajaii. Along with the butternut squash, Brus, a piquant fermented ricotta cheese, is traditionally used in the filling. In the recipe below, ricotta cheese and a sharp tangy pecorino are substituted to achieve similar results.

Dough

4 cups (500 g) all-purpose flour, plus more as needed

¾ cup (6 fl. oz. / 180 ml) water

½ cup (4 fl. oz. / 120 ml) extra-virgin olive oil

Kosher salt

Filling

1 medium butternut squash (about 2.5 pounds / 1.14 kg)

3 tablespoons (1.5 fl. oz. / 45 ml) extra-virgin olive oil

Kosher salt and freshly ground black pepper

2 tablespoons chopped marjoram

1 cup ricotta

½ cup grated piquant pecorino cheese

2 eggs, plus 1 egg white

¾ cup canola oil, for frying

Make the dough: In the bowl of an electric mixer fitted with a dough hook, mix the flour, water, olive oil, and 1 tablespoon salt on low speed until they come together, 8 to 10 minutes. Turn the dough out onto a lightly floured surface and knead the dough until smooth and elastic, about 2 to 3 minutes. Set aside, covered with a kitchen towel.

Heat the oven to 425°F (220°C). Peel the butternut squash, cut in half, and scoop out the seeds. Cut the squash into 1-inch cubes, toss with 2 tablespoons olive oil, a generous pinch of salt and pepper, and 1 tablespoon of marjoram, and roast in the oven until tender, about 30 minutes. Remove the butternut squash from the oven, mash with a fork, and set aside to cool. Lower the oven temperature to 200°F (100°C)

In a large bowl, mix together the butternut squash with the ricotta, pecorino, 2 eggs, 1 tablespoon marjoram, the remaining 1 tablespoon olive oil, and salt and pepper to taste until fully combined.

Divide the dough into 4 pieces. Using a pasta machine, roll the dough out, starting at the widest setting and ending with the second to thinnest setting. Lay out one sheet of pasta and drop tablespoons of filling down one side of the pasta sheet at 1-inch intervals. Brush all around the filling with the egg white and then fold the pasta over the filling. Gently press out any air between the filling and the dough. With a pastry cutter or knife, cut the ravioli into squares and place on a lightly floured sheet pan. Finish the remaining ravioli in the same fashion.

In a heavy cast-iron pan or 10-inch straight-sided skillet, heat the canola oil over medium-high heat until shimmering. Place 4 to 6 ravioli in the oil and cook, turning, until golden brown and puffy, about 3 minutes per side. Drain on a sheet pan lined with paper towel and keep warm in the oven while you fry the rest of the ravioli.

SERVES 8

Making barbajaii

Barbajaii ravioli ready for frying

Oven-Roasted Cornish Hens

GALLETTI ACCOMODATI

Game birds often replace the common chicken at the Italian table. The small fowl are appreciated for their moist and juicy meat, while larger chickens are reared more for their eggs than for consumption and are reserved for making long-simmered soups and stocks.

3 tablespoons (1½ fl. oz. / 45 ml) extra-virgin olive oil

3 Cornish hens (about 2 pounds each / 900 g), cut in half, backbones and breastbones removed

Kosher salt and freshly ground black pepper

1 medium yellow onion, cut into fine dice

2 cloves of garlic, peeled and sliced

1 tablespoon chopped thyme, plus more for garnish

1 tablespoon chopped marjoram

1 tablespoon all-purpose flour

1½ cups (12 fl. oz. / 340 ml) red wine

¼ cup (2 fl. oz. / 60 ml) water

½ cup (4 fl. oz. / 120 ml) homemade chicken broth (see page xi) or canned low-sodium broth

Heat the oven to 375°F (190°C).

Heat 2 tablespoons of olive oil in a large ovenproof casserole pan over medium-high heat. Season the Cornish hens with salt and pepper and add them to the pan in batches, searing on both sides until deep golden brown, 10 to 12 minutes total. Remove from pan and set aside on a plate.

Reduce the heat to medium, add the onion and garlic to the pan, and sauté until tender but not browned, about 5 minutes. Add the herbs and the Cornish hens to the pan, transfer to the oven, and roast until cooked through, about 30 minutes, or until a meat thermometer registers 165°F (75°C). Remove the Cornish hens from the pan and place on a platter.

Meanwhile, make a roux: In a small skillet, mix the remaining 1 tablespoon olive oil and the flour and cook until golden brown. Set aside to cool.

Prepare the sauce: Place the casserole pan back on the stove, over medium-high heat. Add the red wine, and reduce to ¼ cup. Add the water and chicken broth to the pan and simmer 2 minutes. Add the roux, whisking constantly until fully incorporated. Simmer the sauce until it has thickened enough to coat the back of a spoon, about 2 minutes. Season to taste with salt and pepper and strain through a fine mesh sieve.

Serve each person half a Cornish hen drizzled with the sauce and garnish with fresh thyme.

SERVES 6

Rabbit with Olives and Pine Nuts

CONIGLIO ALLA LIGURE

Briny olives, delicate pine nuts, and floral marjoram are quintessential ingredients in the Ligurian repertoire. This simple braised rabbit dish is redolent of these classic flavorings.

Add ¼ cup of olive oil to a heavy casserole pan and place over medium heat until shimmering. Season the rabbit pieces with salt and pepper and add to the pan in batches, searing on all sides until deep golden brown, about 10 to 12 minutes. Remove to a plate and set aside.

Lower heat to medium and add the onion to the pan, sautéing until tender but not browned, 6 to 8 minutes. Add the pine nuts and olives and sauté for 2 to 3 minutes. Deglaze the pan with the white wine and let simmer until reduced by half, about 5 minutes. Add the chicken broth and place the rabbit back in the pan with the herbs and a teaspoon of salt.

Cover the pan and lower the heat, letting simmer until the rabbit is cooked through and fork-tender, 50 to 60 minutes. Season to taste with salt and pepper. Serve on a platter, sprinkled with marjoram.

SERVES 6

¼ cup (2 fl. oz. / 60 ml) extra-virgin olive oil

2 rabbits, each cut into 8 pieces (about 2 pounds each / 900 g each)

1 medium yellow onion, cut into fine dice

¼ cup pine nuts

¾ cup mixed small black and green olives such as niçoise and picholine, pitted

1 cup (8 fl. oz. / 240 ml) dry white wine

1 cup (8 fl. oz. / 240 ml) homemade chicken broth (see page xi) or canned low-sodium broth

2 tablespoons chopped marjoram, plus more for garnish

1 tablespoon chopped thyme

Kosher salt and freshly ground black pepper

Chilled Zabaglione
ZABAIONE FREDDA

6 large egg yolks

½ cup (100 g) granulated sugar

2 tablespoons (1 fl. oz. / 30 ml) white wine

2 tablespoons (1 fl. oz. / 30 ml) dry Marsala

1 cup (8 fl. oz. / 240 ml) heavy whipping cream

3 cups fresh mixed berries or ¼ cup crushed amaretti cookies

Zabaglione is a warm egg custard laced with Marsala and often served over fresh berries. Diego lightens up this classic with fresh whipped cream and serves it chilled, resembling an airy mousse.

Whisk together egg yolks and sugar until pale yellow and thickened. Add the white wine and Marsala and continue to whisk until well incorporated.

Heat water in a double boiler over low heat to a gentle simmer. Place egg yolk mixture in the top of the double boiler and whisk constantly until the mixture has doubled in volume and has thickened to light foamy custard, 5 to 8 minutes. Remove from heat and let cool.

Whip the cream either by hand or with an electric mixer until stiff peaks form. With a rubber spatula fold the cream into the zabaglione. Spoon the custard into individual glass bowls and chill until ready to serve.

Serve with either mixed berries or amaretti cookies.

SERVES 6

ROSSESE

In the calcium-rich white soil in the mountains surrounding Terre Bianche grows the red Rossese grape. Its ability to flourish nowhere in the world but this isolated area enhances its charm and mysticism. The Rossese vines have been in Paolo's family for generations, and the grapes are crushed to make a dry red wine that is produced in limited quantity and is not available for export. To experience this unique wine it is best to travel to Terre Bianche and drink a bottle with one of Diego's superb meals.

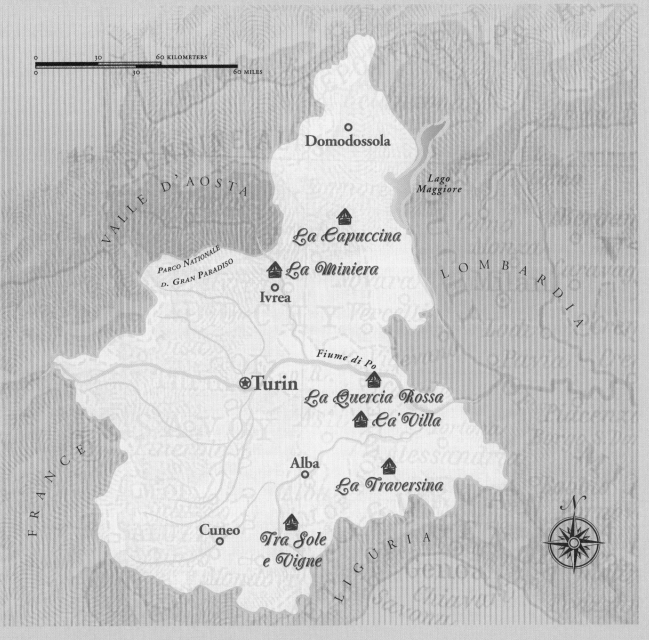

0   30   60 KILOMETERS

0   30   60 MILES

Domodossola

VALLE D'AOSTA

LOMBARDIA

Lago Maggiore

La Capuccina

PARCO NATIONALE D. GRAN PARADISO

La Miniera

Ivrea

Fiume di Po

Turin

La Quercia Rossa

Ca'Villa

Alba

La Traversina

FRANCE

Cuneo

Tra Sole e Vigne

LIGURIA

N

Piemonte is a geographically diverse region that offers remarkably changing landscapes, from the rolling hills of the Langhe, to the plains of the Po River Valley, to dramatic snow-peaked mountain ranges. This amazing natural beauty has molded a great culinary tradition, an elegant and refined cuisine retaining French characteristics from when the region was ruled by the Savoy dynasty. From these varied terrains come a rich palette of ingredients, all of which are highlighted in classic and modern Piemontese cooking.

The Langhe's powerhouse wines and world-famous producers bring to its fertile hills throngs of wine aficionados from all over the globe. The agriturismo movement has surged here, providing guests a gourmet vacation and the opportunity to experience vineyard life. Meals at the farms allow wineries to showcase their wines and pair them with multiple-course dinners. Numerous antipasti, which begin an evening, are typical of Piemontese dining culture and usually include an abundance of seasonal vegetables. Insalata Russa (Russian salad) epitomizes the richness and decadence of Piemontese cooking, combining numerous vegetables with hard-boiled eggs, tuna fish, and spices, all bound together with mayonnaise. Home to the white truffle, Langhe tables in fall offer the unearthed pungent delicacy, with thin shavings added to simple dishes to bring out the mushroom's distinct taste. Tajarin, a rich yellow pasta made from an egg-yolk dough, turns especially luxurious when enhanced by a slice of white truffle. Piemontese beef, from the meat of white cattle referred to as "Razza Piemontese," is a prized commodity due to a low fat content and extreme tenderness. To accentuate its superior flavor and quality, a classic preparation serves it raw, minced and dressed with a light vinaigrette.

The extensive flatlands of the Po River Valley run through the central core of Piemonte, and the floodplains produce more rice than any other region in Italy. Its characteristic nutty, toothy, textural grain is a favorite for risotto, most commonly made by pouring small amounts of meat broth into the cooking rice, which absorbs the simmering liquid. The Piemontese bring the rice dish to another level with risotto al Barolo, adding the full-bodied regional wine to the broth, which imparts a ruby-red hue to the finished dish. Topped with softened mountain butter and handfuls of grated cheese, this creamy first course symbolizes the wealth of top-notch ingredients in the Piemonte kitchen.

While the big reds of Piemonte—Barolo, Barbera, and Barbaresco—have achieved liquid gold prestige, many lesser-known wines' under-the-radar status allows for greater value, such as the slightly effervescent Fresia and the light-bodied Dolcetto. Though they are often overshadowed, Piemonte also produces some terrific whites, such as the minerally Erbaluce, the mellow and easy drinking Gavi, and the more full-bodied Arneis. From the town of Asti comes the sweet but not too sweet Moscato d'Asti, whose low alcohol levels make it a perfect accompaniment for dessert.

CHAPTER 4
❧ TRA SOLE E VIGNE ❧

The Manzone family's agriturismo offers food and wine lovers the opportunity to indulge in serious Piemontese cuisine while imbibing some of the most recognized wines in the world. Set atop a sloping hill, with row after row of manicured vines extending to the valley below, the vineyard has been producing superior wines since 1843. On their land, the Manzones harvest native red grapes for their wines, white truffles form beneath the earth where poplars grow, and groves of hazelnut trees flourish, all providing materials for the Tra Sole e Vigne kitchen.

The Manzones' strong family unit and their dedication to their land have brought prosperity to the estate. The two brothers, Giuseppe and Elio, handle all facets of wine production, while their families come together to run the agriturismo. Recently opened, Tra Sole e Vigne represents a new chapter in the family's history, brought about by travelers desiring the opportunity to eat, sleep, and drink among their vines. The Manzones' high standards are applied to their agriturismo and their sense of hospitality reflects this. The opulent dining room, rich with white linen tablecloths, decorative drapes, and a large bay window with a breathtaking vista of the vineyard and countryside, perfectly suits the decadent Piemontese cuisine. Chef Alberto Manzone and his mother, Lucia, prepare dinners for guests in typical Langhe fashion, with an abundance of antipasti setting the stage for the evening. Marco Manzone, both sommelier and waiter, offers

Manzone family of Tra Sole e Vigne

discourse and knowledge about his family's wines, and hearty Manzone wines not only accompany meals, but also are used profusely in the family's recipes. No hesitation is given to uncorking the family's best wines for cooking: a deep red risotto made with Barolo is a specialty of the house, as is a Piemontese beef stew whose preparation includes two different types of hearty red wine. Second helpings are always encouraged, and Lucia doesn't need to twist too many arms. The family's decision to open Tra Sole e Vigne has taken their vineyard to another level of devotion. Their commitment to its success is evident in the hard work the Manzones set out for themselves. This is at no time more apparent than when, at the end of the night, long after all of the guests have gone to bed, Giuseppe and Elio remain in the kitchen to wash dishes.

Langhe-Style Peppers with Salsa Verde
PEPERONI CON SALSA VERDE

In the summer and fall months, the local markets are ripe with extraordinarily large and vibrantly colored bell peppers, whose sweetness lends them to a host of different recipes. These sweet bell peppers spread with a pungent variation of salsa verde are a mainstay at Tra Sole e Vigne, where guests are presented a large assortment of antipasti each night.

Heat the oven to 400°F (200°C).

Rub peppers with 1 tablespoon of the olive oil and place on a sheet pan. Roast in the oven until browned and tender, about 30 minutes, turning halfway through. Remove from oven and immediately place in a plastic bag or a bowl covered with plastic wrap. Let rest for 20 minutes.

Soak the bread in 2 tablespoons of red wine vinegar for 30 minutes.

Mince the parsley, anchovy fillets, garlic, hard-boiled egg and yolk, and tuna. Mix all ingredients together in a bowl. Chop the bread very fine and stir into the parsley mixture. Add ¼ cup olive oil, season with salt and pepper to taste, and add the remaining tablespoon of red wine vinegar.

Remove peppers from the bag or bowl, peel the skin from the peppers, and remove the seeds. Cut the peppers into strips about 2 inches thick.

Spread 1 tablespoon of the filling over each pepper strip. Drizzle with the remaining tablespoon of olive oil and serve at room temperature.

SERVES 6

2 red bell peppers

2 yellow bell peppers

6 tablespoons (3 fl. oz. / 90 ml) extra-virgin olive oil

¼ cup of stale Italian bread, crust removed and cut into ¼-inch cubes

3 tablespoons (1½ fl. oz. / 45 ml) red wine vinegar

1½ cups flat-leaf parsley

5 anchovy fillets

1 peeled clove of garlic

1 hard-boiled egg, plus 1 hard-boiled egg yolk

3 ounces (85 g) Italian tuna packed in olive oil, drained

Kosher salt and freshly ground black pepper

Sweet Piemontese peppers

Beef Tartare
CARNE CRUDA

1 pound (450 g) filet mignon

1 tablespoon finely chopped anchovy

3 tablespoons (1½ fl. oz. / 45 ml) lemon juice

¼ cup (2 fl. oz. / 60 ml) extra-virgin olive oil, plus more for drizzling

2 tablespoons (1 fl. oz. / 30 ml) olive oil

1 teaspoon Dijon-style mustard

Kosher salt and freshly ground black pepper

2 ounces (60 g) shaved Parmigiano Reggiano

Carne cruda, which translates as "raw meat," is a traditional specialty of the Langhe. Tender meat from the Razza Piemontese cow, the local free-range cattle, is cut into thin slices and then chopped over and over again with a heavy knife until the color turns from deep brownish red to a pinkish red. A lemony anchovy vinaigrette lightly dresses the meat to add a subtle nuance of flavor; the dressing should enhance the meat, not overpower it. This is a true delicacy, and the meat's quality is essential. Check out your local farmers market to source free-range beef.

Cut the filet into thin strips, about ⅛-inch thick. Lay the strips flat on a cutting board and, with a large chef's knife or cleaver, chop the meat rapidly, in a repetitive motion. Begin horizontally, then rotate the board and continue to chop vertically, very, very finely, until the meat changes color from brownish red to a lighter pinkish hue. The total chopping time should be around 15 minutes.

In a small bowl, mix together the anchovy, lemon juice, olive oils, and mustard. Season the meat with salt and pepper and lightly toss the vinaigrette with the meat, adding a little at a time.

Chill until ready to serve. Spoon out a small portion onto a plate and garnish with the Parmigiano Reggiano shavings. Drizzle plate with extra-virgin olive oil.

SERVES 6

Preparing carne cruda

Piemontese Beef Stew
BOCCONCINO DI CARNE

Meat slowly cooked together with robust Piemontese red wine creates a deeply fla-vored beef stew. Tra Sole e Vigne barters its vineyard's wines with a local farmer who raises cattle and cooks the tender meat in a bottle of its own Barbera wine.

3 tablespoons (1½ fl. oz. / 45 ml) extra-virgin olive oil

1 leek, cleaned and cut into ¼-inch half-moon slices

2 medium yellow onions, cut into small dice

2 stalks celery, cut into small dice

2 carrots, peeled and cut into small dice

4 cloves of garlic, peeled and sliced

2 tablespoons minced rosemary

2 pounds (900 g) beef chuck roast, cut into 1-inch cubes

Kosher salt and freshly ground black pepper

1 tablespoon cornstarch

1 bottle (750 ml) full-bodied red wine

1½ cups (12 fl. oz. / 360 ml) canned low-sodium beef broth

3–4 whole cloves

1 teaspoon cinnamon

In a heavy casserole pan, heat olive oil over medium-high heat. Add the leek, onions, celery, carrots, garlic, and rosemary, and sauté until tender and lightly browned, about 10 minutes.

Rinse meat and pat dry. Season with 2 teaspoons salt and ½ teaspoon pepper, toss with cornstarch, and add to the vegetables, continuing to cook until the meat starts to brown.

Raise the heat to high and add the red wine to the pan. Bring to a boil and cook for about 10 minutes to let the alcohol burn off, and reduce slightly.

Add 1 cup of the broth, the cloves, and season lightly with salt and pep-per. Cover the pan, reduce to low heat, and simmer for about 1 hour.

Add the cinnamon, another ½ cup of broth, and continue to cook until the meat is tender, about 45 minutes to an hour. Taste the sauce for season-ing and adjust if necessary.

SERVES 6

Hiking through the Vineyards of Barolo

The Langhe region of southwest Piemonte arguably produces some of the finest wines in Italy. Barolo, perhaps the most refined and certainly the most recognized, comes from the Nebbiolo grape, grown on sloping hills that proliferate throughout the region. I Sentieri del Barolo (the Barolo Trails) are a network of well-marked hiking trails through these vineyards. The trails' signature red-and-white painted stripes guide hikers through stunning countryside dotted with ancient castles, medieval villages, and vineyards that seemingly never end. La Morra and Novello are two of the main towns the trails meander through and are perched on hilltops with commanding views. Barolo, the town from which the wine takes its name, lies down in the valley, where charm and quaintness pave the way to the town's majestic castle, which today houses a museum, wine store, and tasting room. Local *tabacchi,* easily recognized by their black-and-white letter T signs, sell maps that clearly mark the numerous trails.

A day spent trekking the hilly terrain can build quite an appetite. Find respite in the numerous wine bars and trattorias in several towns along the trail, which offer traditional Langhe cuisine accompanied by wines from vineyards you may have recently walked through. A plate of local cheeses or a salami panino with a glass of local wine provides the necessary boost to continue hiking. Agnolotti (a meat ravioli), braised Piemontese rabbit, and a shared bottle of Barolo, on the other hand, could transform any reserved energy into blissful relaxation and a bus ride back to your accommodations. I Sentieri del Barolo allow wine lovers a chance to walk and breathe among the fruit of their passion and provides a unique opportunity to connect with the origins of some of the world's best wines.

Stuffed Baked Peaches
PESCHE AL FORNO

4 large firm but ripe peaches

3 large egg yolks

½ cup (100 g) granulated sugar

¼ cup (20 g) Dutch-process cocoa powder

¼ cup (20 g) ground amaretti cookies

This is a great dessert for entertaining: The peaches can be prepared ahead of time and then thrown in the oven while your guests linger over dinner. Make sure to use sweet ripe peaches that are still firm enough to retain their shape while baking.

Heat the oven to 375°F (190°C).

Cut the peaches in half and discard the pits. Hollow out some of the flesh and set aside.

In a blender, add the egg yolks, sugar, cocoa powder, amaretti cookies, and reserved peach flesh and puree until well combined.

Stuff the hollowed peaches with the cocoa filling and place on a sheet pan. Bake in the oven for 20 minutes or until tender. Serve warm.

SERVES 8

CHAPTER 5

La Traversina

It's no real wonder that Rosanna Varese and Domenico Puppo's agriturismo has gained international recognition as a unique and charming destination in southern Piemonte. Ivy-covered walls and magnificent flower gardens create a Hansel-and-Gretel atmosphere. English travelers interested in the more than four hundred different varieties of plants and flowers in the gardens especially frequent Traversina. Guests convene for breakfast and dinner in an open room off of the kitchen, sitting at long and narrow old wooden tables. Rosanna and Domenico seat their company by nationality and language, assuring conversation with guests from all over the world. Family-style meals are served in courses, with Rosanna and Domenico joining everybody for dinner. With their dog, Ollie, sleeping under the table and the open kitchen exposed to diners, these casual meals provide a unique opportunity to experience the Italian life of the dinner table.

Rosanna refers to her cooking style as simple, preferring to tend her flowers rather than spend all day in the kitchen. Because of Traversina's close proximity to Liguria, Rosanna's cooking embodies elements from both regions. Domenico's garden provides many of the staples used in her dishes, especially a particular strain of tomato, handed down in Domenico's family for generations and the only one of its kind in all of Italy. Deep red, round, and weighing more than one kilogram on average,

it is distinctive for its incredible strong tomato essence. Domenico proudly claims that its weight is all flavor, without all of the water typical of the fruit. A small variety of local Piemontese wines flows freely through dinner as well. Summer and fall months find rooms at Traversina hard to come by, and the bustling dining room is filled with jovial guests night after night. With different cultures, languages, and people from all parts of the world united and bonded by good food and drink, it is no wonder that Traversina is a special place.

One of the four hundred varieties of flowers at La Traversina

Puff Pastry with Mortadella and String Beans

PASTA SFOGLIA CON MORTADELLA E FAGIOLINI

Creamy, nutmeg-flecked, snow-white béchamel has deep roots in northern Italian cuisine and its use is widespread through every region. This simple dish is a testament to Rosanna's preference for uncomplicated dishes that demand little work in the kitchen, allowing her to spend more time in her garden.

4 ounces (115 g) trimmed string beans

2 ounces (60 g) thinly sliced mortadella

1 recipe béchamel (see page x)

¼ cup grated Parmigiano Reggiano

Kosher salt and freshly ground black pepper

1 pound (450 g) store-bought puff pastry

Bring 4 quarts of salted water to a boil. Add the string beans in the water and cook until tender, 2 to 3 minutes. Drain and submerge in a bowl of ice water. Remove the beans from the water and dry on kitchen towels. Cut the string beans into ¼-inch pieces.

Chop the mortadella very fine and mix with the string beans, béchamel, and Parmigiano Reggiano. Season to taste with salt and pepper.

Heat the oven to 425°F (220°C).

Roll out the puff pastry on a lightly floured surface until ¼ inch thick. Cut into 4-inch rounds using a cookie cutter or glass. Place on a sheet pan lined with parchment paper and prick all over with a fork. Scoop 2 tablespoons of the string bean–béchamel mixture into the center of each round. Bake until puffed and golden brown, about 20 minutes. Remove from the oven and let rest about 10 minutes prior to serving.

SERVES 8

Pasta with Saffron Sauce
PENNE CON SUGO ALLA ZAFFERANO

*Pungent and pricey saffron transforms ordinary pasta into something exquisite,
while gently heating the saffron allows it to infuse and meld with the cream sauce.*

In a 10-inch skillet sauté the onion and the pancetta together, until the onion
becomes tender and the pancetta becomes a little crispy, about 5 minutes.
Add the cream to the pan, along with the saffron, and cook over medium-
low heat, being careful not to boil the cream.

Meanwhile, bring a 6 quart pot of salted water to a boil and cook penne
until al dente, following cooking instructions on the box. Drain the pasta,
toss immediately with the saffron sauce, and add the marjoram. Season to
taste with salt and pepper. Serve with grated Parmigiano Reggiano.

SERVES 4

1 white onion, cut into fine dice

8 ounces (225 g) pancetta, cut into
small dice

1 cup (8 fl. oz. / 240 ml) heavy
cream

2 teaspoons saffron

1 pound (450 g) boxed penne

2 tablespoons chopped marjoram

Kosher salt and freshly ground
pepper

½ cup grated Parmigiano Reggiano

Rosanna cooking dinner

Frozen Chocolate Ricotta Cream Cake
TORTA FREDDA DI RICOTTA AL CIOCCOLATA

5 ounces (145 g) chocolate wafer cookies, preferably Nabisco

²/₃ cup plus 1 tablespoon (120 g) granulated sugar

5 tablespoons (2½ oz. / 75 g) unsalted butter, melted

1 cup (8 fl. oz. / 240 ml) heavy cream

13 ounces (368 g) ricotta

1 tablespoon Dutch-process cocoa powder, plus more for dusting

Ricotta is perhaps the most widely used cheese throughout all of Italy. In this recipe, Rosanna incorporates it into a frozen dessert, proving the versatility of the fresh cheese and its ability to be used in both savory and sweet dishes.

In the bowl of a food processor, pulse the chocolate wafers and 1 tablespoon of sugar into fine crumbs. Add the melted butter and pulse until well combined. Press crumb mixture firmly on the bottom of a 9-inch springform pan.

In the bowl of an electric mixer fitted with the whisk attachment, whip the cream until stiff peaks form. Set aside.

Combine ²/₃ cup sugar, ricotta, and cocoa powder and beat with a hand-held mixer until the mixture is smooth and creamy, about 3 minutes. With a rubber spatula, gently fold the whipped cream into the ricotta mixture.

Pour the ricotta filling evenly over the crumb base, cover with plastic wrap, and place in the freezer for at least three hours.

Remove the dessert from the freezer 15 minutes prior to serving. Release it from the springform pan and lightly dust the top with cocoa powder. Cut into wedges and serve.

SERVES 8–10

Ricotta cake

Tilling the fields

CHAPTER 6
⤷ CA' VILLA ⤶

Marco Villa's agriturismo in the Monferrato region of Piemonte makes trendy boutique hotels in any international city look out of style. An architect for a German firm, Marco has a keen eye for detail, and his design for Ca' Villa makes obvious the amount of time spent restoring the farmhouse and his desire to cater to a sophisticated international crowd. Rustic elements from the 1726 structure—brick vaulted ceilings, exposed knotty hand-hewn beams, and the farm's original cantina—are set against a backdrop of sleek lines, abstract paintings, and modern amenities including a large pool, a red-clay tennis court, and an open patio with huge white umbrellas overlooking rolling hills. Marco's agriturismo offers a haven for tourists seeking a more active holiday, and Ca' Villa's city-chic feel in the bucolic Piemontese countryside creates an idyllic setting of comfort and relaxation.

Marco bought the abandoned building in 1999 and immediately planted hazelnut trees, hoping to restore the villa into an agriturismo one day. Six years later, with a bountiful hazelnut production, a completely renovated farmhouse, and a top-notch chef, Ca' Villa opened its doors for business.

For Marco, finding a chef who shared a similar vision for the agriturismo was vital. When long-time friend Franco Piumatti, a native of the Langhe, closed his restaurant in nearby Alba, Marco knew he was a perfect fit for the type of cuisine he aspired to serve in his restaurant. With a deep respect for the traditional classics of his region and an intense passion for innovation, Franco has a unique approach to cooking. In his updated, modernized kitchen, Franco shines, using cutting-edge appliances to prepare time-honored dishes. While Franco incorporates as much of the farm's own honey, hazelnuts, fruit, and vegetables as he can into his creations, he fiercely insists on sourcing only the absolute best ingredients from his native region. Rather than braising meats slowly in a covered pot on the stove, Franco puts his fancy technological oven to work, sealing meats in a vacuum sealer and then placing them in an extremely low oven for hours, resulting in a melt-in-your-mouth texture packed with flavor. Current with food trends from all over the world, Franco makes a Moscato wine gelée, which he uses to garnish a caramelized red-onion risotto. His single large raviolo with a runny egg yolk tucked into a spinach and ricotta filling exemplifies his pasta-making skills and always receives rave reviews from the dining room. Marco and Franco's forward-thinking approach and inventive ways keep Ca' Villa at the forefront of progressive trends, yet their respect for the historic past and the roots of their culture ensures the farm's warmth and charm.

Eggplant and Yellow Pepper Terrine
TERRINA DI MELANZANE E PEPERONI GIALLI

This terrine exhibits the fresh flavors of the Italian summer bounty. The grilled eggplant lends a smoky taste that rounds out the sweetness of the pepper puree. Once cut into slices, the terrine's layering of colors is as pleasant to the eye as to the palate.

3 yellow bell peppers

¼ cup (2 fl. oz. / 60 ml) extra-virgin olive oil

2 eggplants (aubergines), cut into lengthwise strips

Kosher salt and freshly ground black pepper

1 large egg

1 cup ricotta

½ cup chopped basil

1 cup grated Parmigiano Reggiano

Heat the oven to 425°F (220°C). Rub the peppers with 2 tablespoons olive oil and roast in the oven until tender, about 30 minutes, flipping the peppers over halfway through the cooking time. Immediately place in a plastic bag and seal. Let rest 20 minutes. Reduce the oven temperature to 375°F (190°C)

Heat the grill to medium heat. Brush eggplant strips with the remaining olive oil and sprinkle with salt and pepper. Grill until tender, about 4 minutes per side.

Peel the skins off the peppers and remove the seeds. In a food processor, puree the peppers, egg, ricotta, basil, and Parmigiano Reggiano until smooth and thick. Season to taste with salt and pepper.

Line a 9 × 5 × 3-inch loaf pan with enough parchment paper to fold over the top (it is easiest if you dampen the paper) and then place a layer of eggplant strips to cover the bottom. Add a thin layer of the pepper puree, and alternate between layers of eggplant and pepper puree, ending with the pepper puree.

Meanwhile, bring 4 cups of water to a boil. Fold the top of the parchment paper over the terrine, and place in a 9 × 13-inch baking dish. Put the baking dish in the oven, and pour the hot water into the dish until it reaches half way up the loaf pan side. Bake the terrine until the filling is slightly puffed and set, about 55 minutes. Let the terrine cool completely in the water bath, peel back the parchment paper, and invert onto a large plate. Carefully lift pan away from the terrine.

Cut the terrine into ¼-inch-thick slices and serve at room temperature.

SERVES 6

Carpaccio with Gorgonzola Sauce, Pears, and Walnuts

CARPACCIO CON GORGONZOLA, PERE E NOCI

The Gorgonzola cheese sauce gives a classic dish a new twist. Served alongside the pear salad, the carpaccio makes a great appetizer for fall and winter months. It is essential to purchase fresh, quality meat from a reputable butcher for this recipe.

Wrap the filet in plastic wrap and place in the freezer for at least 1 hour, until it is nice and firm. With a very sharp carving knife, slice the meat as thin as you can get it, about ⅛ inch thick. Place the slices between two pieces of plastic wrap and gently pound with a mallet until the meat is as thin as possible, almost translucent. (Alternatively, have your butcher cut it on a slicer.)

Mix the pears together with a teaspoon of lemon juice, the walnuts, and a pinch each of salt and pepper.

Use a double boiler to combine the Gorgonzola and mascarpone. Stir until the cheese has melted, and thin with the milk.

Lay three slices of the carpaccio on each serving plate, brush lightly with olive oil, drizzle with the remaining teaspoon of lemon juice and season lightly with salt and pepper. Place 2 tablespoons of the pear and walnut mixture in the center of each plate and drizzle lightly with the Gorgonzola sauce.

SERVES 6

12 ounces (340 g) filet mignon or 2 ounces (60 g) per person

2 pears, peeled, cored, and cut into ¼-inch dice

2 teaspoons lemon juice (10 ml)

½ cup chopped walnuts

Kosher salt and freshly ground black pepper

2 ounces (60 g) Gorgonzola

4 ounces (115 g) mascarpone

2 tablespoons (1 fl. oz. / 30 ml) whole milk

2 tablespoons (1 fl. oz. / 30 ml) extra-virgin olive oil

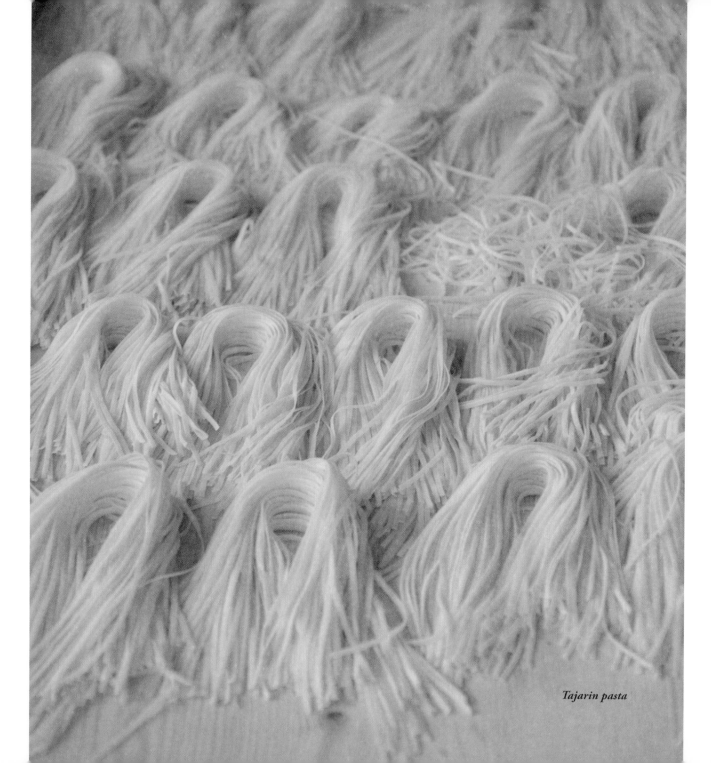

Tajarin pasta

Tajarin with Sunchoke, Leek, and Sausage

TAJARIN CON SUGO DI TOPINAMBUR, PORRI,
E SALSICCIA

Tajarin is a delicacy from Piedmont; the rich egg-yolk pasta at one time symbol-
ized wealth. Today it is often accompanied by shavings of the prized white truffle,
but Chef Franco dresses his pasta with a leek, sunchoke, and sausage ragu. If
time is an issue, a store-bought fresh tagliatelle complements the sauce and can
substitute for the fresh tajarin.

Make a well in the flour and add the egg yolks, eggs, pinch of salt, and olive
oil to the center. With a fork, lightly beat the eggs and then gradually pull
the flour into the egg mixture. Mix the flour and eggs together until well
combined. Knead dough until it becomes smooth and elastic. Cover the
dough and let rest for 1 hour.

Using a pasta machine, prepare the dough. Cut the dough into 6 pieces
and cover with a towel. Pass one piece at a time through the pasta machine.
Starting on the widest setting, pass the dough through the pasta machine several times until the dough is smooth and elastic. Lower the setting on the
pasta machine one notch at a time and pass dough through twice on each
setting, finishing on the last (thinnest) setting. Lay the dough on a flat surface
sprinkled lightly with flour and let the dough dry slightly. It should still be a
little tacky and pliable or it will not cut properly. Pass the dough through the
tagliatelle cutter on the pasta machine. Place the cut pasta on a sheet pan or
rack and twist into little nests. Leave to dry at least 1 hour prior to cooking.

Melt 2 tablespoons of butter with 1 tablespoon olive oil in a 10-inch
sauté pan over low heat and add leeks. Cover the pan and cook leeks slowly,
stirring occasionally until very tender, about 45 minutes.

In a separate 12-inch sauté pan, melt 2 tablespoons butter over medium-
high heat and cook the sunchokes until browned but still retaining some

Pasta

2 3/4 cups (500 g) semolina flour

15 large egg yolks, plus 2 large eggs

Kosher salt

1/2 tablespoon (1/4 fl. oz. / 7.5 ml)
extra-virgin olive oil

Sauce

4 tablespoons (2 oz. / 45 g)
unsalted butter

1 tablespoon (1/2 fl. oz. / 15 ml)
extra-virgin olive oil

5 leeks, cleaned and cut into thin
slices

12 ounces (340 g) sunchokes
(Jerusalem artichokes), scrubbed
and cut into medium dice

4 ounces (115 g) pancetta, cut into
fine dice

1 pound (450 g) sweet pork sausage, removed from casing

1/2 cup (4 fl. oz. / 120 ml) white vermouth

8 ounces (225 g) cherry tomatoes,
cut into quarters

Kosher salt and freshly ground black
pepper

1 cup (8 fl. oz. / 240 ml) homemade chicken broth (see page
   xi) or canned low-sodium broth,
   warmed
1 pound (450 g) tajarin pasta

crunch. Add a tablespoon of water to the pan if it becomes too dry. Remove sunchokes from the pan and set aside.

Add the pancetta and the sausage to the pan and cook over medium-high heat until the meat browns. Add the vermouth and cook until reduced to dry. Add the leeks to the pan with the sausage mixture along with, the cherry tomatoes, season with salt and pepper to taste, and cook about 5 minutes. Add the chicken broth and the sunchokes to the pan and cook another 5 minutes.

Bring 6 quarts of salted water to a boil. Add the pasta into the water, and stir to prevent the pasta from sticking or clumping together. Cook the pasta at a rolling boil until tender, 2 to 3 minutes. Drain well and toss immediately with sauce.

SERVES 6–8

SUNCHOKES

Marco and Franco host special dinners throughout the year, focusing on a particular specialty of the area and serving five-course dinners paired with wines, all centered around one ingredient. On one occasion they used a tuber called the topinambur (sunchoke, or Jerusalem artichoke). In the late summer, yellow flowers sprout throughout Ca' Villa's fields signifying the arrival of the sunchoke, which grows beneath the ground. Franco highlighted the artichoke-like flavor of the root vegetable in every course, including ravioli with a sunchoke filling and a rolled and roasted rabbit stuffed with sunchokes and white truffles.

Risotto with Caramelized Onions and Gorgonzola

RISOTTO CON CIPOLLE CARAMELLATE E GORGONZOLA

On the vast plains of the Po River Valley, fields of Arborio, Carnaroli, and Vialone rice flourish. These rices are used primarily for making risotto. Sweet red onions caramelized in port and the Gorgonzola cheese that melts into this risotto at the end create a true gastronomic delight.

6 tablespoons (3 oz. / 90 g) unsalted butter

3 thinly sliced red onions

Kosher salt and freshly ground black pepper

1 cup (8 fl. oz. / 240 ml) ruby port

1 medium yellow onion, cut into fine dice

2 cups Arborio rice

½ cup (4 fl. oz. / 120 ml) dry vermouth or white wine

1 quart (32 fl. oz. / 960 ml) homemade chicken broth (see page xi) or canned low-sodium broth

¼ cup grated Parmigiano Reggiano

4 ounces (115 g) crumbled Gorgonzola

In a heavy 10-inch sauté pan, melt 3 tablespoons of butter over medium heat. Add the red onions and stir to coat with the butter. Cook for about 5 minutes to let soften. Sprinkle with a pinch of salt, cover the pan, and reduce the heat to low. Continue to cook for about 30 minutes, stirring occasionally. Raise the heat to medium-high and add the port. Simmer the onions and let the port reduce until completely dry, about 25 more minutes.

Meanwhile, make the risotto. In a heavy 12-inch straight-sided sauté pan, add 2 tablespoons of butter and the yellow onion and sauté over medium heat until the onion is tender and translucent but not browned, 8 to 10 minutes. Add the rice and stir to coat the rice with the butter. Cook the rice until opaque, 2 to 3 minutes. Add the vermouth, and let reduce until dry.

Heat the chicken broth in a small saucepan, almost to a boil. Add the broth, one ladle at a time, to the risotto, stirring constantly with a wooden spoon until the broth has been completely absorbed by the rice. Continue to ladle broth into the risotto in the same manner, one ladle at a time, and continue stirring until the rice is al dente and creamy, about 15 minutes.

Stir in the remaining tablespoon of butter, the Parmigiano Reggiano, and the caramelized onions.

To serve, spoon the risotto into shallow bowls and sprinkle the top with the Gorgonzola cheese.

SERVES 6–8

Spinach, Ricotta, and Egg Yolk Raviolo
RAVIOLO BERGESE

6 ounces (170 g) spinach

10 tablespoons (5 oz. / 130 g) unsalted butter

Kosher salt and freshly ground black pepper

8 ounces (225 g) ricotta

¼ cup grated Parmigiano Reggiano, plus more for garnish

¼ teaspoon freshly grated nutmeg

1 teaspoon lemon zest

1 recipe basic pasta dough

12 jumbo egg yolks, egg whites reserved

Franco pays homage to the late great Italian chef Nino Bergese, aptly naming this dish after him. Spinach and ricotta cheese are combined to make a border for the jumbo-size egg yolk that takes center stage in this oversized raviolo. The pasta is cooked very gently, so the yolk is soft and runny when cut into, blending harmoniously with the butter sauce.

Remove the tough stems from spinach and clean by rinsing in cold water. In a 12-inch sauté pan over medium heat, melt 2 tablespoons of butter; add the spinach and cover to wilt, 3 to 5 minutes. Remove the cover and let the spinach dry out a little, then season with ½ teaspoon salt and ¼ teaspoon pepper.

In the bowl of a food processor, combine the ricotta, Parmigiano Reggiano, nutmeg, lemon zest, spinach, and a pinch each of salt and pepper, and puree until smooth. Fill a pastry bag fitted with a round tip with the ricotta mixture.

Making raviolo

Raviolo ready for cooking

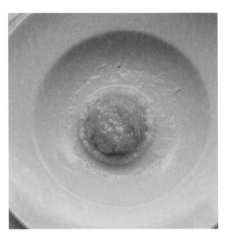
Plated raviolo

Divide the dough into 4 pieces. Using a pasta machine, roll the dough out, starting at the widest setting and ending with the second to thinnest setting. Lay out one sheet of pasta and pipe the ricotta mixture into circles on the dough, 1 inch wide and ½ inch tall. Place one egg yolk in the center of each ricotta circle. With a pastry brush, brush egg white onto the dough around the filling. Use another sheet of dough to cover the egg yolk and ricotta filling, being careful not to break the yolk. Press the dough together and make sure to remove all air from inside. Cut out the ravioli with a round fluted cookie cutter.

Bring 6 quarts of salted water to a soft boil. Gently place the ravioli in the boiling water, cook for 3 minutes, and then remove with a slotted spoon. Reserve ¼ cup of the pasta water.

In a 2- or 3-quart saucepan, melt the remaining 8 tablespoons butter until it begins to foam. Whisk in the reserved pasta water and cook for 1 minute to emulsify the liquids.

Place one raviolo on each individual plate, drizzle with the butter sauce, and sprinkle with grated Parmigiano Reggiano. Serve immediately.

YIELDS 12

Lemon Chicken

POLLO AL LIMONE

3/4 cup (6 fl. oz. / 180 ml) lemon juice

1/2 cup (4 fl. oz. / 120 ml) extra-virgin olive oil

1 pound (450 g) chicken tenders

Kosher salt and freshly ground black pepper

All-purpose flour, for dredging

3 tablespoons (1½ oz. / 45 g) unsalted butter

5 anchovy fillets

1 tablespoon (10 g) capers

1 tablespoon chopped flat-leaf parsley

Plain chicken tenders get a big flavor kick after a soak in a lemon marinade, while anchovies and capers make a pungent sauce, which dresses up the white meat.

In a medium-size bowl, whisk together the lemon juice and olive oil. Add the chicken tenders to the bowl, cover with plastic wrap, and marinate in the refrigerator for 8 hours.

Remove the chicken from the bowl and reserve the marinade. Season the chicken with 1 teaspoon salt and ¼ teaspoon pepper and dredge in the flour to coat evenly, shake off any excess flour.

Melt the butter in a 12-inch skillet over medium-high heat. Once it begins to foam, cook the chicken until rich golden brown, 4 to 5 minutes per side. Remove the chicken from the pan and place on a serving platter. Add the anchovies, capers, and reserved marinade to the pan and cook 2 to 3 minutes. Drizzle the sauce over the chicken tenders and garnish with parsley.

SERVES 4

Stuffed Veal Rolls
ROLLATINI DI VITELLO

Stracchino, a soft, mild cow's-milk cheese, is easily spreadable and used as a filling for many Italian specialties. Here the cheese is added to the filling for the veal and then whisked into the sauce at the end to add body. If stracchino is unavailable, substitute quark or any other soft, pliable cow's-milk cheese.

Heat oven to 425°F (220°C).

Place veal on a flat surface and season with salt and pepper. Place a piece of prosciutto down on each piece of veal, followed by a dollop of stracchino cheese, spreading the cheese out with a knife. (Reserve 2 tablespoons cheese.) Fold the sides of the veal in toward the center, then roll veal up lengthwise. Tie the bundle with kitchen string. Continue with the remaining veal pieces.

Heat the olive oil in a 12-inch sauté pan over medium-high heat. Dredge the veal rolls in flour, shaking off any excess flour, and sear the veal on all sides, until golden brown, 3 to 4 minutes. Remove the veal from the pan and set aside on a plate. Add the garlic and bay leaves to the pan and sauté until the garlic is golden brown, 1 to 2 minutes. Add the white wine and let reduce by half. Return the veal to the pan and place in the oven to finish cooking, 5 to 7 minutes.

Remove veal from oven and place on a serving platter, snipping the kitchen string. Strain the pan juices through a fine mesh sieve into a small saucepan. Place over medium heat and bring up to a boil. Whisk in reserved stracchino cheese until smooth. Spoon the sauce over the veal rolls and serve immediately.

SERVES 4–6

12 veal scallops (about 1½ pounds, 675 g), pounded out ⅛ inch thick

Kosher salt and freshly ground black pepper

8 ounces (225 g) thinly sliced prosciutto di Parma

8 ounces (225 g) stracchino cheese

2 tablespoons (1 fl. oz. / 30 ml) extra-virgin olive oil

All-purpose flour, for dredging

2 peeled and sliced cloves of garlic

3 bay leaves

1 cup (8 fl. oz. / 240 ml) dry white wine

Roasted Pork Tenderloin with Grape Sauce
FILETTO DI MAIALE CON SUGO D'UVA

Piemontese grapes tend to go toward making one thing: wine. But here the sweet delicate flavors of the grapes pair perfectly with the tenderness of the pork. Just don't forget to pair it with a crisp white wine.

4 tablespoons (2 oz. / 60 g) unsalted butter

1 tablespoon (½ fl. oz. / 15 ml) extra-virgin olive oil

2 pork tenderloins, 1–1 ¼ pounds (500–750 g) each

Kosher salt and freshly ground black pepper

1 cup (6 oz. / 168 g) red or green grapes (or a mixture of the two), cut into quarters

1 tablespoon honey mustard

1 tablespoon (½ fl. oz. / 15 ml) warm water

1 tablespoon chopped thyme

Heat the oven to 350°F (180°C).

In a large ovenproof sauté pan, heat 2 tablespoons of butter with 1 tablespoon oil over medium-high heat. Season the pork tenderloins with salt and pepper. Sear the pork on one side until golden brown, about 5 minutes, then flip over. Place a few pats of butter on top of pork and finish cooking in the oven, 25 to 30 minutes, or until a meat thermometer reads 140°F (60°C). Remove pork from the oven and place on a cutting board. Let the meat rest for 15 minutes.

Meanwhile, make the sauce: Place the sauté pan, with the juice from the pork, back over medium heat. Add the grapes, and a pinch of salt and sauté until they release their juices, 3 to 5 minutes. Add the mustard, warm water, and thyme to the pan and cook 1 minute. Season to taste with salt and pepper.

Cut the pork into medallions, and spoon the grape sauce over the pork. Serve immediately.

SERVES 4–6

Plated dish: pork with grapes

Chocolate Hazelnut Soufflé
SUFFLÈ DI CIOCCOLATO E NOCCIOLA

Hazelnuts are the chief agricultural product at Ca' Villa and chocolate and hazelnuts are a heavenly match, especially when they are used to make a billowy soufflé.

7 tablespoons (3½ oz. / 100 g) unsalted butter, at room temperature

⅔ cup (130 g) superfine sugar (castor sugar)

3½ ounces (100 g) toasted hazelnuts, peeled

2 eggs, at room temperature, separated

Table salt

3½ ounces (100 g) high-quality bittersweet chocolate

Vanilla ice cream, for serving

Heat the oven to 425°F (220°C). Prepare 5 individual ramekins by buttering them and then sprinkling the bottom and sides with a little bit of sugar.

Puree the hazelnuts with 2 tablespoons (28 g) of sugar until they form fine crumbs.

With an electric mixer, whip egg whites and a pinch of salt until soft peaks form. Gradually add 1 tablespoon (14 g) of sugar and continue to whip until stiff peaks form, being careful not to overbeat the egg whites.

Cut the chocolate into small, equal-size pieces and place in the bowl of a double boiler (bain-marie) until melted. Remove from heat and set aside to cool.

In a large mixing bowl, beat the remaining ½ cup (90 g) sugar with the egg yolks until pale yellow and very thick, 2 to 4 minutes. Add the butter and continue to beat until fully combined. Gradually add the ground hazelnuts and continue to beat together until incorporated. Gently stir in the chocolate.

Gently fold the egg whites into the chocolate-hazelnut mixture in three additions. Pour the batter into the prepared ramekins, until about three-quarters full.

Lower the oven to 175°F (80°C) and bake the soufflés for 30 minutes, or until they have risen above the ramekin rims and have set. Serve immediately with a scoop of vanilla ice cream.

SERVES 5

Chocolate hazelnut soufflé

La Quercia Rossa landscape

CHAPTER 7

La Quercia Rossa

A working farm since the 1700s, Quercia Rossa prides itself on its agrarian principles. Today it is run by Laura Vigone, her son Matteo, and her brothers and sisters. Wine and hazelnuts are the chief products, with rows of vines intermixed with hazelnut groves extending into a broad valley beneath the agriturismo. Guests at the farm are encouraged to help with the harvests, fulfilling anyone's dream of picking grapes at an Italian vineyard. For those preferring not to get their hands dirty, small wooden tables are scattered about the property, perfect for sharing one of Quercia Rossa's wines and taking in a landscape of gentle hill-like waves of churned dirt intermixed with verdant green fields and farmland.

Quercia Rossa offers a level of service unique to agriturismo dining. Long, elaborate dinners take center stage for an entire evening of dining at an unhurried pace. Matteo presents diners each course from a wooden cart he wheels out of the kitchen. Guests are served heaping portions of pasta from large sauté pans, with blocks of Parmesan at every table for grating. Meat courses are carved tableside by Matteo, who proposes a pairing of one of Quercia Rossa's seven types of wine. A vegetable cart follows with salad and an array of the farm's vegeta- bles, often grilled and marinated with Ligurian olive oil specially made for the farm. Dessert abounds with sinful delights, with the cart piled high with an abundance of homemade cakes, tortes, and puddings.

The home-style cooking of Quercia Rossa comes from an all-women kitchen spanning generations. At first glance, Teresa, the main cook, embodies the stereo-typical strong Italian female chef, hardened by years of strenuous work feeding the masses. But after working in her kitchen, you see that she exudes a sweet humble-ness beneath the facade, which lends itself to her style of cooking. With patience and utmost care, she crafts agnolotti (a type of small ravioli filled with white ragu), braises pork shoulder in red wine until it's meltingly ten-der, and breaks down a rabbit for stew in seconds flat. In addition to preparing for dinner, the kitchen keeps busy making products to sell in the farm store. Quercia Rossa's abundance of hazelnuts led Laura and Teresa to develop a secret recipe for chocolate spread that surpasses any other Italian chocolate-hazelnut condiment on the market. As generous as the two may be, they are unwilling to part with their recipe, so anyone wishing to indulge in this treat must visit the agriturismo personally.

Grapes ready for crushing (right)
Grape harvest (below)

Stuffed Zucchini Flowers
FIORI DI ZUCCA RIPIENI

Zucchini flowers are often served stuffed with a host of different ingredients and fried until crisp and golden brown. At Quercia Rossa, the cooks use a rich stuffing of prosciutto and zucchini and flatten the flowers as they fry to make them extra crispy.

Rinse the zucchini flowers in cold water and remove the stems from the bottoms and insides of the flowers.

Sauté the zucchini in an 8-inch skillet with the olive oil until tender, 6 to 8 minutes. Let cool slightly.

Make the stuffing by mixing together the prosciutto, the Parmigiano Reggiano, ½ cup bread crumbs, 1 egg, the zucchini, and the melted butter and season with salt and pepper.

Stuff each zucchini flower with 1 tablespoon of filling and gently press down to flatten.

Gently beat the remaining 2 eggs in a small bowl. Dip the zucchini flowers into the eggs and then coat with the remaining ¾ cup bread crumbs.

Heat the oven to a 200°F (90°C). In a 10- or 12-inch skillet, heat the canola or vegetable oil over medium-high heat until shimmering. Add the zucchini flowers, in batches, and fry on both sides until deep golden brown, 2 to 3 minutes per side. Remove to a sheet pan lined with paper towels and keep warm in the oven while you fry the remaining flowers. Serve warm.

SERVES 6

12 large zucchini flowers

1 small zucchini (courgette), cut into fine dice

1 tablespoon (½ fl. oz. / 15 ml) extra-virgin olive oil

2 ounces (60 g) minced prosciutto

¼ cup grated Parmigiano Reggiano

1¼ cups (185 g) bread crumbs

3 large eggs

2 tablespoons (1 oz. / 30 g) unsalted butter, melted

Kosher salt and freshly ground pepper

1 cup (8 fl. oz. / 240 ml) canola or vegetable oil

Penne with Roasted Pepper Sauce
PENNE CON SUGO DI PEPERONI

This creamy roasted pepper sauce has only the slightest hint of cream. It gets its richness from the pureed peppers.

2 yellow bell peppers

2 red bell peppers

2 tablespoons (1 fl. oz. / 30 ml) extra-virgin olive oil, plus more for brushing

2 peeled cloves of garlic

1 pound (450 g) boxed penne

¼ cup (2 fl. oz. / 60 ml) heavy cream

Kosher salt and freshly ground pepper

1 tablespoon minced oregano

¼ cup grated Parmigiano Reggiano

Heat an oven to 425°F (220°C). Brush peppers with olive oil and roast in oven until tender, about 30 minutes, turning halfway through the cooking time. Place immediately in a plastic bag and let rest 20 minutes. Peel peppers, remove seeds, and cut into thin slices.

In a 10-inch sauté pan heat 2 tablespoons olive oil and sauté garlic until golden brown. Add the peppers and cook for about 5 minutes to combine the flavors.

Bring 6 quarts of salted water to a boil. Cook the pasta, following the instructions on the box, until al dente, then drain in a colander.

Meanwhile, puree the peppers in a food processor or blender and return to the sauté pan. Add the cream, season with salt and pepper to taste, and heat the sauce through. Toss the pasta with the sauce and sprinkle with oregano and Parmigiano Reggiano. Serve immediately.

SERVES 6

Pork Braised in Red Wine
STRACOTTO DI MAIALE

Stracotto, which translates as "overcooked," refers to a cooking method in which tougher cuts of meat are slowly braised in red wine. Stracotto is most commonly made with beef, but at Quercia Rossa the cooks prefer to use pork from local pigs. They marinate the pork butt overnight in house-made Barbera wine and then use it as the braising liquid, creating a meltingly tender and flavorful dish.

Rinse the pork and pat dry. Season the pork generously with salt and pepper.

In a large casserole pan, combine the vegetables, herbs, pork, and wine and let marinate at least 8 hours (and up to 24 hours) in the refrigerator, covered. Turn meat halfway through marinating time.

Remove the pork from the refrigerator and let sit for 1 hour to bring up to room temperature. Place pan on the stove over medium-high heat. Bring the contents up to a boil, reduce heat to low, and cook at a gentle simmer for about 2 hours, or until the pork is fork-tender.

Remove the meat from the pan and place on a cutting board. Remove the bay leaves from the pan and continue cooking to reduce the liquid by half. Puree the vegetables in a blender with the liquid to finish the sauce, and season to taste with salt and pepper. Slice the meat and drizzle with the sauce.

SERVES 4

3½ pounds (1 kg / 586 g) Boston butt or pork shoulder

Kosher salt and freshly ground black pepper

1 onion, cut into medium dice

1 stalk celery, cut into medium dice

1 carrot, peeled and cut into medium dice

¼ cup chopped flat-leaf parsley

2 bay leaves

2 tablespoons chopped thyme

1 bottle (750 ml) Barbera wine or other full-bodied red wine

Braised Duck Legs
COSCIA D'ANATRA

Teresa uses both the breasts and legs for this recipe, but we have had better success with the legs. The dark meat can stand up to long cooking times without drying out, and it's a refreshing alternative to the ubiquitous chicken.

4 large duck legs (about 8 oz. each / 900 g)

1 tablespoon chopped rosemary

1 tablespoon chopped basil

1 tablespoon chopped sage

3 bay leaves, chopped fine

Kosher salt and freshly ground pepper

8 thin slices pancetta

2 tablespoons (1 fl. oz. / 30 ml) extra-virgin olive oil

1 medium yellow onion, cut into small dice

2 stalks celery, cut into small dice

2 carrots, peeled and cut into small dice

1 cup (8 fl. oz. / 240 ml) white wine

2 cups (16 fl. oz. / 480 ml) home-made chicken broth (see page xiii) or canned low-sodium broth, plus a little more, if needed

Heat the oven to 375°F (190°C).

Rinse duck legs and pat dry with paper towels. Place duck legs skin side down on a cutting board and trim the legs of excess fat. Butterfly and bone the legs, trying to keep the meat intact, and gently pound out with a meat mallet. (Alternatively, have your butcher debone the legs.)

Combine the chopped herbs. Season the duck legs with salt and pepper, sprinkle each with 1 teaspoon of the herb mixture, and then place 2 slices of pancetta on the legs over the herb mixture. (Reserve some herb mixture for garnish.) Roll the duck legs up lengthwise and tie with kitchen string. Season the bundles with salt and pepper.

Heat a heavy casserole pan over medium heat. Add the duck bundles and cook slowly to render some of the fat, about 10 minutes per side. Remove duck bundles from pan, place on a dish, and drain off all but 1 tablespoon of the duck fat from the pan.

Add olive oil, onion, celery, carrots, and a pinch of salt to the casserole pan and cook over medium heat, until the vegetables are tender. Raise the heat to high and add the white wine, scraping up any browned bits from the pan with a wooden spoon. Add the chicken broth and bring up to a boil. Return the duck bundles to the pan, cover tightly, and place in the oven. Cook until the legs are tender, 1½ to 2 hours. Remove from the oven and set duck bundles aside and let rest for 15 minutes.

Meanwhile, puree the contents of the casserole pan in a blender, adding a little more broth if necessary. Season to taste with salt and pepper.

Remove the kitchen string from the duck bundles and carve the duck into thin slices. Fan out over individual plates, drizzle with sauce, and sprinkle with a pinch of the fresh herb mixture.

SERVES 4

Plucking feathers from duck breast

Stuffed duck with pancetta

Braised Rabbit with Stewed Peppers
CONIGLIO CON PEPERONATA

Sweet late-summer red and yellow peppers bring out the best in this dish. Stewed in tomatoes and onion, they make a perfect bed for braised rabbit drizzled with a white wine sauce.

2 rabbits, (about 2 pounds each / 900 g each) cut into 8 pieces each, saving organs

1 tablespoon (½ fl. oz. / 15 ml) white wine vinegar

2 cups (16 fl. oz. / 480 ml) cold water

Kosher salt and freshly ground pepper

5 tablespoons (3 fl. oz. / 75 ml) extra-virgin olive oil

1 tablespoon chopped rosemary

1 tablespoon chopped sage

1 tablespoon ground bay leaves, plus 3 whole bay leaves

1 medium yellow onion, cut into fine dice

1 stalk celery, cut into fine dice

1 carrot, peeled and cut into fine dice

1 cup (8 fl. oz. / 240 ml) white wine

1 cup (8 fl. oz. / 240 ml) homemade chicken broth (see page xi) or canned low-sodium broth

Place the rabbit pieces in a large bowl. Add the white wine vinegar and cover with the cold water. Let rest for about 10 minutes. Drain rabbit and pat pieces dry with a paper towel.

Season the rabbit pieces with salt, pepper, 2 tablespoons olive oil, and the chopped herbs. In a heavy casserole pan, heat the remaining 3 tablespoons of olive oil over medium-high heat. Add the rabbit in batches and brown on all sides, 8 to 10 minutes. Remove rabbit from pan and set aside.

Lower the heat to medium and add the onion and 3 bay leaves to the pan. Sauté until the onions begin to tenderize, about 7 minutes. Add the carrot and celery to the pan and continue to cook until tender and lightly browned, about 10 minutes.

Raise the heat to high, add the white wine, and simmer until reduced by half. Add the chicken broth and bring to a boil. Add the rabbit pieces and reserved organs, reduce the heat to low, cover, and simmer until the rabbit is tender, about 40 minutes.

Meanwhile, prepare the peperonata: In a large sauté pan, combine 2 tablespoons of olive oil and the onion and cook over low heat until tender and beginning to brown, about 20 minutes. Add the garlic and the pepper strips and cook for another 15 minutes. Add the crushed tomatoes and vegetable broth and cook for another 15 minutes. Season to taste with salt and pepper and add the fresh basil leaves.

Remove rabbit from the casserole pan and set aside on a plate. In a blender or with a handheld immersion blender, puree the contents of the casserole pan until smooth to make the sauce.

Spoon the peperonata onto a large serving platter, place the rabbit pieces over the peppers, and drizzle with the sauce.

SERVES 6

For the peperonata

2 tablespoons (1 fl. oz. / 30 ml) extra-virgin olive oil

1 large sweet yellow onion, cut into thin slices

2 peeled and sliced cloves of garlic

2 yellow bell peppers, cut into 1/4-inch strips

2 red bell peppers, cut into 1/4-inch strips

1 1/2 cups crushed tomatoes

1/2 cup (4 fl. oz. / 120 ml) vegetable broth (see page xii) or water

Kosher salt and freshly ground black pepper

1/4 cup torn basil leaves

Meringue
MERINGATA

3 large egg whites

1 cup (200 g) granulated sugar

Pinch of table salt

1 teaspoon (5 ml) vanilla extract

1 cup (8 fl. oz. / 240 ml) heavy cream

Every night at Quercia Rossa, a dessert cart loaded with sweets makes its way around the dining room. It has become a favorite among locals, who come for the variety and abundance of tempting treats, which Laura changes frequently. One staple, however, is her meringata, whose light pillowy whipped cream and crunchy meringue cookie bits have everyone taking second helpings.

Heat the oven to 200°F (90°C). Line a sheet pan with parchment paper.

Place the egg whites, sugar, and salt in the bowl of an electric mixer and set over a pan of gently simmering water. Whisk the egg whites until the sugar dissolves and the egg whites start to thicken, 2 to 4 minutes. Attach the bowl to the mixer, fit it with the whip attachment, and beat on medium-high speed until soft peaks form. Gradually add the vanilla, and continue to whip until stiff peaks form.

Place the meringue in a pastry bag fitted with a ½-inch round tip and pipe 2-inch rounds onto the parchment-lined sheet pan. Bake for 1½ to 2 hours, or until the meringues are pale in color and fairly crisp. Turn off the oven, open the door a crack, and leave the meringues in the oven to finish drying overnight. Roughly chop the meringues into medium-size pieces.

In the bowl of an electric mixer fitted with the whip attachment, beat the whipped cream into stiff peaks.

Spoon a layer of whipped cream into the bottom of 8 individual ramekins. Add a layer of meringue pieces and then top with another layer of whipped cream. Sprinkle the tops with a tablespoon each of meringue pieces and chill in the refrigerator until ready to serve.

SERVES 8

CHAPTER 8
⚜ LA MINIERA ⚜

We decided to visit La Miniera because we knew that it would be an unusual experience in Piemonte, if not in all of Italy. Run by a Jewish couple that is proud of its Jewish-Italian heritage, La Miniera serves an authentic cuisine that represents a very small minority of the country's population. Roberta Ana and her husband purchased a once-thriving mineral mine in the Piemontese hills in 1991. They slowly restored the mine into a working farm, transforming the rocky soil into vegetable gardens, planting several varieties of fruit trees around the property, and building a small pen for raising animals. Today, guests sleep in the former workers' dorms and eat meals in the house where the mine director lived and had his office. The farm's unique history, as well as a cuisine not easily found in the rest of Italy, make La Miniera a destination for those seeking an alternative getaway in northern Piemonte.

Meals are enjoyed in a tiny dining room in a house filled with paintings, photographs, and nature sculptures. It is evident where Roberta's passion lies, and her cooking reflects her unyielding love for all things wild. An active voice in preserving her culture, Roberta has published cookbooks about the cuisine that is both rooted in Jewish heritage and adapted to the Italian philosophy of seasonality and availability. Her food primarily utilizes the bounty of her garden, with vegetables prepared in countless manners, placating any carnivore's palate

Autumn squash

with their complex flavors. Course upon course of vegetable sformati, purees, salads, and soups parade out of La Miniera's kitchen. Couscous replaces the ubiquitous pasta and is a refreshingly light course when mixed with vegetables and served at room temperature in summer months. Fowl, including duck, turkey, and goose, are La Miniera's primary meats, and a cured goose "prosciutto" is one of Roberta's specialties. Desserts always highlight the fruit grown around the farm, such as giant blueberries, linden berries, cherries, kiwis, and fresh purple and green figs, which grow everywhere on the property. Meals at La Miniera offer the opportunity to savor foods practically impossible to find outside of private homes in Italy, and they embody a cuisine created through religion by a people preserving the traditions of their lost homeland.

Eggplant Turnovers
BOREKITAS

The dough for these turnovers is simple to make and easy to roll out, making the turnovers a great addition to your repertoire of finger foods. Serve these as a snack for your family or as a hors d'oeuvre at your next gathering.

Dough

¼ cup (2 fl. oz. / 60 ml) canola oil

¼ cup (2 fl. oz. / 60 ml) water

1¼ cups (175 g) all-purpose flour

Kosher salt

Filling

1 large eggplant (aubergine)

¼ cup (2 fl. oz. / 60 ml) olive oil

1 peeled and sliced clove of garlic

Kosher salt and freshly ground
    pepper

2½ ounces (70 g) crumbled feta
    cheese

1 tablespoon grated Parmigiano
    Reggiano

2 tablespoons chopped thyme

Pinch of crushed red pepper flakes

1 large egg yolk, beaten

1 tablespoon (15 g) sesame seeds

Make the dough: Stir together the oil and water in a medium-size bowl and then gradually mix in the flour and a pinch of salt. Stir the dough until it comes together and then gently knead until smooth and soft. Set aside to rest, covered, at least 1 hour.

Peel the eggplant and cut into ¼-inch cubes. Place cubes in a strainer and sprinkle generously with salt. Let rest 30 minutes to draw out the moisture and bitterness. Blot dry with a paper towel.

Heat olive oil in a 12-inch skillet over medium heat until shimmering. Add the eggplant and cook until it is tender and golden brown, about 10 minutes. Add the garlic slices, season to taste with salt and pepper, and continue to cook 2 minutes more. Drain the eggplant on a dish lined with paper towels and let cool.

In the bowl of a food processor, combine the eggplant, feta cheese, Parmigiano Reggiano, thyme, red pepper flakes, and 1½ teaspoons sesame seeds. Pulse until the mixture is roughly pureed.

Roll the dough out to ¼ inch thick and cut out round discs using a cookie cutter or glass that is 3 inches wide. Place a tablespoon of filling in the center of each disc. Fold the dough into half moon shapes and press the edges together with the tines of a fork to seal. Brush the top of the pastry with the beaten egg yolk and then sprinkle with the remaining sesame seeds. Place on a sheet pan and bake in a 350°F (180°C) oven until golden brown.

YIELDS ABOUT 3 DOZEN TURNOVERS

Eggplant in the garden

Leek Puree with Asparagus Mold
CREMA DI PORRI CON SFORMATO DI ASPARAGI

Similar to a soufflé but lacking the characteristic airiness, sformato takes its name from the method in which it is served: "outside of its mold." The leek and potato cream is a nice base for the asparagus "sformato." Other vegetables can be used to flavor the sformato depending on the season.

4 leeks (8 oz. / 225 g), cleaned and
    cut into ¼-inch slices

4 Yukon Gold potatoes, peeled and
    cut into ¼-inch slices

2 tablespoons (1 oz. / 30 g) unsalted
    butter

1 quart (32 fl. oz. / 920 ml) water

1 cup (8 fl. oz. / 240 ml) heavy cream

Kosher salt and freshly ground black
    pepper

½ cup grated Parmigiano Reggiano

30 ¼-inch cubed pieces French
    baguette

1 tablespoon (½ fl. oz. / 15 ml)
    extra-virgin olive oil

Sformato

1 tablespoon bread crumbs

1 pound (450 g) asparagus

1 tablespoon (½ fl. oz. / 15 ml)
    extra-virgin olive oil

1 peeled and sliced clove of garlic

7 large eggs

½ cup (4 fl. oz. / 120 ml) whole milk

½ cup grated Parmigiano Reggiano

1 tablespoon chopped thyme

1 tablespoon chopped flat-leaf parsley

1 tablespoon chopped chives

Kosher salt and freshly ground
    black pepper

In a 4- to 6-quart saucepan, combine the leeks, the potato slices, and the butter. Cover with the water and add 1 tablespoon of salt. Bring the water up to a boil, then lower to a simmer and cook until the vegetables are tender, about 15 minutes. Transfer to a blender and add the cream and Parmigiano Reggiano. Puree until smooth. Season to taste with salt and pepper.

Heat the oven to 350°F (180°C).

Make the croutons: Toss the baguette pieces with a tablespoon of olive oil and bake in the oven until golden brown and crispy, 5 to 7 minutes.

Meanwhile, make the sformato: Oil 6 individual ramekins and sprinkle with bread crumbs to coat the inside.

Cut the asparagus on the bias into ⅛-inch pieces. In a sauté pan, heat 1 tablespoon of olive oil. Add the garlic and the asparagus and cook over medium heat until tender, about 10 minutes.

In a bowl, gently beat the eggs with the milk. Stir in both types of grated cheese, the herbs, and the asparagus and season to taste with salt and pepper. Pour mixture into prepared ramekins and then place 5 croutons in each ramekin. Bake in the oven for 25 to 30 minutes, or until golden brown and puffed slightly. Remove from the oven and let cool.

Ladle 6 ounces of the leek puree into a shallow bowl and then invert a sformato into the center of the puree. Serve hot.

SERVES 6

Vegetable Couscous Salad
COUSCOUS CON VERDURE

Couscous is small granular semolina pasta that was introduced into Italy by way of the Middle East. This recipe exhibits both Roberta's Jewish and Italian heritage.

Mix together the chili powder, cinnamon, ground ginger, garlic powder, and coriander in a small bowl.

Heat 1½ tablespoons of olive oil in a small nonstick skillet over low heat. Add the spice mixture and cook until fragrant, 1 to 2 minutes. Remove from heat and let cool.

In a 2- or 3-quart saucepan, combine the water, the spice mixture, and a pinch of salt and bring up to a boil. Pour the couscous into the boiling water, cover, and remove from heat. Let stand 5 minutes, covered.

Meanwhile, sauté the onion and the eggplant in a nonstick sauté pan with 3 tablespoons of olive oil, over medium-high heat, until the eggplant is crispy, 8 to 10 minutes. Season with salt and pepper, then remove to a paper towel to drain. Add 1 tablespoon of olive oil to the pan and cook the zucchini until golden brown and slightly crispy. Drain on paper towels.

Transfer the couscous to a large bowl and fluff with a fork. Stir in the tomatoes, chickpeas, zucchini, eggplant, and onions until well-mixed.

Add 2 tablespoons of lemon juice, 1 tablespoon of olive oil, and the fresh herbs. Fold in gently. Refrigerate until ready to serve, or serve at room temperature.

SERVES 6

1 teaspoon chili powder

1 teaspoon cinnamon

¼ teaspoon ground ginger

¼ teaspoon garlic powder

½ teaspoon ground coriander

6½ tablespoons (3½ fl. oz. / 95 ml) extra-virgin olive oil

1¾ cups (14 fl. oz. / 420 ml) water

8 ounces (225 g) couscous

1 medium yellow onion, cut into small dice

1 small eggplant (aubergine), peeled and cut into ¼-inch cubes

Kosher salt and freshly ground black pepper

1 small zucchini (courgette), cut into ¼-inch slices

8 ounces (225 g) quartered cherry tomatoes

1 cup (165 g) chickpeas

2 tablespoons (1 fl. oz. / 30 ml) lemon juice

2 teaspoons chopped mint

1 tablespoon chopped flat-leaf parsley

Goat cheese–stuffed zucchini rolls

Zucchini Roll
INVOLTINI DI ZUCCHINE

Pink peppercorns add a hint of spice and floral flavor to the zucchini rolls. Use a mild goat cheese to not overpower the delicacy of the zucchini and herbs.

Heat the grill to medium heat. Brush the zucchini strips with olive oil and add salt and pepper to taste. Grill zucchini until tender, about 4 minutes per side.

Combine all of the fresh herbs. Stir 1 tablespoon of olive oil into the goat cheese to soften.

Assemble the zucchini rolls: On a clean work surface put ½ tablespoon of goat cheese, sprinkle with 1 teaspoon of the hazelnuts, and then add another ½ tablespoon of the goat cheese. Sprinkle with another ½ teaspoon of the hazelnuts, then 1 tablespoon of the herb mixture and ¼ teaspoon of the pink peppercorns. Wrap a strip of zucchini around the cheese mixture and drizzle with olive oil. Finish with the remaining ingredients in the same manner. Transfer the zucchini rolls to a serving platter and serve at room temperature.

SERVES 8

2 zucchini (courgettes), cut lengthwise into strips

Extra-virgin olive oil, as needed

Kosher salt and freshly ground black pepper

2 tablespoons chopped flat-leaf parsley

2 tablespoons chopped mint

1 tablespoon chopped basil

1 tablespoon chopped marjoram

8 ounces (225 g) fresh goat cheese

½ cup finely chopped toasted and peeled hazelnuts

2 tablespoons whole pink peppercorns

Carrot, Fennel, Apple, and Raisin Salad

INSALATA DI CAROTA, FINOCCHIO, MELA, E UVA SECCA

Roberta serves this salad in the colder months, when fresh lettuce is unavailable. If you have a mandoline, use it to slice the fennel paper-thin, and shred the carrots on a box grater to achieve a softer texture from the two crunchy vegetables.

1 head fennel

1 red apple

4 peeled and grated carrots

¼ cup (30 g) golden raisins (sultanas)

Kosher salt and freshly ground black pepper

3 tablespoons (1½ fl. oz. / 45 ml) red wine vinegar

1 teaspoon Dijon-style mustard

½ cup (4 fl. oz. / 120 ml) extra-virgin olive oil

Slice the fennel and apple into paper-thin slices on a mandoline or with a sharp knife. In a large bowl, mix together the fennel, apple, carrots, and raisins and season to taste with salt and pepper.

In a small bowl, whisk together the red wine vinegar and mustard. Gradually whisk in the extra-virgin olive oil until emulsified. Toss the vinaigrette with the salad and serve.

SERVES 4

A flock of curious geese

Gianluca shaping bread

CHAPTER 9

La Capuccina

After two unsatisfying careers in the textile industry, Gianluca and Raffaella abandoned everything to create a new life for themselves in the Piemontese countryside. The couple began their dream by restoring Gianluca's family's house into a working farm and agriturismo. With little knowledge about agriculture, they found that each step was a learning process, and through trial and error, the couple slowly learned how to live off their land. Their herd of goats has grown through the years, as have their vegetable gardens, their collection of cows, and their chicken coops. Currently they are constructing a laboratory for the production of cheese, continuing their progress toward an impressive degree of sustainability.

The development of Gianluca's cooking mirrors La Capuccina's agrarian growth. He has taken small steps to teach himself how to cook at a professional level. His ambition and an intense desire to retain his region's food heritage have developed into an obsession with the Slow Food movement. This quest has led him to seek advice from older generations, and he has learned from them the secrets of the past. Gianluca's ricotta gnocchi is a dish redolent of history. In times past, a type of ricotta was made from nonpasteurized full-fat milk brought to a slow boil, mixed with vinegar, and strained. Unlike commercial ricotta, which is often bland and used to bring out subtleties in other ingredients, Gianluca's cheese explodes with flavor, offering a completely different texture

La Capuccina's cheese comes from goats like these.

and taste. Today, Slow Food recognizes La Capuccina's efforts and hosts dinners there, honoring the preservation of local dishes. La Capuccina also boasts an incredible all-local wine list. In a region dominated by power wines from the Langhe, many know little about other wine-producing areas in Piemonte. Gianluca and Raffaella stand proudly behind the wines of their neighbors, many of whom they know personally, and offer in-depth knowledge about each of them. Recently awarded "agriturismo of the year" by one of Italy's most respected food journalists, Gianluca and Raffaella are two very proud and humble owners whose naïveté has grown into experience and triumph.

Bean Soup with Cotechino
ZUPPA DI FAGIOLI CON COTECHINO

8 ounces (225 g) pinto beans

2 tablespoons (1 fl. oz. / 30 ml) extra-virgin olive oil

1 yellow onion, cut into ¼-inch slices

1 stalk celery, cut into medium dice

1 carrot, peeled and cut into medium dice

2 tablespoons chopped flat-leaf parsley

1 tablespoon chopped thyme

1 bay leaf

1 cup (8 fl. oz. / 240 ml) crushed canned tomatoes

1 quart (32 fl. oz. / 960 ml) home-made chicken broth (see page xi) or canned low-sodium broth

Kosher salt and freshly ground black pepper

1 cup (8 fl. oz. / 240 ml) whole milk

8 ounces (225 g) kielbasa

Cotechino is a fresh sausage made from fatback pork and pork rind. It originates from Emilia-Romagna, but it is now found on menus throughout northern Italy. Since cotechino is difficult to find outside of Italy, we have substituted kielbasa in the recipe below. Though hardly Italian, the smoky fresh flavor of kielbasa pairs well with the bean soup. But if you can get your hands on cotechino, give it a whirl.

Soak the beans in cold water, covered in the refrigerator, overnight.

In a 4-quart saucepan, heat 2 tablespoons of olive oil over medium-high heat. Add the onion and sauté until it becomes translucent, 4 to 5 minutes. Add the carrot and the celery and continue to cook until tender, about 7 minutes, stirring occasionally.

Add the herbs and the crushed tomatoes to the pan and cook 3 minutes. Put the beans in the pan, cover with the chicken broth, and bring up to a boil. Reduce the heat to medium-low and simmer until the beans are tender, 45 minutes to 1 hour. Season to taste with salt and pepper.

Puree the contents of the saucepan and pass through a fine mesh sieve. Return the soup to the saucepan. Gently stir in the milk over low heat and warm through. Adjust seasoning if needed.

Heat the grill or broiler to high heat. Prick the kielbasa with a fork and grill or broil the sausage until brown and blistery, 3 to 4 minutes per side. Cut the kielbasa into thin slices.

Spoon the soup into individual crocks and top with a slice of kielbasa.

SERVES 4

Sugar-Smoked Duck Breast
ANATRA AFFUMICATA ALLO ZUCCHERO

This recipe requires a deft hand in the kitchen and a lot of patience, as it is difficult to make, but it is fully worth the effort. The trick is not burning the sugar, which would impart a burnt flavor to the meat. When cooked properly, the duck retains a smoky sweet flavor with subtle hints of spice.

With a sharp chef's knife score the duck skin into a ½-inch crosshatch pattern, and season both sides of the breasts generously with salt and black pepper.

With heavy-duty foil make a square pouch and add the sugar, cloves, cinnamon sticks, coriander, white peppercorns, and juniper berries. Place the foil pouch in the bottom of a 7-quart pan, cover with a perforated pan or steamer basket, and cover with a lid. Place over medium-low heat.

Once the sugar starts to caramelize and begins to smoke, add the duck breast, skin side down on the perforated pan, and cook for 20 minutes. Turn the duck breast over and continue to cook another 10 minutes, or until the duck is medium rare. Remove from heat and chill in the refrigerator for at least one hour.

Carve the duck into thin slices and serve as an antipasto or over a bed of greens.

SERVES 4

1 1-pound (450 g) boneless duck breast

Kosher salt and freshly ground black pepper

3 pounds (1.5 kg) granulated sugar

10 whole cloves

2 cinnamon sticks

1 tablespoon whole coriander

1 tablespoon whole white peppercorns

1 tablespoon lightly crushed juniper berries

Ricotta and Spinach Gnocchi
GNOCCHI DI RICOTTA E SPINACI

Gnocchi should be light, airy, and slightly sticky. Too much flour can make them firm and unappetizing. These green-speckled dumplings are best with fresh baby spring spinach, whose tender leaves Gianluca quickly sautés to make a sauce for the gnocchi.

1 pound (450 g) spinach

1 pound (450 g) fresh ricotta

2 large eggs, plus 2 large egg yolks

¾ cup (65 g) grated Parmigiano
Reggiano, plus more for serving

2 cups (250 g) all-purpose flour

3 tablespoons (1½ fl. oz. / 45 ml)
extra-virgin olive oil

1 peeled clove of garlic

Kosher salt and freshly ground black
pepper

Wash and clean the spinach. Bring 4 quarts of salted water to a boil. Add half of the spinach and cook for 2 to 3 minutes. Drain in a colander and then submerge the spinach in an large bowl filled with ice water. Drain the spinach again and squeeze out all of the excess water.

Mince the spinach as fine as possible with a pinch of salt. In a large bowl, mix together the ricotta, eggs, egg yolks, Parmigiano Reggiano, minced spinach, and flour. Mix together until a dough forms and knead until smooth. Cover with plastic wrap and let rest in the refrigerator, about 30 minutes.

Remove the dough from the refrigerator and cut it into 4 even pieces. Roll each piece out into a 1-inch-thick rope. Cut each rope with a pastry cutter or knife into ¼-inch pieces.

In a large sauté pan, heat 3 tablespoons of olive oil over medium heat, along with the garlic clove. Lightly brown the garlic and then discard from the pan. Roughly chop the remaining spinach and add it to the pan. Cook until the spinach is wilted and bright green, 2 to 3 minutes. Season to taste with salt and pepper.

Bring 6 quarts salted water to a boil. Drop the gnocchi into the boiling water and cook until they rise to the surface, 1 to 2 minutes. Remove with a spider or slotted spoon. Toss them with the sautéed spinach and add a heaping amount of grated Parmigiano Reggiano. Serve in a large bowl.

SERVES 4

Fresh-made ricotta cheese

Chicken Roulade
INVOLTINI DI POLLO

Stewing cabbage brings out a subdued sweetness in the vegetable. Stuffing the breast with the cabbage puree and wrapping it in foil ensures a moist interior, which also benefits from being topped with the roasted garlic aioli. Gianluca presents this to La Capuccina's guests as an appetizer to begin his multi-course dinners.

Garlic aioli

1 whole head of garlic

1 tablespoon (½ fl. oz. / 15 ml) extra-virgin olive oil

2 tablespoons (1 fl. oz. / 30 ml) lemon juice

1 egg yolk

Pinch of kosher salt

1 cup (8 fl. oz. / 240 ml) canola oil

Chicken

4 large skinless boneless chicken breasts (about 2 pounds / 900 g)

2 tablespoons (1 fl. oz. / 30 ml) olive oil, plus more as needed

1 yellow onion, cut into fine dice

1 stalk celery, cut into fine dice

1 carrot, peeled and cut into fine dice

1 head green cabbage, shredded

1 tablespoon chopped thyme

2 tablespoons chopped flat-leaf parsley

½ cup (4 fl. oz. / 120 ml) water

3 tablespoons (1½ fl. oz. / 45 ml) heavy cream

Kosher salt and freshly ground black pepper

Heat the oven to 425°F (225°C).

Make the aioli: Slice the top off the head of garlic, drizzle with olive oil, and wrap in tin foil. Place on a sheet pan and roast in the oven until tender and fragrant, about 45 minutes. Remove from the oven and let cool. Squeeze the garlic cloves from the head into the bowl of a food processor. Add the lemon juice, egg yolk, and salt, and puree until combined. With the food processor running, gradually add the canola oil in a steady stream until the mixture emulsifies and has the consistency of mayonnaise. Place in a bowl and refrigerate until needed.

Meanwhile, prepare the chicken: Butterfly the chicken breasts and pound out as thin as possible without tearing the flesh.

In a 12-inch sauté pan, heat 2 tablespoons olive oil over medium heat and cook the onion, celery, and carrot until tender, about 7 minutes. Add the cabbage, thyme, and parsley and cook until the cabbage begins to soften and wilt, about 5 minutes. Add the water to the pan, reduce the heat to low, cover, and cook until extremely tender, about 45 minutes. Stir occasionally. Add more water to the pan if necessary. Season to taste with salt and pepper. Remove from the heat and let cabbage mixture cool completely.

In the bowl of a food processor, combine the cabbage mixture and the heavy cream. Season with salt and pepper. Puree the mixture until a thick paste forms. Divide the cabbage mixture in half.

Place each chicken breast on a piece of foil and season with salt and pepper. Spoon 2 tablespoons of the cabbage mixture in the center of the chicken, roll up lengthwise, and wrap in the foil. Continue with the other three breasts and reserve the remaining filling.

Bake the chicken for 30 to 35 minutes, or until the internal temperature reaches 165°F (74°C). Remove from the oven and let cool. Unwrap the chicken from the foil and carve into ½-inch slices.

Meanwhile, heat the reserved cabbage mixture in a small pan until warmed through.

Spoon the cabbage mixture onto a large serving platter, top with the chicken slices, and drizzle with the roasted garlic aioli.

SERVES 4–6

La Capuccina's dining room

Fennel bulbs

Although geographically small, Valle d'Aosta is packed with culinary personality and features an impressive landscape of rugged mountain chains and deep valleys. Picturesque alpine villages dot the region with traditional stone-roofed houses and flowering window boxes.

The pride of Valle d'Aosta are the chocolate-brown cows whose milk produce a creamy Fontina cheese that has achieved international recognition. The characteristic taste comes from milk collected during the spring and summer, when the cows are sent up to pasture high in the mountains and graze in alpine meadows abundant with wild herbs and medicinal grasses. The animals' ability to choose what they eat makes their milk rich, with an elevated fat content that provides Fontina its signature flavor. Also from this milk is produced a sweet and aromatic mountain butter that serves as the base and essential fat for all Valle d'Aostan cooking.

Cured meats, sausages, and salami play an integral role in Valle d'Aosta's culinary repertoire, stemming from a history of impoverishment and long winters. Two specialties popular throughout the region are mocetto, an air-cured meat using beef and goat, and budino, a sausage made with potatoes and beets, and whose characteristic deep-red color can be attributed to a bit of pig's blood added to the mixture. Snow-white lardo also joins mocetto and budino on antipasti plates, as well as more typical pork salami. These meats are always accompanied by a flavorful dense rye bread called pane nero, which proliferates in the area since rye flour thrives in the harsh climate.

Bread and vegetable soups thick and bubbling with Fontina cheese, along with gnocchi and steaming polenta, often topped with more Fontina cheese, replace pasta in Valle d'Aosta. Rib-sticking polenta is served alongside rich meat dishes, providing a dense and hearty side dish. Braises make up many second courses and wild game, pork, beef, goose, and veal make for great mountain comfort food. Juniper berries, nutmeg, cinnamon, and cloves season many of the meat dishes and create the unique flavors of Valle d'Aostan cooking.

Desserts, often simple affairs, include fruits that grow in the area and pound cakes with plump berries. Apple fritters, raspberry sorbet, goat-milk gelato, and chocolate cream are just a few examples of the sweet delights you might encounter at the end of a meal. And almost always present to cap the evening is the signature cheese board, representing Valle d'Aosta's most recognized culinary production.

CHAPTER 10

LES ECUREUILS

A low-lying stone farmhouse offering a stunning panorama, this family-run agriturismo of Glory, Sandra, Piero, and Pepe is reached by a long and winding road that switchbacks up a mountain. Snow-capped peaks abound in every direction, with a valley below dotted with tiny hamlets, ancient castles, and rivers that cascade down from the mountains. A true working farm, Les Ecureuils's seemingly effortless perfection is attained through the family's dedication, passion, and cohesive understanding of the land on which they live. Having restored Les Ecureuils more than twenty years ago with a vision in mind, the family has since brought to life that dream, as the farm is now one of the most recognized agriturismi in northern Italy.

In a region famous for Fontina cheese produced from alpine dairy cows, Les Ecureuils has achieved local acclaim for superb goat cheese that is handmade daily at the farm. Piero studied the fundamental techniques of cheese making at goat farms in nearby France, but his wife, Sandra, has since taken over the production and perfected it. Today she makes more than five different kinds, including a ricotta and an aged semisoft Toma. From her goats' milk, she also makes butter, yogurt, and an over-the-top creamy gelato. While these dairy products are used with abundance in Les Ecureuils's cooking, Piero also sells the cheese throughout the valley at farmers' markets. Its popularity has led several farmers to abandon their cow's-milk cheese

Les Ecureuils's mountain farmhouse

making and switch over to raising goats, hoping to replicate Les Ecureuils's success.

Comfort and warmth emanate from Les Ecureuils's dining room, engulfing guests with an aroma of burning wood and wafts of long-simmering pots in Glory's kitchen. In a cozy, impeccably Valle d'Aostan, room, rustic pine walls adorned with traditional folklore, bucolic wooden furniture, and an ornate porcelain woodstove all complement the hearty rib-sticking fare. Serious alpine dishes include goat cheese gnocchi tossed with intensely rich mountain butter, pork stew heavily spiced with herbal juniper berries, and the farm's own dried blood sausage. Glory also makes her own goose sausage, skinning the bird, grinding its meat with lard and spices, and stuffing it back into the fatty skin. The true mountain cuisine of Les Ecureuils has brought accolades from journalists all over the world, strengthening the family's original ideas and philosophies on cooking and feeding its guests. What comes from the farm and what can be produced in the mountain climate is the base of the cooking. The result is a cuisine forged from the necessity of enduring long winters—perfect for enticing guests to ski or take a hike and explore the natural beauty of the Valle d'Aosta.

Les Ecureuils's alpine goats

Heating goat milk and separating curd from whey

Ladling cheese into molds

Weighing down cheese to shed moisture and make compact

Aging cheese in cantina

Rye bread soup, veal in cartoccio, walnut celery salad, and crema di Cogne

Rye Bread Soup
ZUPPA DI PANE NERO

This soup is a must-try, especially on a harsh winter evening, since it is nourishing and full of sustenance to warm your bones.

In a 4-quart saucepan, add the rye bread to the chicken broth and bring up to a boil. Add the Fontina and goat cheese and stir constantly with a spoon until the cheese begins to melt. Season to taste with salt and pepper. With an immersion blender or in a blender, puree the soup until smooth.

In a 10-inch skillet over medium heat, sauté the shallots in butter until they are tender and just beginning to brown, about 7 minutes. Add the juniper berries, and continue to cook until fragrant, 1 to 2 minutes.

Ladle the soup into individual crocks or bowls and spoon the shallots and juniper berries on top. Serve immediately.

SERVES 4

6 ounces (170 g) rye bread, cut into
½-inch cubes and toasted

1 quart (32 fl. oz. / 960 ml) homemade chicken broth (see page xi)
or canned low-sodium broth

4 ounces (115 g) shredded Fontina
cheese

2 ounces (60 g) crumbled goat
cheese

Kosher salt and freshly ground black
pepper

2 shallots, cut into fine dice

1 tablespoon (½ oz. / 15 g) unsalted
butter

1 teaspoon lightly crushed juniper
berries

MARKET DAY IN AOSTA

Every weekend, Piero loads his van with Les Ecureuils's cheese and heads down to the region's capital of Aosta. In the main piazza, surrounded by historic buildings and with mountains looming in the distance, local farmers hold a weekly market. It is a great opportunity for Piero to show off his family's unique variety of cheeses—ricotta, Toma, and a fresh spreadable cheese mixed with herbs and spices—as they were the first in the valley to produce cheese from goat milk. Aosta's market allows farmers to mingle with city dwellers, stimulating the economies of Valle d'Aosta's small family farms, which proliferate throughout the alpine region.

Goat Cheese Gnocchi with Walnut Butter Sauce

GNOCCHI DI FORMAGGIO DI CAPRA CON BURRO E NOCI

Goat-milk ricotta is one of the many types of cheese produced at Les Ecureuils. It is drier and more dense than cow's-milk ricotta, and its pungent tangy flavor mixes well with the walnut butter sauce. Goat-milk ricotta is not always readily available; for similar results, mix fresh goat cheese with cow's-milk ricotta.

1 cup (125 g) all-purpose flour, plus
    more for dusting

12 ounces (340 g) goat-milk ricotta
    or 1 cup (210 g) soft goat cheese
    mixed with ¾ cup (150 g)
    cow's-milk ricotta

6 tablespoons (3 oz. / 90 g) unsalted
    butter

⅓ cup (40 g) chopped walnuts

1 tablespoon chopped thyme, plus
    more for garnish

Kosher salt and freshly ground
    black pepper

Mix together the flour and goat-milk ricotta, and knead until a nice soft dough forms. Cut the dough into 4 even pieces. Roll each piece out into a 1-inch-thick rope and cut each rope, with a pastry cutter or knife, into ¼-inch pieces. With your thumb, roll each piece of cut dough against the back of a handheld cheese grater. Place the gnocchi on trays dusted lightly with flour and place in the refrigerator.

Bring 6 quarts salted water to a boil. Drop the gnocchi into the boiling water and cook until they rise to the surface, 1 to 2 minutes. Remove with a spider or slotted spoon. Reserve ¼ cup of pasta water.

Meanwhile, melt the butter in a 12-inch sauté pan. Once it begins to foam, add the walnuts and thyme. Sauté a few minutes, until the butter begins to brown and the walnuts are lightly toasted, 2 to 3 minutes. Whisk in the reserved pasta water and season to taste with salt and pepper.

Toss the gnocchi in the butter sauce, sprinkle with some fresh thyme, and serve.

SERVES 6

Glory shaping goat cheese gnocchi

Goat cheese gnocchi

Polenta with Spinach
POLENTA CON SPINACI

2 quarts (64 fl. oz. / 1.89 L) water

1 tablespoon kosher salt

1 pound (450 g) spinach

2 cups (310 g) stone-ground polenta

3 tablespoons (1½ oz. / 45 g)
  unsalted butter

4 ounces (115 g) shredded Fontina
  cheese

Stone-ground polenta is the preferred variety in Italy. Its toothy texture and nutty flavor is unrivaled by any of the mass-produced varieties. At Les Ecureuils, Glory cooks it with wild nettle, a prickly bitter green that grows wild in the mountains. The addition of the greens to the polenta water enhances the flavor of the dish and gives the cornmeal mush a pleasant vibrant color. In the recipe below, we substitute spinach, but any leafy green could work.

Bring the water up to a boil in a heavy-bottomed 6-quart pan over medium-high heat. Add the salt and the spinach, and cook until the spinach is tender. With an immersion blender, puree the spinach in the water until completely smooth. Bring the spinach water back up to a boil.

In a steady stream, gradually add the polenta, whisking constantly to prevent lumping. Lower the heat to medium-low and stir the polenta constantly with a wooden spoon, until the polenta is creamy and soft, about 45 minutes. Stir in the butter and Fontina, and continue to stir until the cheese has melted and is fully incorporated. Serve immediately.

SERVES 6

Pork Stew with Red Wine and Juniper Berries
CARBONATA DI MAIALE

Juniper trees proliferate in the mountainous region of Valle d'Aosta, and their medicinal-flavored berries appear in many of the classic dishes of the region.

In a 6-quart pan, melt the butter over medium heat. Add the onions and sauté until tender and beginning to brown, about 10 minutes.

Season the pork with 1 tespoon salt and ¼ teaspoon white pepper. Toss the pork loin with the flour and then add it to the onions. Brown the meat on all sides. Add the wine, spices, and juniper berries to the pot. Bring the wine to a boil, cover, and lower the heat to medium-low. Cook at a gentle simmer, stirring occasionally, until the meat is tender, 40 to 45 minutes. Season to taste with salt and pepper and serve with polenta with spinach.

SERVES 6

4 tablespoons (2 oz. / 60 g) unsalted butter

2 red onions, cut into small dice

2½ pounds (1.14 kg) pork loin, cut into 1-inch cubes

¼ cup (32 g) all-purpose flour

Kosher salt

1 teaspoon freshly ground white pepper

1 bottle (750 ml) dry red wine

1 teaspoon ground cloves

1 teaspoon ground cinnamon

1 teaspoon ground nutmeg

3 tablespoons lightly crushed juniper berries

Polenta with spinach (see page 104), for serving

Vinegar Chicken
POLLO SOTT'ACETO

1 yellow onion, cut into ½-inch slices

1 stalk celery, cut into ½-inch pieces

1 carrot, peeled and cut into ½-inch pieces

1 bay leaf

3 sprigs flat-leaf parsley

2 sprigs plus 1 teaspoon chopped thyme, plus more for garnish

1 whole chicken, 3–4 pounds (1.5–2 kg)

½ cup (4 fl. oz. / 120 ml) canola oil

6 cloves of garlic, peeled and sliced thin

2 red onions, cut into thin slices

½ cup (4 fl. oz. / 120 ml) white wine vinegar

Kosher salt and freshly ground black pepper

1 teaspoon chopped rosemary

1 teaspoon chopped sage

1 teaspoon crushed red pepper flakes

1 large zucchini (courgette)

3 tablespoons (1½ fl. oz. / 45 ml) extra-virgin olive oil

1 head Boston lettuce

This very tasty dish is extremely refreshing in the summertime. At Les Ecureuils, fresh river trout is interchanged with the chicken, which is equally delicious. Give it a try by poaching trout in the same liquid, but remember to shorten the cooking time and reduce the amount of liquid.

Add 4 quarts of water to a pot along with the yellow onion, celery, carrot, bay leaf, parsley, and thyme sprigs and bring to a boil over medium-high heat. Add the chicken and return to a boil, then reduce the heat to low and gently poach the chicken until cooked through, about 45 minutes.

In a 12-inch sauté pan, heat the canola oil over medium-high heat. Add the garlic and onions and cook until tender, about 5 minutes, being careful not to burn the garlic. Add the vinegar to the pan and continue to cook for another 5 minutes. Season to taste with salt and pepper.

Shred the chicken and spread the pieces out in a shallow baking dish. Season with salt and pepper and sprinkle with the chopped herbs and red pepper flakes. Spoon the onion mixture over the chicken. Cover and refrigerate at least 1 day.

Heat the grill to medium heat. Cut the zucchini into ¼-inch rounds on the bias. Brush with 2 tablespoons of extra-virgin olive oil and season with salt and pepper. Grill zucchini until tender, about 4 minutes per side.

Clean the Boston lettuce in cold water, dry on paper towel or kitchen towels, and tear into pieces. Toss the lettuce with 1 tablespoon extra-virgin olive oil. Arrange the lettuce on a large serving platter, spoon the chicken over the bed of lettuce, and then fan the zucchini pieces around the perimeter. Garnish with some fresh thyme leaves.

SERVES 6

CHAPTER 11

❧ MAISON ROSSET ❧

From its facade, Maison Rosset could easily be over-looked as a typical Italian trattoria in the historic center of a small town. Nothing could be farther from the truth. An agriturismo in every regard, Maison Rosset prides itself on the fact that nearly everything served in its restaurant is grown or raised on its mountain farm. In the agriturismo's fourteen-year existence, the Rosset family has established a dedicated and loyal following of Valle d'Aostans, who fill the lively dining room nightly. For centuries, the property existed as an urban farm with animals, gardens, and barns fitting into the landscape of the town. When the restaurant opened, it brought a de-mand and need for more space to raise animals, so they were relocated to a farm in the country. Today, the entire property has been converted for self-sufficient produc-tion. The old barns are now individual rooms for pro-ducing wine, cheese, pasta, and gelato, and also house a separate sterile space for butchering the farm's animals. A large vegetable garden out back is all that remains of the original farm.

Elena, the backbone of both the kitchen and the farm, proudly claims that sugar, flour, oil, and salt are the only items used in her kitchen that are not of the farm's own production. Dairy cattle are the pride and joy of Maison Rosset, and they roam freely in the alpine mountains in summer, feasting on wild herbs, medici-nal plants, and green grass. Their creamy and rich cheese

Alpine cows

plays a dominant role in the farm's recipes, particularly in a velvety sauce liberally ladled over steaming polenta. Steadfast traditionalists, the Rossets cook polenta every night, slowly stirring the ground corn over an antique wood-fired stove specifically made for the yellow por-ridge. They also use the farm's original wood-fired oven to bake their black bread, which they serve with honey and lard, as well as to slow-roast beef brined in an herbal infusion. Camillo Rosset, the dining room's sole waiter, gregariously and effortlessly runs a warm and relaxing environment. The soft, woodtoned room heated by two large fireplaces sets the stage for an evening of hearty food and is perfect for cold Valle d'Aostan winters.

Homage to Valle d'Aostan Mountain Cattle

Valle d'Aosta's pungent and exceptionally rich Fontina cheese has earned international recognition and is the region's most popular culinary export. The prized cheese is made from the milk of dairy cows that spend the summer months feeding in the mountains, consuming fresh flowers and alpine grass. This summer diet produces high-quality milk essential to Fontina cheese's characteristic flavor.

Every autumn, locals celebrate the movement of their cherished livestock from the mountains down into the valley with a grand procession called La Desarpa. With flowered wreaths adorning their heads and large leather cowbells hanging from their necks, the cows parade directly through town squares and centers, where they are enthusiastically welcomed home from their summers at pasture. A large festival follows, with music, villagers dressed in traditional garb, and regional specialties, including a warmed mulled wine known as *vin brûlé*.

La Desarpa kicks off another time-honored Valle d'Aostan event, in which these huge dairy cattle engage in a type of cow sumo wrestling known as the Combat des Reines. Several cows are placed in a large arena and face off against one another by locking horns. It's a fierce contest of sheer dominance, and winners are the beasts that can outlast their opponents. A series of regional heats throughout the valley leads up to the finale in late October, where the queen of the valley will be determined in front of thousands of spectators. Queen of the valley is a highly respected title that the winner will wear proudly throughout the year, when she leads her herd back into the mountains for summer grazing.

Celery and Walnut Salad
INSALATA DI SEDANO E NOCE

The crunch from the celery, walnuts, and apples is refreshing and satisfying, making this salad a great alternative to leafy green varieties.

Cut the celery, apple, and cheese into ½-inch pieces, and combine with the walnuts. Whisk together the lemon juice and olive oil and toss with the salad. Season to taste with salt and pepper.

SERVES 4

10 stalks celery

1 Golden Delicious apple

2 ounces (60 g) Fontina cheese

2 ounces (60 g) chopped walnuts

1 tablespoon (½ fl. oz. / 15 ml)

¼ cup (2 fl. oz. / 60 ml) extra-virgin
 olive oil

Kosher salt and freshly ground
 black pepper

Sylvie with Fontina cheese

Tomatoes with Parsley Aioli
POMODORI CON SALSA AL PREZZEMOLO

This recipe yields a large amount of aioli, which is a great condiment to keep in your refrigerator. For the recipe below, make sure to use native tomatoes in peak season. This combination is so delicious that you won't be able to stop slicing tomatoes, perfect for a quick and easy summer appetizer or as a side to accompany grilled fish.

1 cup flat-leaf parsley, packed

1 clove garlic, peeled and roughly chopped

2 large eggs

2 teaspoons (10 ml) lemon juice

Pinch of crushed red pepper flakes or cayenne pepper

1 cup (8 fl. oz. / 240 ml) canola oil

4 large ripe tomatoes

Kosher salt and freshly ground black pepper

In a blender, combine parsley, garlic, eggs, lemon juice, a pinch of salt, and red pepper flakes and puree until smooth. With the machine still running, gradually add the oil in a steady stream, until the mixture reaches a thick and creamy mayonnaise consistency.

Cut tomatoes into thick slices, season with salt and pepper, and drizzle with the aioli. Serve at room temperature.

SERVES 6

Rye Bread Toast with Lard and Honey
TARTE DES SALASSES

Lardo is a cured pork fat that is seasoned with herbs and spices and stored in marble containers for at least six months. The tender snow-white fat has a surprisingly sweet and aromatic flavor that melts in your mouth when combined with warm honey toast. Although prosciutto is vastly different from lardo, its salty porky flavor also complements the sweetness of the honey and rye, so it makes a fine substitute.

6 slices rye bread, ¼ inch thick

2 tablespoons honey

2 tablespoons (1 oz. / 30 g) unsalted butter, softened and cut into pieces

6 slices lardo or prosciutto

Heat the oven to 350°F (180°C). Place the bread on a sheet pan and toast in the oven until golden brown, about 10 minutes.

With a whisk, whip together the honey and the butter until creamy. With a pastry brush, spread the honey butter mixture on the warm bread. Lay 1 slice of lardo or prosciutto on top.

SERVES 6

Curing lardo

Vegetable Soup with Ditalini Pasta
ZUPPA DI VERDURE CON DITALINI

Vegetable soup is a staple in any Italian cook's repertoire. Maison Rosset's is served piping hot with a generous slice of wood oven–baked crusty bread and their homemade butter.

3 plum tomatoes

1 large yellow onion, cut into small dice

2 stalks celery, cut into small dice

2 carrots, peeled and cut into small dice

1 bunch Swiss chard, roughly chopped

2 Yukon Gold potatoes, cut into small dice

¼ cup chopped flat-leaf parsley

1 tablespoon chopped sage

1 Parmigiano Reggiano rind

Kosher salt and freshly ground black pepper

1 cup ditalini pasta

Grated Parmigiano Reggiano, for serving

Cut an x into the bottom of each plum tomato. Bring a large pot of salted water to a boil and blanch the plum tomatoes for 30 seconds. Drain tomatoes and immediately submerge in ice water. Remove the skin from the tomatoes, cut them in half, and remove the seeds. Cut the tomatoes into ¼-inch pieces.

In a stockpot, combine all of the vegetables, the herbs, and the cheese rind. Cover with 3 quarts (96 fl. oz. / 2¾ L) of water and bring to a boil.

Lower the heat, season with a little salt and pepper, and simmer for 1 hour.

Remove the cheese rind from the soup and discard. With an immersion blender (or in a blender) puree the soup until it is smooth and creamy. The soup should not be too thick; add water if needed.

Return the soup to a boil and add the ditalini pasta. Cook until the pasta is al dente. Adjust seasoning if needed.

Serve with some grated Parmigiano Reggiano and slices of warm crusty bread.

SERVES 4

Simmering vegetable soup

Veal Chop Cooked in Parchment Paper
COSTOLETTE DI VITELLO IN CARTOCCIO

4 tablespoons (2 oz. / 60 g) unsalted butter

4 bone-in veal loin chops, 1-inch thick (about 2½ to 3 pounds total / 1.13 to 1.36 kg)

Kosher salt and freshly ground black pepper

8 ounces (225 g) mixed wild mushrooms, cleaned and trimmed

1 peeled clove of garlic

2 tablespoons chopped flat-leaf parsley

2 tablespoons (1 fl. oz. / 30 ml) extra-virgin olive oil

4 ounces (115 g) prosciutto di Parma, sliced paper-thin

1 large egg, lightly beaten

In cartoccio is a cooking technique in which food is baked inside a paper pouch. The steam created inside the pouch keeps the meat moist and allows all of the flavors to meld together. A packet is presented to each diner and opened tableside, engulfing guests in the succulent aromas that were trapped within.

Heat 2 tablespoons of butter in a 12-inch sauté pan over medium-high heat. Season the veal chops all over with salt and pepper and sear, in batches, until a rich golden brown, 3 to 4 minutes per side.

Cut the mushrooms into thin slices. Mince the garlic with the parsley. In a 12-inch skillet, melt the remaining 2 tablespoons of butter over medium-high heat. Add the mushrooms to the skillet along with the garlic and parsley mixture. Cook until tender and the mushrooms have released their liquid, 5 to 7 minutes. Season lightly with salt and pepper.

Heat the oven to 400°F (190°C).

Cut 4 pieces of parchment paper into the shape of a heart four times the size of the veal chops (1 heart per chop). Brush the paper with olive oil. Place 1 slice of prosciutto just left of the center of the heart, top with 1 tablespoon of the mushroom mixture, and place the veal chop on top. Then spoon another 1 tablespoon of the mushroom mixture over the veal chop, and cover with another slice of prosciutto. Brush around the veal chop with the egg. Fold the right side of the heart over the veal chop and crimp together the two edges of the paper to seal the parchment and make a pouch. Brush each pouch with olive oil, place on a sheet pan, and bake for 10 minutes. Remove from the oven and let pouches rest 5 to 10 minutes.

Serve each diner an individual pouch, cutting the paper open with a sharp knife.

SERVES 4

Apple Fritters
FRITELLE DI MELE IN PASTELLA

Warm apple fritters have "comfort food" written all over them. They make a perfect afternoon snack on a crisp fall day or a great dessert with a scoop of good-quality vanilla ice cream.

In a small bowl, macerate the minced apple with the lemon zest, 1 tablespoon sugar, and 1 teaspoon cinnamon, for 15 to 20 minutes.

In a medium-size bowl, whisk together the egg whites, milk, vanilla, ½ cup sugar, and 2 teaspoons cinnamon, until well combined and frothy. Stir in the flour ¼ cup at a time, until you have a thick pourable batter.

Heat the oven to 200°F (90°C). In a heavy sauté pan, heat the canola oil until shimmering. Drop spoonfuls of batter into the oil and cook until deep golden brown. Drain on paper towels and place in oven to keep warm while frying the remaining fritters. Sprinkle with the remaining teaspoon of cinnamon. Serve warm.

YIELDS 2 DOZEN

1 peeled and minced Golden
   Delicious apple
1 teaspoon lemon zest
½ cup plus 1 tablespoon (90 g)
   granulated sugar
1 tablespoon ground cinnamon
3 large egg whites
1 cup (8 fl. oz. / 240 ml) whole milk
1 teaspoon vanilla
2 cups (250 g) all-purpose flour
½ cup (4 fl. oz. / 120 ml) canola oil

Winter night at Plan de la Tour

CHAPTER 12

PLAN DE LA TOUR

Plan de la Tour, which translates as "field of the tower," is in an open meadow, surrounded by mountains and next to a historic ruin of a noble family's castle. Rosario and Letizia's agriturismo radiates typical characteristics of Valle d'Aostan mountain chalets. Rustic knotty pine and flat gray stones are the raw materials taken from the valley for the agriturismo's construction. Rosario, a mason by trade, built much of the agriturismo himself and erected a stone tower that rises through the living room, standing not only as the farm's centerpiece but also as a symbol of a new era of prosperity for the property. The barn replicates the alpine style of the agriturismo and houses the farm's cows, goats, pigs, sheep, rabbits, and chickens. Cheese and butter are made in a sterile room inside the barn, where fresh milk gets pumped into vats to begin the cheese making process. Summer months bring the cows outside to graze in the fields of fresh grass in front of the agriturismo, affording guests great photo opportunities with the rugged Alps as their backdrop.

True comfort foods that nourish and replenish the soul are Letizia's bread and butter. A mother of three boys, her maternal instincts show in her cooking and her love for bringing pleasure to the table. The farm is somewhat isolated and in an area known for winter storms, so Letizia prefers to cook what's available locally and from her farm. Her simple dishes are classics from the nearby picture-perfect town of Cogne. Gargantuan portions come piled high in matching terra-cotta crocks, placed before guests with gusto and abundance. A bubbling cauldron of rice and cheese with hunks of softened stale bread hidden beneath the surface exemplifies a cuisine based on stretching a few ingredients into something delicious. Gnocchi made from mountain-grown potatoes and coated with a toothsome sauce made from the farm's Toma cheese also make their way to the table in the colder months. Summertime brings more variety and freshness to the kitchen, and a lighter fare is dished out to the throngs of tourists invading the area. Whether dining in front of a blazing fire or a setting summer sun, guests of Letizia and Rosario are guaranteed a meal prepared with passion that evokes the season at Plan de la Tour.

Caramelized Chestnuts with Prosciutto
CASTAGNE CARAMELLATE CON PROSCIUTTO

Chestnuts and prosciutto are a classic Valle d'Aostan pairing that typically begins meals in the colder months. Honey adds a hint of sweetness that subdues the strong cured flavor of the ham.

4 tablespoons (2 oz. / 60 g) unsalted butter

4 sage leaves

½ pound (225 g) fresh chestnuts, boiled and peeled

3 tablespoons honey

4 ounces (115 g) prosciutto, sliced paper-thin

Melt the butter in a 8-inch sauté pan over medium heat. Add the sage leaves and the chestnuts, cover, and cook for about 10 minutes, stirring occasionally. Remove the cover from the pan, add the honey, and cook another 5 minutes, or until the chestnuts start to caramelize.

Place chestnuts in a small bowl in the center of a serving platter and spread the prosciutto around the chestnuts on the platter. Serve while the chestnuts are still warm.

SERVES 4

THE CASTLES OF VALLE D'AOSTA

Aside from stunning, dramatic natural beauty, Valle d'Aosta impresses with numerous well-maintained castles, which proliferate in the tiny region and stand testament to a feudal history. Plan de la Tour ("field of the tower") takes its name from a crumbling castle tower which sits in a pasture of the agriturismo. Today, cows graze lazily beneath the ivy-covered ruin, ignorant of its noble and historic past.

Gnocchi with Toma Cheese Sauce
GNOCCHI CON FORMAGGIO DI TOMA

Toma ("Tomme" in French) is a semi-hard cow's-milk cheese that is mild and creamy when young and that grows sharp and pungent as it ages. Use a younger Toma for the velvety cheese sauce in this recipe.

Bring 6 quarts of salted water to a boil. Add the gnocchi to the pot and cook until they begin to rise to the surface of the water, about 2 minutes. Drain the gnocchi well.

Heat the heavy cream gently in a 3-quart saucepan, over medium heat, until just boiling. Add the Toma cheese and whisk to melt and incorporate. Season with salt and white pepper to taste.

Spoon some of the sauce into the bottom of a large serving bowl, add the gnocchi, and toss to coat. Spoon more sauce over if necessary. Serve immediately.

SERVES 6–8

1 recipe potato gnocchi (see page ix)

3/4 cup (6 fl. oz. / 180 ml) heavy cream

7 ounces (215 g) Toma cheese, cut into small cubes

Kosher salt and freshly ground white pepper

Chocolate Custard from Cogne
CREMA DI COGNE

Crema di Cogne is a mix between a pudding and chocolate milk. The consistency is neither solid nor thin, but that of a thick shake without the ice cream.

2 cups (16 fl. oz. / 480 ml) heavy cream

2 cups (16 fl. oz. / 480 ml) milk

5 tablespoons sugar

6 ounces (170 g) high-quality bittersweet chocolate

4 large eggs

In a 4-quart saucepan, combine the heavy cream, milk, sugar, and chocolate. Cook over medium-low heat, stirring occasionally, until the chocolate melts and the sugar dissolves. Remove from heat and, with a whisk, whip the cream mixture vigorously until frothy and slightly cooled.

Whisk in the eggs one at a time. Place the pan back on the stove, over low heat, and stir constantly with a heat-proof spatula until the mixture has thickened, but do not allow to boil. Remove from heat.

Pour the cream into 6 individual glasses. Chill in the refrigerator at least 4 hours and up to 24 hours.

Serve with a hazelnut tuille (see page 122).

SERVES 6

Crema di Cogne chocolate dessert

Hazelnut Tuille
TEGOLE ALLE NOCCIOLE

3 tablespoons (1½ oz. / 45 g)
  unsalted butter

2 ounces (60 g) hazelnuts, toasted
  and hulled

½ cup (100 g) sugar

¼ cup (25 g) all-purpose flour

2 large egg whites

These cookies are easy to make and fun to work with. Spread the batter out in a thin, even layer, and when the cookies come out of the oven, immediately remove them from the sheet pan and form them into different shapes (or leave them in their original forms). The cookies are only pliable when still warm.

Heat the oven to 350°F (180°C). Melt 1½ tablespoons of butter in a small saucepan over low heat. Grind the hazelnuts with 1 tablespoon of sugar until fine crumbs form.

In a large bowl, whisk the egg whites until frothy and thickened. Gradually add the remaining sugar, continuing to whisk. Then whisk in the flour and the melted butter, mixing until combined. Gently fold in the ground hazelnuts.

Butter two parchment-lined sheet pans with the remaining butter. Drop the cookie dough by rounded tablespoons onto the sheet pans, leaving ample space between the cookies. Wet the tip of your finger and smooth the dough into oval shapes.

Bake in the oven for about 15 minutes, or until golden brown.

Remove the cookies from the sheet pan immediately using an offset spatula, and place on a rack to cool. To shape the cookies, curve them over a rolling pin while they are still warm.

YIELDS 1 DOZEN

Just-baked tegole cookies

Cascina Caremma's row of farmhouses

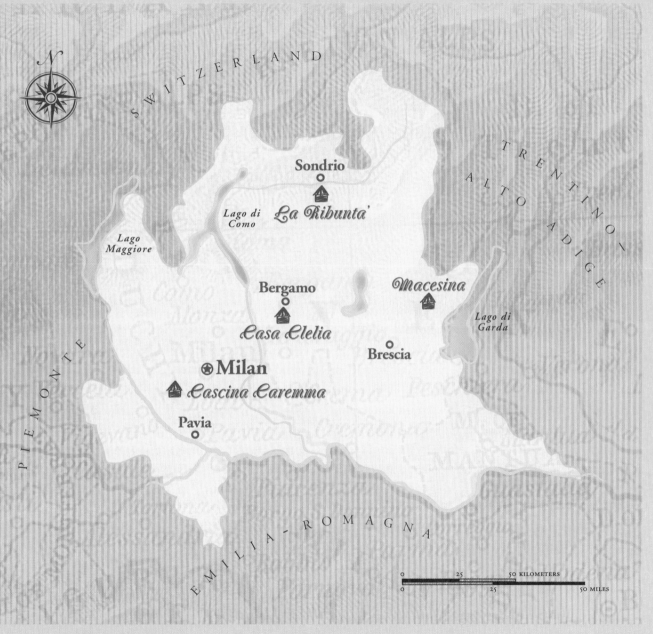

SWITZERLAND

TRENTINO/ ALTO ADIGE

Sondrio

Lago di Como

La Ribunta'

Lago Maggiore

Bergamo

Macesina

Lago di Garda

Casa Clelia

Brescia

Milan

Cascina Caremma

Pavia

PIEMONTE

EMILIA- ROMAGNA

| 0 | 25 | 50 KILOMETERS |
| 0 | 25 | 50 MILES |

Industrious, hard-working Milan has given Lombardian cuisine a bad name. Italy's most fast-paced and modern city pulses with activity, and its inhabitants are often accused of being too consumed with their careers to appreciate the pleasures of eating and drinking. While there may be some truth to this stereotype, the same cannot be said for the other ten provinces of Lombardia, which bring a wealth of culinary riches to the region's table.

Large open fields of rice and corn dominate the landscape of central Lombardia. Their cultivation gave rise to the numerous risotto dishes recognized throughout the region, as well as to the Lombardian love for dense yellow polenta, which acts as a sponge for succulent juices when accompanying meat courses. Pigs are also raised in great numbers, and Lombardians are touted as great salami makers. Their salami's particular taste and richness is attributed to the addition of the leg of the pig, which is commonly cured for prosciutto in other regions. Historically, large-scale farming has played an important economic role throughout the region, and it continues to today, with Lombardia's agricultural production ranking among the highest in all of Italy. Large farmhouses known as cascine dotted the countryside, part of a type of feudal system in which landowners and farmers coexisted together, living and working under the same roof. Today, many of these cascine have been restored to splendor and are open as agriturismi, offering a glimpse into Lombardian agrarian life.

The clear, still waters of Lombardia's lakes are perhaps the biggest draw for foreigners. Elegant villas behind closed gates pique curiosity about their possible movie-star owners, while quaint towns beckon with their open piazzas and restaurants with views. Fresh locally caught fish from these lakes have also made their mark on Lombardian cuisine, and today many species are farmed because of the high demand for their sweet freshwater taste. Warm air generated from lake waters lends a Mediterranean feel to the region and provides an optimal environment for producing top-notch extra-virgin olive oil, which, along with regional butter, is the main cooking fat.

Lombardia also boasts extraordinary mountains in its northern quarter, known as the Valtellina. Here exists another Lombardia, with Swiss influences both in cuisine and culture. A harsh climate led to the cultivation of buckwheat flour and its strong taste prevails in numerous local dishes. Deep purple air-dried beef, named bresaola, is another local gastronomic specialty rapidly gaining worldwide recognition. While Lombardian wines get little notice in world markets, the Valtellina produces a bottle-fermented sparkling wine, made using Champagne methods, that rivals some of France's best bubblies.

Lombardia's chief export, for which the food world owes its gratitude, is the region's many great cheeses. The delicious stink of Gorgonzola, eye-watering sharp provolone, the incredible melting cheese called Taleggio, and sinful full-fat mascarpone are only a few of Lombardy's contributions to the cheese board. While headstrong Milan bustles, competing on the global market, the rest of Lombardia sits back, basking in the abundance of regional pleasures at its fingertips.

Chapter 13

Cascina Caremma

Only thirty kilometers away from the dense urban chaos of Milan, Cascina Caremma's unspoiled position in Ticino National Park beckons city dwellers to a country retreat immersed in peace and tranquility. What began as a risky endeavor by Gabrielle Corti and his wife twenty years ago has evolved into a miniature self-sustaining village, with organic farming its fundamental philosophy. Eighty-eight acres of cultivated fields are spread among the low-lying plains whose fertile soil and humid climate produce corn, peas, barley, rye, wheat, and rice. Vines and small vegetable patches, as well as wild medicinal herbs, are found throughout the farm and free-range pigs live in the fields. All of these products, whether used to feed the animals, therapeutically at the farm's spa, or as the base for the restaurant's dishes, directly connect all facets of life at Cascina Caremma to the land. With an extreme respect for the land and tradition, Gabrielle has made his once-abandoned farm a self-sufficient environment complete with guest rooms, a beauty spa, a farm store, a restaurant, a butchery room, an open-air renovated hayloft for banquets and celebrations, a soccer field, and individual rooms for company meetings. In addition, Gabrielle has plans for a farm classroom where he will teach future generations the importance of self-sufficiency and organic farming. He also hopes to build a brewery for making beer from the farm's own barley and hops, as well as a laboratory for

making cheese. Perhaps what is most impressive about this agriturismo is that, among all the modern conveniences, practically everything exists because of an equilibrium with its surroundings. This low-impact approach toward living off the land ensures productive and fruitful harvests for years to come at Cascina Caremma.

What began as a small dining room with Gabrielle doing all of the cooking has morphed into a five-cook kitchen that practically never stops. Open for lunch and dinner as well as catering weddings and corporate meetings held at the farm, Cascina Caremma retains its personality through dishes prepared with the farm's own ingredients. Strictly seasonal and cooking only regional and classic Lombardian recipes, Cascina Caremma is a heightened dining experience, booked practically full every night of the week. Beginning the evening are numerous plates of antipasti: A vegetable strudel made with the farm's own whole-wheat flour and fried risotto cakes display the versatility with which raw ingredients are transformed into inventive finished dishes. Risotto and pasta, both from the farm's bounty, make up the first course,

and two meat courses follow, always with a side of polenta. This stone-ground corn has a unique texture that is both smooth and coarse. Gabrielle attests that it is some of the best in Italy because of the traditional method in which it is made: ground with giant stone wheels. Cascina Caremma's passion and dedication bring thousands of guests to the farm each year. For a brief moment in their lives, they experience a time-honored lifestyle nearly extinct in today's fast-paced world.

Corn stalks of Cascina Caremma

Whole-Wheat Strudel with Butternut Squash and Leek
STRUDEL INTEGRALE DI ZUCCA E PORRI

Strudels are most often seen on the dessert table, but at Cascina Caremma, a savory strudel is always included in the army of antipasti plates. Whole-wheat flour comes from one of the many grains that flourish at the farm and is used to make a nutty, buttery dough.

Make the dough: In the bowl of an electric mixer fitted with the paddle attachment, combine the flour, salt, and butter and mix on low speed until the dough forms coarse crumbs the size of hazelnuts. Gradually add the water in a steady stream until the dough just comes together. Turn the dough out onto a sheet of plastic wrap, flatten into a disc, and refrigerate for at least 1 hour.

Heat the oven to 425°F (220°C).

Cut the butternut squash in half, remove the seeds, and rub with olive oil. Place skin side up on a sheet pan. Roast in the oven until tender, 40 to 45 minutes. Remove from the oven and set aside to cool. Reduce the oven temperature to 375°F (190°C).

In a 12-inch sauté pan, melt butter over medium-low heat. Add the leeks and cook until extremely tender but not browned, 15 to 20 minutes.

Spoon the flesh from the butternut squash into a large bowl and mash until smooth. Mix in the leeks, parsley, cheese, and extra-virgin olive oil and season to taste with salt and pepper.

Remove the dough from the refrigerator. Roll out into a rectangle on a lightly floured surface until ¼ inch thick. Spread the filling down the center of the dough, and then fold the edges of the dough over, enclosing the filling like an envelope. Place dough on a sheet pan lined with parchment paper. Bake in the oven until deep golden brown and firm, 25 to 30 minutes.

Let cool. Cut the strudel into slices and serve at room temperature.

SERVES 8

Dough
2¼ cups (280 g) whole-wheat flour
Pinch of table salt
16 tablespoons (8 oz. / 230 g) European-style unsalted butter, cold and cut into pieces
⅓ cup (3 fl. oz. / 80 ml) ice water

Filling
1 medium butternut squash
1 tablespoon (½ fl. oz. / 15 ml) extra-virgin olive oil
2 tablespoons (1 oz. / 30 g) unsalted butter
3 leeks, cleaned and cut into slices
¼ cup chopped flat-leaf parsley
½ cup grated Grana Padano cheese
1 tablespoon (½ fl. oz. / 15 ml) extra-virgin olive oil
Kosher salt and freshly ground black pepper

Potato Croquettes with Taleggio Cheese Sauce
CROCCHETTE DI PATATE CON FONDUTA DI TALEGGIO

At Cascina Caremma, guests are served an onslaught of appetizers. This is just one of the many that make their way to the table nightly. The creaminess of the potato croquette is extra decadent with the velvety Taleggio cheese sauce.

Croquettes

1 pound (450 g) russet potatoes, peeled and quartered

Kosher salt and freshly ground black pepper

2 tablespoons (1 oz. / 30 g) unsalted butter

½ cup (4 fl. oz. / 120 ml) heavy cream

2 large eggs, plus 2 egg yolks

½ cup grated Parmigiano Reggiano

2 tablespoons chopped flat-leaf parsley

¼ cup (30 g) all-purpose flour

¼ cup (30 g) bread crumbs

2 cups (16 fl. oz. / 480 ml) vegetable oil

Fonduta

¾ cup (130 g) cubed Taleggio cheese

½ cup (4 fl. oz. / 120 ml) whole milk

1 egg yolk

Pinch of white pepper

Place the potatoes in a 6-quart saucepan and cover with cold water. Place over medium-high heat and bring to a boil. Add 1 tablespoon salt and simmer until tender, about 15 minutes. Drain the potatoes and then either pass through a ricer into a medium-size bowl or mash well with a hand masher. Stir in the butter, heavy cream, 1 whole egg, egg yolks, Parmigiano Reggiano, and parsley. Mix well to combine and season to taste with salt and pepper. Cover and place in the refrigerator for at least 1 hour.

Place the flour and bread crumbs in separate dishes and lightly beat the remaining egg in a shallow bowl. Spoon up some of the potato mixture and form into a 1-inch round ball. Roll in the flour, then dip in the egg, and then coat with the bread crumbs. Set aside on a sheet pan and continue making croquettes in this fashion until all the potato mixture is gone; you should have 8 croquettes. Refrigerate for at least 30 minutes before frying.

Meanwhile, soak the Taleggio cheese in the milk for about 20 minutes. In a small saucepan, combine the milk, Taleggio, and egg yolk. Warm over low heat and stir continuously to melt the cheese. Be careful not to allow the mixture to boil, or the cheese will separate. Add the white pepper.

Heat the oven to 200°F (90°C). Heat 2 cups of vegetable oil over medium heat until shimmering. Add the potato croquettes in batches and fry until golden brown all over, about 5 minutes. Remove the croquettes to a sheet pan lined with paper towels to drain and place in the oven to keep warm while you fry the remaining croquettes.

Serve each of the croquettes with a dollop of fonduta.

YIELDS 8 CROQUETTES

Pork Stew with Prunes and Pine Nuts
BOCCONCINI DI MAIALE CON PRUGNE E PIGNOLI

At Cascina Caremma this dish is made with wild boar and served beside the farm's own stone-ground polenta. If available, substitute wild boar for the pork; the flavor will be a little stronger, but it works well with the sweet prunes.

Heat the oven to 300°F (150°C).

Season the pork all over with 1 teaspoon salt and ½ teaspoon pepper. In a large heavy-bottomed casserole pan, add 2 tablespoons olive oil over medium heat and brown pork on all sides until a rich golden brown, about 10 minutes. Remove the pork to a plate lined with paper towels to drain the fat, and pour off all but 1 tablespoon of the fat from the pan.

Add 1 tablespoon of oil to the pan. Add the onion, celery, carrot, and a pinch of salt and sauté until tender and starting to brown, about 7 minutes. Add the white wine and bring up to a boil, scraping any browned bits from the pan with a wooden spoon.

Return the pork to the pan, adding the bay leaf and chicken broth, and bring to a boil. Cover, leaving the lid slightly ajar. Reduce the heat to low and cook until the meat is fork-tender, 1¾ to 2 hours.

Toast the pine nuts in a the oven for 3 or 4 minutes. Add the toasted pine nuts and the prunes to the pork and continue to cook 15 minutes more. Ladle into shallow bowls and serve immediately.

SERVES 6

3 pounds (1⅓ kg) Boston butt, trimmed of excess fat and cut into 1-inch cubes

Kosher salt and freshly ground black pepper

3 tablespoons (1½ fl. oz. / 45 ml) extra-virgin olive oil

1 medium yellow onion, cut into medium dice

1 stalk celery, cut into medium dice

1 carrot, peeled and cut into medium dice

¾ cup (6 fl. oz. / 180 ml) white wine

1 bay leaf

3 cups (24 fl. oz. / 720 ml) home-made chicken broth (see page xi) or canned low-sodium broth

¼ cup (35 g) pine nuts

4 ounces (115 g) prunes

Saffron Risotto with Sausage and Kale

RISOTTO ALLO ZAFFERANO CON SALSICCIA
E CAVOLO NERO

The combination of saffron and risotto was fashioned in Lombardy, and the region's most recognized rice dish, risotto alla Milanese, uses the spice judiciously for both color and flavor. This risotto adds saffron threads to the classic pairing of sausage and leafy kale for a great fall first course.

1 quart (32 fl. oz. / 960 ml) homemade chicken broth (see page xi)
or canned low-sodium broth

1 large pinch saffron threads

2 tablespoons (1 fl. oz. / 30 ml)
extra-virgin olive oil

1 yellow onion, cut into small dice

½ pound (225 g) sweet Italian
sausage, casing removed and
crumbled

1 cup (8 fl. oz. / 240 ml) full-bodied
red wine

1 bunch kale, cut into 1-inch ribbons,
plus more for garnish

2 cups Arborio rice

1 cup (8 fl. oz. / 240 ml) white wine

Kosher salt and freshly ground black
pepper

3 tablespoons (1½ oz. / 45 g) unsalted butter

¼ cup grated Parmigiano Reggiano

Heat the chicken broth with the saffron in a 4-quart saucepan over medium heat. Bring up to a boil, then lower the heat and keep warm.

In a 12-inch straight-sided sauté pan, warm the olive oil over medium heat. Add the onion and a pinch of salt, then sauté until tender and translucent, about 7 minutes. Add the sausage to the pan, stirring occasionally, and sauté until browned, about 5 minutes. Add ½ cup red wine to the pan and simmer until reduced to dry, about 10 minutes.

Add the kale to the pan and cook until wilted, about 10 minutes. Add the rice to the pan and toast, 2 to 3 minutes. Pour in the white wine and the remaining ½ cup of red wine, bring to a boil, and reduce until dry.

Add the broth to the pan one ladle at a time, to cover the rice, stirring constantly with a wooden spoon until the broth has been completely absorbed by the rice. Continue to ladle broth into the risotto in the same manner, one ladle at a time, stirring continuously, until the rice is al dente and creamy, about 15 minutes. Season to taste with salt and pepper.

Stir in the butter and the grated cheese and garnish with a tablespoon of finely chopped raw kale. Serve in individual shallow bowls.

SERVES 4

Adding saffron broth to cooking risotto

Mixed-Grain Butter Cookies
PAN MEJIN CASCINA CAREMMA

2 tablespoons (20 g) fine cornmeal

¼ cup (40 g) whole-wheat flour

¼ cup (40 g) all-purpose flour

3 tablespoons (1½ oz. / 45 g) un-salted butter

¼ cup (50 g) granulated sugar

1 egg yolk

Pinch of salt

1 tablespoon (½ fl. oz. / 15 ml) Marsala

½ teaspoon baking powder

¼ teaspoon baking soda

Grains are one of the primary agricultural products at Cascina Caremma, and this recipe uses and exhibits some of those prized resources. The pan mejin is a delicate cookie with a rich buttery flavor and a crunchy texture, best served with afternoon tea or a glass of chilled sweet wine.

In the bowl of an electric mixer fitted with the paddle attachment, mix together all of the ingredients until they begin to come together and form a dough. Scrape the dough out onto a clean work surface and shape into a round disc. Wrap in plastic wrap and chill in the refrigerator at least 1 hour.

Heat the oven to 350°F (180°C).

Remove the dough from the refrigerator. Lightly dust a work surface with flour. Roll out the dough until ¼ inch thick. Cut out cookies using a small round cookie cutter. Place on a parchment-lined sheet pan and bake for 12 minutes, or until set and lightly browned. Remove from the oven and with an offset spatula transfer the cookies on a rack to cool.

YIELDS 1 DOZEN

IL TICINO PARK

Milan's urban sprawl, with its overpopulation, congestion, and smog, makes Ticino National Park a gem of natural rural beauty only thirty minutes from the city center. The rapidly flowing Ticino River slices through its core, and with it brings wildlife, lush landscapes, and plenty of water to hydrate the fertile rice fields in the vast plains of the park. Cascina Caremma lies in the heart of this thriving ecosystem, which provides the agriturismo with an abundant bounty of grains, vegetables, and wild herbs.

CHAPTER 14

La Ribunta'

Valtellina, the most northern part of Lombardia, spans a deep valley, flanked on both sides by imposing mountain chains that connect Italy to Switzerland. The Valtellina boasts a populace proud of its mountain heritage and a culture decisively different from that found in the towns surrounding the region's lakes, that of the Lombard plains, or the fast-paced life of Milan. Here, at the base of a mountain above the Ada River, Fabio and Kika enthusiastically welcome guests into their home and agriturismo. A true gourmet and a lover of the region's fine red wines, Fabio sprinkles his promotion of his region's cuisine with historical facts about the antique farming tools that adorn the dining room. He also boasts an exceptional palate and is a judge on a regional board for local cheeses. Ribunta's small farm consists of a diverse vegetable garden and small pens in which chickens, ducks, and rabbits are raised for the restaurant.

Twenty kilometers from La Ribunta', Fabio and Kika's apple orchard flourishes in the fall months. The fruit is picked and stored in the couple's temperate cantina beneath the agriturismo. The apples are stacked in wooden boxes amid an impressive wine cellar, jars of the farm's preserves, wheels of aging local Bitto and Casera cheeses, homemade lard, and bresaola (a regional air-cured beef) dangling from wooden dowels.

Valtellina mountain cuisine greatly differs from that of the rest of Lombardy. Out of La Ribunta's kitchen emerge dishes that are one part typical Valtellina and another part Kika's concoctions. Standard cold-weather staples include buckwheat and rye flours, cabbage, potatoes, butter, lard, and rich creamy cheese. A traditional dish that incorporates nearly all of these ingredients is pizzoccheri, a type of pasta made from buckwheat flour, whose heavy, dense consistency and rich Casera cheese sauce offered energy and endurance during the harsh winters. Taroz, a type of potato puree with fresh green and yellow beans, lots of butter, and even more cheese, stands out as a fortifying side dish, suitable for vigorous alpine activity. Pork tenderloin with a crispy outer crust from a dredging in chestnut flour and strange-sounding but delicious blueberry risotto are Kika's whimsical creations, developed from what her farm brings to her pantry. With Fabio as waiter and sommelier offering profound knowledge about local wines, the husband-and-wife team at La Ribunta' brings to life Lombard mountain culture.

Buckwheat Cheese Fritters
SCHIAT

Schiat means "toad" in Valtellinian dialect: Once fried, these cheese fritters resemble frog legs. As unappetizing as this may sound, these delicious treats are difficult to stop eating.

8 ounces (225 g) Casera cheese (or substitute Gruyère), cut into ½-inch cubes

1¼ cups (150 g) buckwheat flour

¾ cup (100 g) all-purpose flour

Kosher salt

1 tablespoon (½ fl. oz. / 15 ml) grappa

1⅛ cups (9 fl. oz. / 270 ml) water

2 cups (16 fl. oz. / 480 ml) canola oil

Place the cheese on a plate lined with parchment paper and cover with another piece of parchment. Place in the freezer until the cheese is cold throughout, about 40 minutes.

Mix together the flours and ½ tablespoon salt. Add the grappa. Stir in enough water to make a pancake-like batter.

Heat the canola oil in a heavy 3-inch-deep sauté pan over medium-high heat until shimmering. Dip the cheese into the batter and then spoon some batter and 1 cube of cheese into the hot oil. Fry until deep golden brown and puffed. Drain on a paper towel and sprinkle with a pinch of salt. Continue frying the rest of the cheese. Serve immediately.

SERVES 6

Testing batter for frying cheese

Fried cheese

Green and Yellow Wax Bean Casserole
TAROZ

This hearty vegetable dish could easily make for a full meal. Potatoes and fresh green and yellow beans are fortified with lots of cheese and butter. Mashing them all together makes for a rib-sticking dish suited for cold Valtellina winters.

8 ounces (225 g) yellow wax beans

8 ounces (225 g) string beans

1 pound (450 g) Yukon Gold
   potatoes

3 tablespoons (1½ oz. / 45 g)
   unsalted butter

1 tablespoon chopped sage

4 ounces (115 g) shredded Casera
   cheese (or substitute Gruyère)

Kosher salt and freshly ground black
   pepper

Trim the beans and cut in half. Peel the potatoes and cut into quarters and then ¼-inch-thick slices.

Place the potatoes in a 6-quart saucepan and add cold water to cover and 1 tablespoon of salt. Bring the water to a boil, then lower the heat, simmering gently for about 7 minutes. Add the beans to the boiling water and continue to cook until the potatoes are tender, 5 to 7 minutes longer.

Melt the butter in a small saucepan and then add the sage. Cook until the butter becomes golden brown.

Drain the potatoes and the beans and then return to the pan. With a wooden spoon or the bottom of a ladle, mash together the potatoes and the green beans until slightly broken up. Place the potato mixture in a serving bowl and stir together with the cheese. Pour the hot butter over and stir together until the cheese has melted and holds together all of the ingredients. Season to taste with salt and pepper. Serve immediately.

SERVES 4

Pork Tenderloin with Chestnut-Flour Coating

FILETTO DI MAIALE IN CROSTA DI FARINA DI CASTAGNE

The chestnut flour creates a tasty crust that seals in the juiciness of the pork. Combined with the honey, it adds a distinct flavor profile that complements the meat. Chestnut flour is often found in specialty food stores, especially Italian markets.

1 pork tenderloin (1½–2 pounds / 500–900 g)

Kosher salt and freshly ground black pepper

¼ cup (55 g) chestnut flour

4 tablespoons (2 oz. / 60 g) unsalted butter

½ cup (4 fl. oz. / 120 ml) white wine

1 tablespoon (½ fl. oz. / 15 ml) honey

1 tablespoon chopped sage

¼ cup (2 fl. oz. / 60 ml) homemade chicken broth (see page xi) or canned low-sodium broth

Heat the oven to 400°F (200°C).

Salt and pepper the pork tenderloin. Dredge in the chestnut flour. Melt 2 tablespoons butter in a large ovenproof sauté pan, add the pork tenderloin, and sear on all sides until browned, 2 to 3 minutes per side. Place the pan in the oven until the pork is cooked through and registers 150°F (65°C) on a meat thermometer, about 20 minutes.

Transfer the pork to a cutting board and let rest. Place the pan back on the stove over medium-high heat, Add white wine to the pan and scrape up any browned bits with a spoon. Reduce the wine by half and then add the honey and the sage, and cook until the honey is dissolved, 1 to 2 minutes. Add the broth and reduce by half, then whisk in the remaining 2 tablespoons of butter. Season to taste with salt and pepper. Cut the pork into medallions, place on a serving platter, and drizzle with the sauce.

SERVES 4

Duck Breast with Apples
PETTO D'ANATRA CON MELE

Fruit is a common accompaniment to duck, as the sweet undertones of the fruit complement the fatty gaminess of the bird.

2 1-pound (900 g) duck breasts

Kosher salt and freshly ground black pepper

1 yellow onion, cut into fine dice

2 Golden Delicious apples, peeled, cored, and cut into fine dice

½ cup (4 fl. oz. / 120 ml) white wine

¾ cup (6 fl. oz. / 180 ml) homemade chicken broth (see page xi) or canned low-sodium broth

1 tablespoon (½ oz. / 15 g) unsalted butter

1 tablespoon chopped thyme

2 tablespoons chopped sage

With a sharp knife, score the skin of the duck breasts into a ½-inch cross-hatch pattern. Season all over with salt and pepper. Cook the duck, skin side down, over medium-low heat in a heavy-bottom sauté pan. Slowly render the fat from the skin without moving the breasts. Carefully pour off some of the fat as it accumulates. Cook until the skin is rich golden brown and crispy, 20 to 25 minutes. Remove all but 2 tablespoons of the fat from the pan. Turn the duck breasts over, raise the heat to medium, and continue to cook until the duck breasts are golden brown and medium-rare, 3 to 4 minutes (or until an instant-read thermometer registers 135°F (57°C). Transfer the duck skin side up to a cutting board and let rest.

Add the onions and the apples to the sauté pan and season with salt. Cook until tender, 7 to 10 minutes, then add the white wine and reduce until almost dry. Add the broth and reduce by half, then stir in the butter and the herbs.

Carve the duck into slices and serve with the apple and onion salsa.

SERVES 4

La Ribunta' apples

CENTRALFRUTTA
BOLOGNA - ITALIA

AGING BITTO CHEESE

In Fabio's cantina, among hundred of wine bottles and various types of hanging salami, is his proud collection of aging Valtellina cheeses. Bitto and Casera are two of the valley's most recognized agricultural products and they are used extensively in traditional recipes. Bitto is an aged and robust cheese made in the mountains in summer, using milk from cows who spend their summers grazing in the alpine meadows. Casera is milder and is produced year-round at lower elevations. At La Ribunta', some of the cheeses Kika uses to give a pungent bite to her cooking are more than twenty years old.

Valtellina mountain cheeses

CHAPTER 15
CASA CLELIA

A seventeenth-century stone farmhouse, Casa Clelia is tucked away from the bustling environs surrounding it and immersed in woods, with gardens, orchards, and stables making up the farm. Rosanna, Casa Clelia's forward-thinking proprietor, restored the manor house with green, environmentally-sensible materials and methods. Solar panels and a wood-fired burner provide most of the energy used at the bustling agriturismo. Individual rooms each have their own style and decor, yet all share the same intimacy and rustic aesthetic, with warm wood tones, satin fabrics, and exposed stone walls. Two dining rooms with exposed beams, barrel vaults, simple antique furniture, and fireplaces make for an unpretentious and embracing environment. A large organic vegetable garden and sheep, chickens, pigs, and cows are the farm's production, making for versatile and interesting Lombardian cuisine.

Remo has been Rosanna's chef for the last five years and he possesses a sound knowledge of Lombardian specialties. His four-man kitchen works efficiently to create nightly tasting menus that feature a large mixed antipasto plate, two primi (one of which is always risotto), two meat courses, a vegetable, and dessert. Organic vegetables and Casa Clelia's own meats provide an excellent base for Remo's cooking. His Bergamo-style ravioli, named for the nearby two-tiered medieval town, is loaded with ground beef and pork and blended with sweet amaretti cookies and raisins. The result is a play of savory and sweet, reflec-

tive of the city it is named after, where vast differences between the upper medieval center and lower more modern town work together to create a harmonious urban environment. Remo's professional capabilities also come out through intricate desserts, and a mousse made from sparkling Prosecco and persimmons shows off his talents. Casa Clelia's multiple-course meals provide satiation rather than fullness, allowing diners to indulge in all that the farm and chef have to offer. The kitchen also keeps busy making marmalades, conserves, and jarred marinated vegetables, all of which are for sale and presented in a rustic wooden hutch in the agriturismo's lobby. Casa Clelia provides an agriturismo experience that retains the character and charm of yesteryear while moving forward to embrace an ecological future, forging a harmonic environment with lots of good sensible eating.

Savoy cabbage

Risotto with Red Cabbage and Taleggio Cheese

RISOTTO CON CAVOLO ROSSO E TALEGGIO

Taleggio cheese and Grana Padano cheese both hail from the Lombardy region. Taleggio is creamy and soft with a mild flavor and is good on a cheese plate, as a base for a cheese sauce, or stirred into risotto to enhance the creaminess of the rice. Grana Padano is a hard, sharp cheese that is usually grated over pasta, soup, and risotto.

In a large 12-inch skillet over medium heat, sauté ½ cup of onion in 1 tablespoon butter and 1 tablespoon olive oil. Cook until the onion becomes tender, 5 to 7 minutes. Add the red cabbage and continue to cook until it begins to soften, about 10 minutes. Season with salt and pepper. Raise the heat to high and pour in the red wine. Bring to a boil, then reduce the heat to low and cook slowly until the wine has reduced completely. Remove skillet from heat.

Meanwhile, in a 12-inch straight-sided sauté pan, add 1 tablespoon olive oil, 1 tablespoon butter, and remaining onion and sauté over medium heat until tender and translucent. Add the rice to the pan, coat it with the olive oil and butter, and cook until slightly toasted, about 2 minutes. Add the white wine and reduce to dry.

Pour the chicken broth into a 3-quart saucepan and bring to a boil. Remove from heat and keep warm. Add a ladle of the broth to cover the rice, and stir continuously until the broth has reduced to below the rice. Add another ladle of broth to cover, and continue cooking the rice in this manner for about 10 minutes, stirring continously. Add the cabbage and continue to cook, adding broth one ladle at a time, until the rice is al dente, 10 minutes.

Add the Taleggio and the Grana Padano. Stir until the cheese is melted and well combined. Adjust seasoning if needed, and serve with some fresh parsley sprinkled on top.

SERVES 4–6

1 large yellow onion, cut into fine dice

2 tablespoons (1 oz. / 30 g) unsalted butter

2 tablespoons (1 fl. oz. / 30 ml) extra-virgin olive oil

1 head red cabbage, shredded

Kosher salt and freshly ground black pepper

1½ cups (12 fl. oz. / 340 ml) red wine

2 cups Arborio rice

1 cup (8 fl. oz. / 240 ml) white wine

1 quart (32 fl. oz. / 960 ml) homemade chicken broth (see page xi) or canned low-sodium broth

4 ounces (115 g) Taleggio cheese, cut into pieces

2 tablespoons grated Grana Padano cheese

1 tablespoon chopped flat-leaf parsley

Bergamo-Style Ravioli
CASONCELLI ALLA BERGAMASCA

Casa Clelia sits ten minutes outside of Bergamo, and many of the dishes served there are influenced by the small medieval city. Amaretti, the almond-laced cookies, originate from Lombardy and play an integral role in its cuisine. They are found in many meat fillings, creating a play on sweet and savory.

5 tablespoons (2½ oz. / 75 g) unsalted butter

1 yellow onion, cut into small dice

1 peeled and sliced clove of garlic

12 ounces (340 g) ground beef

8 ounces (225 g) ground pork

Kosher salt and freshly ground black pepper

1½ cups (12 fl. oz. / 340 ml) red wine

1 tablespoon lemon zest

1 ounce (30 g) amaretti cookies, broken up into small pieces

1 cup (125 g) bread crumbs

2 tablespoons (25 g) raisins

3 tablespoons (1½ fl. oz. / 45 ml) whole milk

¼ cup grated Grana Padano or Parmigiano Reggiano

1 recipe basic pasta dough (see page viii)

4 ounces (115 g) cubed pancetta

1 tablespoon chopped sage

Add 2 tablespoons of butter to a large sauté pan over medium heat. Add the onion and garlic and sauté, being careful not to burn the garlic, until tender, 5 to 7 minutes. Add the ground meat, season with salt and pepper, stir occasionally to break up the meat, and brown, about 10 minutes. Add the red wine and cook slowly over medium-low heat, reducing the wine until dry. Add the lemon zest and the amaretti cookies, and stir well to combine.

Moisten the bread crumbs and the raisins in the milk. Add to the meat mixture and stir well to combine. Pulse all of the ingredients together in a food processor until roughly combined. Stir in the grated cheese.

Divide the dough into 4 pieces. Using a pasta machine, start at the widest setting and end with the second to thinnest setting as you roll out the dough. To form the ravioli, cut the sheets of dough into 3-inch circles with a glass or cookie cutter. Place a spoonful of filling in the center of each round. Fold the dough over the filling, pressing out any air, to make a crescent-moon shape. Then press down on the flat side of the crescent moon to form a dip in the center.

Bring 6 quarts of salted water to a boil.

Meanwhile, sauté the pancetta in a medium-size sauté pan over medium heat, until it renders some of its fat and begins to cook, but do not allow it to become crispy. Remove some grease from the pan, if necessary, and add the remaining butter. Once melted and beginning to foam, add the sage leaves.

Drop the ravioli in the boiling water and cook until they begin to float to the top and are tender, 2 to 3 minutes. Drain the ravioli and add them to the pan with the pancetta and sage. Toss to coat and season to taste with salt and pepper. Serve immediately.

SERVES 6–8

Shaping Bergamo-style ravioli

Herb-Encrusted Rack of Lamb with Roasted Potatoes, Peppers, and Pancetta

COSTATA D'AGNELLO CON ERBE, PATATE, PEPERONI, E PANCETTA

Lamb is a specialty of Lombardia, and a favorite is agnello da latte, which translates as "suckling lamb." Slaughtered at one to three months old, the lamb is sweet, tender, and aromatic.

2 large Yukon Gold potatoes, cut into wedges

1 red bell pepper, cut into ¼-inch strips

3 ounces (85 g) pancetta, cut into small dice

¼ cup plus 2 tablespoons (5 fl. oz. / 150 ml) extra-virgin olive oil

Kosher salt and freshly ground black pepper

2 frenched racks of lamb (8 ribs and 1–1½ pounds each / 450–675 g)

1 tablespoon (½ oz. / 15 g) unsalted butter

1½ cups (187 g) bread crumbs

2 tablespoons minced flat-leaf parsley

1 tablespoon lemon zest

¼ cup grated Parmigiano Reggiano

1 peeled and minced clove of garlic

¾ cup (6 fl. oz. / 180 ml) red wine

Heat the oven to 425°F (220°C).

Toss the potatoes, peppers, and pancetta with ¼ cup of olive oil. Season with salt and pepper and roast in the oven until the potatoes are golden brown and crispy, 40 to 45 minutes.

Season the racks of lamb with salt and pepper. Heat 2 tablespoons of olive oil and 1 tablespoon of butter in a 12-inch ovenproof skillet over medium-high heat. Sear the lamb until rich golden brown, about 3 minutes per side. Remove from the heat and set aside.

In a shallow dish, mix together the bread crumbs, parsley, lemon zest, cheese, and garlic. Coat the racks of lamb with the bread crumb mixture. Return to the skillet fat side up and roast in the oven for 12 to 15 minutes, until medium-rare—135°F (57°C) on a meat thermometer. Remove the lamb from the skillet, and let rest at least 10 minutes before carving.

Make a pan sauce with the drippings from the lamb. Place the skillet over high heat, deglaze with the red wine, scraping up any browned bits with a wooden spoon, and cook until reduced by half. Carve the racks of lamb into individual chops.

Spoon the potato medley in the center of individual dinner plates, fan four chops per plate over the potatoes, and drizzle with the pan sauce. Serve immediately.

SERVES 4

Just-born lamb

Lavender chicken

Chicken Breast with Lavender
PETTO DI POLLO ALLA LAVANDA

The pancetta and the chicken skin seal in the meat's juiciness, while the exterior is crisp and fragrant. The lavender bread crumb coating tantalizes the senses.

Heat the oven to 400°F (200°C).

Season the chicken breasts with salt and pepper. Arrange 3 slices of pancetta on the bottom side of each chicken breast and tie with kitchen string. In a large ovenproof skillet, over medium-high heat, heat 2 tablespoons olive oil and sear the chicken breasts on both sides, until the skin side is golden and the pancetta side is somewhat crispy, about 4 minutes per side. Remove chicken breasts from the pan, discard the kitchen string, and set chicken aside.

Briefly pulse together the bread crumbs and the lavender in a small food processor. Lightly coat the chicken breasts with the bread crumb mixture.

Return the chicken to the skillet and cook in the oven skin side up until the chicken is cooked through, about 20 minutes or until an instant thermometer registers 165°F (74°C). Place the chicken on a serving platter.

Prepare a pan sauce: Place the skillet over medium-high heat and add the chicken broth. Bring to a boil, then lower the heat and let simmer for about 5 minutes, until reduced by half. Drizzle the chicken with the sauce and garnish with lavender to serve.

SERVES 4

4 boneless chicken breasts, skin on

Kosher salt and freshly ground black pepper

12 thin slices pancetta

2 tablespoons (1 fl. oz. / 30 ml) extra-virgin olive oil

1 cup (125 g) bread crumbs

2½ tablespoons lavender, plus more for garnish

1 cup (8 fl. oz. / 240 ml) homemade chicken broth (see page xi) or canned low-sodium broth

Crepes with Apples and Gorgonzola
CRESPELLE CON MELE E GORGONZOLA

Crespelle are the Italian version of crepes, and they are used in many preparations throughout the country. At Casa Clelia, the crepes are filled with a sweet Gorgonzola sauce and topped with diced apple salsa. Remo usually serves the crepelle as an appetizer, but they also make an interesting dessert.

6 tablespoons (3 oz. / 90 g) unsalted butter

5 tablespoons (75 g) all-purpose flour

2 cups (16 fl. oz. / 480 ml) whole milk

5 ounces (142 g) crumbled Gorgonzola dolce

¼ cup grated Grana Padano

Pinch of freshly grated nutmeg

Kosher salt and freshly ground white pepper

2 Golden Delicious apples, peeled and cored and cut into small dice

Pinch of cinnamon

1 teaspoon (5 ml) lemon juice

1 tablespoon granulated sugar

1 recipe crepes (see page ix)

Heat the oven to 375°F (180°C).

For the filling: Melt 5 tablespoons of butter in a 3-quart saucepan. Add the flour and stir with a wooden spoon until combined. Cook over medium heat until golden brown, 2 to 3 minutes. Whisk in the milk until smooth and free of lumps, and bring to a boil. Reduce the heat to low and simmer until thickened. Stir in the Gorgonzola, the Grana Padano, and a pinch of nutmeg. Season to taste with salt and white pepper.

Melt 1 tablespoon of butter in a medium-size sauté pan. Add the apples and cook until tender, 3 to 5 minutes. Sprinkle with cinnamon, 1 teaspoon of lemon juice, and sugar, and sauté for 2 or 3 more minutes.

Assemble the crespelle: Fill each crepe with 3 tablespoons of the cheese sauce. Fold in half and then in half again. (They should have a triangular shape.) Place the filled crespelle on a sheet pan, drizzle cheese sauce over the top, and bake in the oven until they are warmed through and the sauce is bubbly, 10 to 12 minutes.

Place crespelle on individual plates, spoon some of the apple mixture over them, and serve warm.

SERVES 6

Chef Remo, left, at home in Casa Clelia's kitchen

Prosecco mousse and peach puree

Prosecco Mousse with Peach Puree
SPUMA DI PROSECCO E PESCHE

Prosecco is a dry sparkling wine hailing from the Veneto; however, it is a favorite libation throughout the country. A classic drink, the Bellini, combines peach nectar with Prosecco and is often imbibed as an aperitivo. Here that same classic pairing comes together in a luscious dessert, with silky Prosecco mousse topping a light peach jelly.

Combine the peaches, sugar, pectin, and vanilla bean (split in half with the pulp scraped) in a medium-size saucepan. Cook over medium-high heat, bringing to a boil, reduce heat to medium-low and simmer for about 15 minutes, until the peaches have broken down. Remove from heat, discard vanilla bean, and let cool. Pour mixture into a blender and puree until smooth. Pour the peach puree into 8 individual glass cups, filling one-third full, and refrigerate.

In the bowl of an electric mixer fitted with the paddle attachment, beat the sugar and egg yolks until pale yellow and thickened, 3 to 5 minutes.

Pour 1 cup (240 ml) of Prosecco into a small bowl. Sprinkle the gelatin evenly over the surface of the Prosecco and let rest 10 minutes. Add the Prosecco to the egg mixture, and stir until well combined. Place the bowl over a pan of barely simmering water over low heat (double boiler) and whisk until the mixture has doubled in volume, about 4 minutes. Remove from the heat and let cool.

Whip the heavy cream until soft peaks form, and fold into the Prosecco mixture. Gradually beat in the remaining ½ cup Prosecco and whip until stiff peaks form. Using a spatula, add a quarter of the whipped cream to the egg mixture and stir together gently. Fold the remaining whipped cream into the mixture until completely combined.

Pour the mousse into the cups over the peach puree, cover with plastic wrap, and return to the fridge to set, at least 4 hours.

SERVES 8

Peach puree

2 pounds (900 g) peaches, peeled, and cut into ½-inch cubes

½ cup (100 g) granulated sugar

1 tablespoon (10 g) pectin

1 vanilla bean

Mousse

1¾ cups (350 g) granulated sugar

12 large egg yolks

1½ cups (12 fl. oz. / 350 ml) Prosecco

½ tablespoon (5 g) powdered gelatin

1 quart (32 fl. oz. / 960 ml) heavy cream

Macesina's restored agriturismo

CHAPTER 16

MACESINA

The bright greens, deep oranges, and golden yellows of Macesina burst with vitality against a dull backdrop of heavy Lombardian haze. An original cascina, where landowners and farmers coexisted, it has been owned for generations by the family of twin sisters Marta and Francesca. Today an immaculately renovated agriturismo has returned the farm to its former splendor. It is hard to imagine the years of formidable work that went into restoring the abandoned building, which now emits warmth and prosperity. In the interior medieval courtyard stands a single knotty olive tree, reflective of the farm's main production and the eternal symbol of peace. Macesina's barns have been converted into functioning rooms of the agriturismo, which surround the courtyard and provide guests a glimpse of what life in the farmhouse community might have been like. Surrounding fields of corn and wheat and five hundred olive trees are the agriturismo's main production, and they flourish in the warm Mediterranean-like air, which blows from nearby Lake Garda.

Francesca, the main cook (with Marta as her sidekick), primarily prepares specialties from Brescia, a quaint historic town twenty minutes away. Risotto, polenta, and local fresh pasta are often served, as well as rich meats, freshwater fish, and game. A good friend of the family, Ital, is an avid hunter and fisherman and often supplies the farm with wild mountain venison, trout, and wild duck. The family's next-door neighbor, Adamello, whose father

once worked tending Macesina's land, raises rabbits, chickens, and capon for the sisters, as well as lending a hand in the fields.

Lombardy has the luxury of producing great butter as well as olive oil, and Francesca uses both in her cooking. Both sisters' husbands, Roberto and Oscar, serve as waiters in the small restaurant, which is open only to guests, and recommend wines from a small list from a producer down the road and offer information about their variety of cheeses, from local farms around the agriturismo. Oscar's brother, president of the local Slow Food faction, has a farm nearby that specializes in honey, which accompanies the cheese course. Macesina's restoration has revitalized not only the farm itself but an entire community, and that community's devotion to promoting its goods is evident in Macesina's nightly meals, abundant with the farm's own ingredients as well as local products.

Spinach Dumplings in a Butter-Sage Sauce
MALFATTI CON BURRO E SALVIA

8 ounces (225 g) ricotta

1 pound (450 g) spinach, blanched
and finely chopped

1 cup (125 g) bread crumbs

1 teaspoon nutmeg

½ cup grated Grana Padano cheese,
plus more for serving

2 eggs

All-purpose flour, as needed

8 tablespoons (4 oz. / 115 g) unsalted
butter

2 tablespoons chopped sage

Kosher salt and freshly ground black
pepper

Malfatti translates as "poorly made," and these large dumplings are cut irregularly. They are a specialty from Brescia in Lombardy and are the region's version of ricotta gnocchi.

In a medium-size bowl mix together the ricotta, spinach, bread crumbs, nutmeg, grated cheese, and the eggs until completely combined.

Generously flour a work surface. Divide the dough into 4 pieces and roll each piece into a log 1 inch thick. With a knife, cut each log into irregular 1-inch dumplings, then toss in flour to cover. Continue making dumplings until all the dough has been used.

Bring 6 quarts of salted water to a boil. Add the dumplings and cook until they begin to float to the top, 2 to 3 minutes. Reserve ¼ cup of pasta water. Drain dumplings well.

In a large sauté pan, melt the butter over medium heat. Add the sage leaves and cook until the butter begins to lightly brown. Whisk in the reserved pasta water until emulsified, then add the dumplings to the butter sauce. Toss to coat and season with salt and pepper to taste. Serve immediately with freshly grated cheese.

SERVES 6

Malfatti ready for cooking

Trout Fillets with an Almond-Butter-Sage Sauce

TROTA ALLE MANDORLE CON BURRO E SALVIA

Macesina is a stone's throw away from Lake Garda, where freshwater fish thrive, so they make up a large portion of the menu. This recipe works equally well with fish like Arctic char or salmon.

4 tablespoons (2 oz. / 60 g) unsalted butter, cut into pieces

15 whole sage leaves, plus more for garnish

4 trout fillets (about 1–1½ pounds / 450–675 g)

Kosher salt and freshly ground black pepper

¾ cup (6 fl. oz. / 180 ml) white wine

¼ cup (55 g) slivered almonds

Lemon wedges, for serving

Butter a nonstick skillet large enough to hold all the fish fillets. Cover the bottom of the skillet with the cut-up pats of butter. Place a sage leaf over each piece of butter. Place the fish fillets, skin side down, over the sage butter, and season with salt and pepper.

Place the skillet, covered, over medium heat. Once the butter begins to sizzle, lift the cover and add the white wine. Re-cover the skillet and cook several minutes. Add the slivered almonds to the skillet and continue to cook until the fish is cooked through, about 3 minutes.

Serve with lemon wedges and whole sage leaves and drizzle with the butter sauce.

SERVES 4

Local fish from nearby Lake Garda

Stuffed Chuck Roast
PUNTA RIPIENA

4 pounds (1.5 kg) chuck roast

Kosher salt and freshly ground black pepper

4 tablespoons (2 oz. / 60 g) unsalted butter

1 tablespoon (½ fl. oz. / 15 ml) extra-virgin olive oil

1 tablespoon chopped thyme

1 tablespoon chopped rosemary

1 tablespoon chopped sage

1 cup (125 g) bread crumbs

8 amaretti cookies, ground

½ cup (4 fl. oz. / 120 ml) whole milk

½ cup grated Parmigiano Reggiano

1 tablespoon freshly grated nutmeg

¼ cup plus 2 sprigs flat-leaf parsley

1 peeled clove of garlic

1 egg

1 large yellow onion, cut into medium dice

2 stalks celery, cut into medium dice

2 carrots, peeled and cut into medium dice

15 whole sage leaves

The stuffing for this roast goes back many generations in Francesca and Marta's family, highlighting the Lombardian love for native amaretti cookies. Here, Francesca grinds them into a bread stuffing, lending a subtle sweetness to the roast. The stuffing that falls out of the meat as it cooks will taste all the better after absorbing the braising liquid.

Rinse the meat and pat dry with paper towels. Slit the center of the meat to form a pocket to hold the stuffing. (Alternatively, have your butcher prepare the pocket for you.) Season the meat, including the inside cavity, with salt and pepper.

In a small sauté pan, melt 1 tablespoon of butter with 1 tablespoon of olive oil over medium heat. Add the thyme, rosemary, and sage and cook for 1 to 2 minutes to release the flavors of the herbs.

Place the bread crumbs in a large bowl with the ground amaretti cookies and dampen with milk. Stir in the grated cheese, nutmeg, and herb butter mixture.

Mince ¼ cup parsley and garlic together and add to the bread mixture. Stir in the egg and season to taste with salt and pepper. Stuff the pocket of the meat with the bread filling. Secure the pocket with toothpicks or by sewing it closed with kitchen string and a needle.

Place the roast in a large heavy-bottomed casserole pan with the onions, celery, carrots, and 2 sprigs parsley. Cover with cold water. Bring to a boil over medium-high heat. Once the pan begins to boil, cover with a lid, reduce the heat to medium-low, and simmer for an hour. Remove the meat from the pan; strain the liquid through a fine mesh sieve and reserve.

Heat the oven to 375°F (190°C).

In a large ovenproof sauté pan, melt 3 tablespoons of butter over medium heat. Add the whole sage leaves and cook for about 3 minutes. Place the meat in the pan along with a ladle of the reserved broth. Transfer to the oven and cook for 1 hour. Add more reserved broth to the pan as needed: there should always be liquid in the pan.

Remove the meat from the oven and let rest 10 minutes. Carve the meat into slices, place on a large serving platter, and drizzle with pan juices.
SERVES 6

Stuffing roast for punta ripiena

Baite di Pra's grazing cows

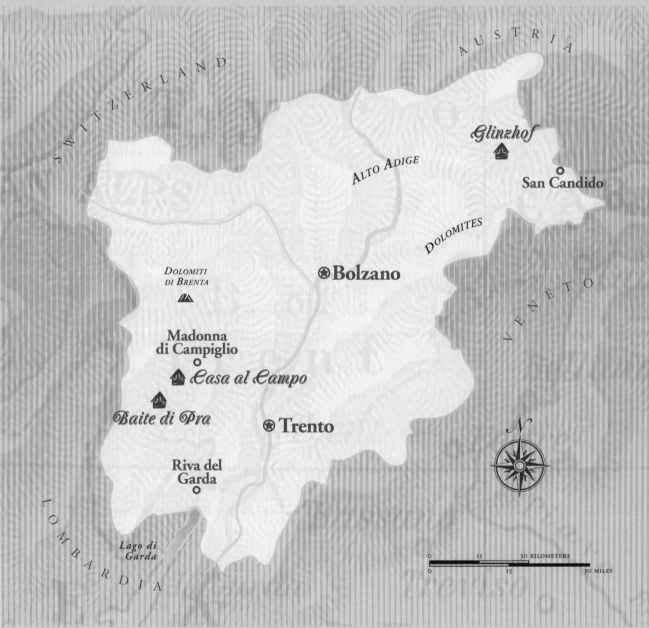

AUSTRIA

SWITZERLAND

Glinzhof

ALTO ADIGE

San Candido

DOLOMITES

Dolomiti di Brenta

⊛ **Bolzano**

VENETO

Madonna di Campiglio

Casa al Campo

Baite di Pra

⊛ **Trento**

Riva del Garda

N

LOMBARDIA

Lago di Garda

0   15   30 KILOMETERS

0   15   30 MILES

Trentino and Alto Adige form a singular region of unrestrained natural alpine beauty. Among the many preserves and national parks exists one of the wildest and most untouched regions in Italy. Trentino–Alto Adige teems with wildlife, abounds with dense old-growth forests, and is home to some of Europe's most spectacular mountain chains. Strained fraternal relationships between the two territories create a world of cultural differences, making Trentino–Alto Adige an exiting place to visit.

Also known as the Sudtirol, Alto Adige was annexed to Italy following the collapse of the Austro-Hungarian empire after World War I, but the German-speaking populace never fully accepted assimilation into Italy. The territory was granted autonomy by the Italian government after World War II, and its inhabitants were allowed to keep German as their official language. To this day, the Sudtirolese feel a closer connection with their former country than with Italy, and they fiercely retain their Austro-Hungarian heritage. Upon crossing the border dividing Trentino from Alto Adige, one enters a Germanic world whose chalet-style architecture, onion-domed churches, Slavic customs, and Austrian wurstel, Wiener schnitzel, and beer halls all stand testimony to a much different Italy.

Trentino, also a part of Austria in the 1800s, willingly joined Italy during the country's unification in the late nineteenth century and fiercely defended its adopted country in World War I. A warm and open population whose personalities lend a Mediterranean feel to Trentino's villages and cities, the people of Trentino have always been at odds with their neighbors, not comprehending their refusal to assimilate into Italian culture.

For the foreigner, however, perhaps the best way to experience and benefit from these cultural nuances is through each region's cuisine. While vast differences are apparent, a common denominator exists in the rugged good eating of both food cultures.

Speck, a smoked pig leg whose characteristic taste comes from juniper and pine smoke, unites both culinary fronts. It sets the table at all meals, whether eaten with cheese for breakfast, as a panino for a simple snack, or piled on an antipasto plate with pickles and vegetables. It also fortifies sauces with a deep flavor base. Hearty bread dumplings, referred to as canederli, originally hailed from Alto Adige but have migrated into the kitchens of Trentino and are now a common first course. Made from beets, spinach, or cheese, and cut into rough cylinder shapes, the dumplings cook in simmering consommé and are served in pairs, floating in the flavorful broth. Heady and lavishly spiced sauerkraut is another staple commonly made in homes throughout Trentino–Alto Adige, and it's a perfect complement to the many pork dishes eaten there. The rugged mountain chains are home to several species of native game, all of which are highly prized for their lean texture and strong taste. A common marinade soaks the meat for several days in red wine, juniper berries, and an assortment of herbs, and then braises it, rendering the tough meat fork-tender. Apples are one of the largest crops cultivated in Trentino–Alto Adige and, recognized for their natural sweetness, they are exported to the rest of Europe. A classic apple strudel brings out the very best of the region's dessert offerings.

While differences in ingredients and cooking styles between the traditional recipes of Trentino and Alto Adige are obvious, an often overlooked division lies in each region's approach toward dining in general. The restaurants at the agriturismi of Trentino are often intimate dining rooms, prix-fixe (with no menu) and open only to overnight guests of the farm. In true Italian fashion, diners begin the evening with numerous antipasti, followed by several courses, and concluding with dessert, coffee, and grappa. Dishes are presented in slow succession and meals can take hours; wine and conversation flow and post-dinner lingering is encouraged. A far different experience sits across the border. Large restaurants, open to the public and often separate from the main farmhouse, are the norm at the agriturismi of Alto Adige. Open to the public and offering a la carte menus, the restaurants exude a more formal ambience. Dinners are quick affairs, with diners often eating only one course, leaving little reason to remain at the table after a meal. In a country where the dining room table stands as the centerpiece of Italian livelihood, this vast chasm of food culture will forever divide the two territories.

Tirolese sheep

CHAPTER 17

Baite di Pra's mountain agriturismo

BAITE DI PRA

When their mountain farm and agriturismo first opened, Michele Ongari and his wife, Patrizia, were unprepared for the recognition they would attain. Baite di Pra was immediately discovered, and it has become a country retreat for city dwellers seeking genuine food among friends and good company in the isolation of the uncontaminated Borzago Valley. With the Adamello mountain glacier as its backdrop, cows lazily grazing in its shadow, and plumes of smoke billowing from the stone farmhouse's chimney, Baite di Pra offers picture-perfect alpine beauty. Two white stucco farmhouses contain the dining room and guest accommodations, each taking rustic cold-weather comfort to a new level. The guest rooms are all named after mountain flowers, and their all-fir construction, painted antique pine hutches, and puffy handmade comforters embrace guests with warmth and mountain hospitality. A similar ambience awaits diners, who convene in a small wood-paneled room crammed with rustic tables and adorned with forged metal lamps, local folk art, and a giant pair of deer antlers. This homey, cozy setting has brought Michele and Patrizia many repeat vacationers who find the soothing tranquility of Baite di Pra the perfect respite from everyday life.

Another main attraction of Baite di Pra is the five-course feasts of regional comfort food prepared by Gianni, the chef. Coming from an unforgiving land, the Trentino diet is one of hearty substance, hatched from what little bounty came from the infertile rocky soil. Gianni's cooking embodies this spirit, and from his kitchen arrive thick stews of beef goulash, large bread dumplings bobbing in meat broth, and delicious wild game soaked in a wine-infused heavily spiced herb marinade for days. Extremely quaffable local wine flows continuously through the meal until dessert, when Michele proudly offers several types of house-made grappa, including one made from the farm's own blueberries. With waves of heat pumping from the wood-fired stove, Vivaldi gently playing in the background, and boisterous conversation filling the small dining room, Baite di Pra comes to life at night. The convivial atmosphere fueled by good food and drink leads to new friendships formed on a shared bond of knowing the special place that is Baite di Pra.

Pickled Onions
CIPOLLE SOTT'ACETO

4 red onions, peeled and cut into
⅛-inch rings

1 tablespoon lightly crushed juniper
berries

1 quart (32 fl. oz. / 960 ml) white
wine vinegar

1 quart (32 fl. oz. / 960 ml) water

2 bay leaves

1 tablespoon black peppercorns

½ cup (100 g) granulated sugar

Pickled vegetables are a common starter at Baite di Pra's table. The sweet and sour flavor profile cleanses the palate, whetting the appetite for the hearty courses that follow.

Place all ingredients in a 6-quart saucepan over medium-low heat. Slowly bring up to a boil and cook for 5 minutes, stirring occasionally. Remove from heat and let the onions cool completely in the liquid. Refrigerate until ready to serve.

SERVES 8

TRENTINO'S NORTH POLE

Trentino-Alto Adige practically transforms into the North Pole in December, when Christmas fairs are hosted in the main towns of the region. Against the backdrop of snow-capped mountains and verdant green pine trees, wooden huts are set up in the main piazzas of towns to resemble miniature Christmas villages. Vendors sell artisanal products of high quality and craftsmanship, all made from local resources. Hearty alpine food and warm vin brûlé add to the convivial holiday atmosphere, lending an air of joy and Christmas spirit unique to Trentino-Alto Adige.

Bread Dumplings in Broth
CANEDERLI ALLO SPECK IN BRODO

These large bread dumplings have their origins in Alto Adige, but they've been adopted by Trentino and are now eaten throughout the entire region. They are simmered and served in broth, which provides nutrients and warmth for cold winters, and the bread-based dumplings have frugal origins, created by the short growing season of Trentino–Alto Adige.

In a large sauté pan, cook the onion with a pinch of salt and the butter until softened and beginning to caramelize, 12 to 15 minutes. Add the bread cubes to the pan and sauté until the bread softens and begins to break down, about 5 minutes.

In a medium bowl mix together the flour and speck, then add the eggs, milk, parsley, and salt and pepper to taste. Add the bread and onions to the flour mixture and stir until well combined. Let rest, covered, in the refrigerator for 15 minutes. Form into 6 large oval-shaped balls.

Bring 6 quarts of salted water to a boil. Drop the canederli into the water and cook until they begin to float to the top, about 5 minutes. Using a slotted spoon, remove canederli from the boiling water and place 1 dumpling each into individual shallow bowls.

Meanwhile, bring the chicken broth to a boil over medium-high heat. Spoon a ladle of broth into each bowl and garnish with chopped chives.

SERVES 6

½ yellow onion, cut into fine dice

3 tablespoons (1½ oz. / 45 g) unsalted butter

5¼ ounces (150 g) stale Italian bread, cut into ¼-inch cubes

¼ cup (30 g) all-purpose flour

3 ounces (85 g) speck, sliced thin and cut crosswise into ⅛-inch strips

2 large eggs

⅔ cup (220 ml) whole milk

1 cup finely chopped flat-leaf parsley

Kosher salt and freshly ground black pepper

2 quarts (64 fl. oz. / 1.89 L) homemade chicken broth (see page xi) or canned low-sodium chicken broth

2 tablespoons chopped chives

Vegetable Strudel
STRUDEL DI VERDURE

Strudel is a common dish in northern Italy. It shows influences from Austrian cuisine and is prepared both in sweet and savory versions. For this recipe, substitute a smoky-flavored ham if speck is unavailable.

1 head savoy cabbage, shredded

1 bunch roughly chopped Swiss chard

1 medium yellow onion, cut into small dice

2 tablespoons (1 oz. / 30 g) unsalted butter

Kosher salt and freshly ground black pepper

3 ounces (85 g) speck, sliced thin and cut crosswise into 1/8-inch strips

1 large sheet store-bought puff pastry

1 cup shredded Asiago cheese

Heat the oven to 400°F (200°C).

Bring 4 quarts of salted water up to a boil. Blanch the cabbage until tender, about 8 minutes. Remove and submerge in a bowl of ice water. Then blanch the Swiss chard until tender, about 3 minutes. Drain and submerge in the ice water. Drain the cabbage and Swiss chard well and squeeze out any excess water.

Sauté the onion in butter in a large sauté pan over medium-high heat until translucent, about 5 minutes. Add the Swiss chard and cabbage and season with salt and pepper to taste. Continue to cook until the cabbage is soft, 12 to 15 minutes. Add the speck and cook 3 minutes more. Remove pan from heat and set aside to cool.

Roll out the puff pastry until 1/4 inch thick. Spoon half the cabbage mixture onto the center of the pastry, then top with 1/2 cup Asiago cheese, the rest of the cabbage, and the remainder of the cheese.

Fold the dough over the filling like an envelope and prick the top with the tines of a fork. Bake in the oven for 35 to 40 minutes or until the dough puffs and is a rich golden brown. Cut into slices and serve warm.

SERVES 6

Smoke-cured mountain bacon

Ricotta dumplings

Ricotta Dumplings with Butter, Pine Nuts, and Raisins

STRANGOLAPRETI

This is Gianni's loose interpretation of a traditional Trentino dish called strangol-apreti, which translates as "priest stranglers." The name refers to priests' often great appreciation for food; these dumplings were said to be so good that priests could not refrain from gorging themselves on them. Usually made with spinach, Gianni's dumplings use only ricotta and are light and delicious. Be sure not to overcook them, as they can melt quickly when added to the pan with the butter sauce.

In a large bowl mix the ricotta with the egg, egg yolk, nutmeg, Parmigiano Reggiano, cornstarch, bread crumbs, and a pinch of salt until completely combined, forming a soft dough. Roll a small amount of the dough to form a 1-inch ball. Place on a sheet pan lightly dusted with flour. Continue forming dumplings, spacing about 2 inches apart on the sheet pan. Cover with wax paper and place in the freezer for at least 1 hour.

Meanwhile, bring 6 quarts of salted water to a boil.

Melt the butter in a small sauté pan. Add the pine nuts and toast lightly, then add the raisins.

Drop the dumplings into the water and cook until they rise to the surface, 2 to 3 minutes. With a slotted spoon, remove the dumplings and place them in the sauté pan with the butter sauce. Toss gently to coat, season to taste with salt and pepper, and serve in individual shallow bowls.

SERVES 6

1 pound (450 g) ricotta

1 large egg plus 1 large egg yolk

½ teaspoon freshly grated nutmeg

½ cup grated Parmigiana Reggiano

1 tablespoon (10 g) cornstarch

½ cup (62 g) bread crumbs

Kosher salt and freshly ground
    black pepper

Flour, for dusting

4 tablespoons (2 oz. / 60 g) un-
    salted butter

¼ cup (30 g) pine nuts

½ cup (60 g) golden raisins
    (sultanas)

Beef Stew with Paprika
GOULASCHSUPPE

Goulash originated in Hungary and made its way into the Italian repertoire when areas like Trentino–Alto Adige were under the influence of the Austro-Hungarian empire. This dish is a favorite at Baite di Pra and nourishes guests on cold autumn nights.

2 tablespoons (1 fl. oz. / 30 ml) extra-virgin olive oil

1 yellow onion, cut into small dice

2 bay leaves

3 pounds (1 kg / 360 g) beef chuck roast, cut into 1-inch pieces

1 cup (8 fl. oz. / 240 ml) red wine

2 cups (16 fl. oz. / 480 ml) canned low-sodium meat broth

3 Yukon Gold potatoes, cut into medium dice

1 tablespoon cumin seeds

1 tablespoon paprika

1 teaspoon crushed red pepper flakes

Kosher salt and freshly ground black pepper

6 slices toasted rye bread

In a heavy casserole pan, heat olive oil over medium heat. Sauté the onions and the bay leaves until the onions are tender and begin to brown, 12 to 15 minutes.

Add the meat to the pan and brown on all sides, about 8 minutes. Pour in the red wine, bring to a boil, and reduce by half. Add the broth. Return to a boil and cover, then reduce the heat to low and simmer for about 1 hour.

Add the potatoes, cumin, paprika, and red pepper flakes. Continue to cook, partly uncovered, over low heat, until the potatoes are tender, about 1 hour.

Serve in individual crocks with a slice of toasted rye bread.

SERVES 6

Veal Shanks Cooked in Beer
STINCO DI VITELLO ALLA BIRRA

At Baite di Pra, pork shanks are used for this recipe. Pork shanks are harder to come by, as they are usually smoked and sold as ham hocks. It is possible to special order pork shanks from your butcher, but the dish is equally delicious with veal shanks. Serve with a side of mashed potatoes or over a bed of polenta.

Heat the oven to 300°F (150°C).

Generously season the veal shanks with salt and pepper. Melt the butter with the olive oil in a heavy casserole pan over medium-high heat, and sear the shanks until deep golden brown, 3 to 5 minutes per side. Remove the shanks from pan and set aside on a plate. Add the vegetables to the pan and cook until tender and beginning to color, 10 to 12 minutes.

Raise the heat to high and pour the beer into the pan. Bring to a boil and simmer for about 10 minutes. Add the broth and return to a boil. Place the shanks back in the pot, along with the bay leaves, sage, rosemary, and juniper berries. Cover the pan and place in the oven. Cook for about 3 hours or until the meat is fork-tender.

Remove the shanks from the sauce and strain the liquid through a fine mesh sieve, discarding the vegetables. Pour the liquid into a small saucepan over medium-high heat, add the cumin seeds, and bring to a boil.

Combine the cornstarch and water to make a slurry. Gradually whisk the slurry into the sauce and simmer until thickened, 2 to 3 minutes. Place the veal shanks on a serving platter and drizzle with the sauce.

SERVES 4

4 veal shanks, 1½ inches thick

Kosher salt and freshly ground black pepper

2 tablespoons (1 oz. / 30 g) unsalted butter

2 tablespoons (1 fl. oz. / 30 ml) extra-virgin olive oil

1 yellow onion, cut into large dice

1 stalk celery, cut into large dice

1 carrot, peeled and cut into large dice

1 leek, light green and white parts only, cleaned and cut into thin slices

3 12-ounce bottles of beer

2 cups (16 fl. oz. / 480 ml) home-made chicken broth (see page xi) or canned low-sodium broth

2 bay leaves

1 tablespoon chopped sage

1 tablespoon chopped rosemary

1 tablespoon lightly crushed juniper berries

1 tablespoon cumin seeds

½ tablespoon cornstarch

1 cup (8 fl. oz. / 240 ml) water

Adamello Park

Baite di Pra's pristine location at the foot of Adamello National Park ensures guests rejuvenating mountain air and a reconnection with nature. The park consists of rugged mountain ranges and glaciers extending into Austria and is home to Italy's largest waterfall. Teeming with wildlife, the park's adopted mascot is the brown bear; sightings are a common occurrence.

Once a part of Austria, Trentino found its Italian ancestry at the fore after World War I, when the Adamello served as a critical strategic border. For three years, hard-fought battles were waged high in the mountain ranges between Italy and Austria. The Italians eventually prevailed and won the territory that today is the Adamello park. An ambitious hike from Baite di Pra leads four hours straight up into the mountains, where World War I cannon wreckage still sits atop perilous peaks, demonstrating how incredibly strenuous and difficult combat must have been at such frigid high elevations. The hike also passes a rifugio, a mountain hut accessible only by foot, which offers hikers beds, food and drink, and a large sundeck overlooking countless peaks and the valley below. Baite di Pra is a mere speck in the distance, and the hike ensures a voracious appetite for hearty alpine cuisine upon returning to the agriturismo.

Carrot Cake
TORTA DI CAROTE

This is not your typical carrot cake. The ground almonds and amaretti cookies add a sweet almond flavor and a bit of crunch.

Heat the oven to 350°F (180°C).

Put the egg whites in a bowl of a standing mixer fitted with the whip attachment. Beat them to stiff (but not dry) peaks. Transfer to a large bowl. Wipe the bowl clean.

Add the egg yolks and the sugar to the bowl of the stand mixer fitted with the paddle attachment and beat together until thick and pale yellow, about 5 minutes. Add the carrot, almonds, and rum and mix until well incorporated. Stir in the amaretti cookies.

Fold in the whipped egg whites in three batches. Pour the batter into a buttered and floured 9 × 12 × 2-inch cake pan.

Bake in the oven until the cake is puffed and golden and a toothpick inserted into the center comes out clean, about 30 minutes.

SERVES 6–8

6 large eggs, separated

1 cup (200 g) granulated sugar

8 ounces (225 g) shredded carrot

2 cups (225 g) ground almonds

1½ tablespoons (¾ fl. oz. / 25 ml) light rum

¼ cup (30 g) ground amaretti cookies

Casa al Campo's valley landscape

Chapter 18
Casa al Campo

Situated in a large open field next to a flowing stream, with panoramic views of pine-covered mountain peaks, Casa al Campo has become a haven for lovers of nature. Opened by the Tisi family in 2002, the agriturismo breathes good feelings, as the family's joy and happiness in running their farm rubs off on all who walk through the doors. Healthy country living meets invigorating mountain air and a plethora of outdoor activities here; guests are enthusiastically encouraged to borrow bikes and explore the paved path that passes the farm and continues deep into the Rendena Valley. Stefano Tisi, a lifelong outdoorsman and cross-country ski instructor, takes guests on wildlife hikes up into the mountains. His local knowledge and deep respect for his native land results in opportunities to view mountain deer and chamois in pristine natural habitats. But however wild and beautiful these animals may be, Stefano is also an avid hunter, and his skills bring an abundance of varied game to Casa al Campo's table.

Claudia Tisi is a perfectionist in every regard. Elegantly plated, never exaggerated, and always delectable are the standards that greet guests nightly in the agriturismo's mountain country dining room. Casa al Campo's own organic garden, pigs, rabbits, and chickens provide most of what gets used in the kitchen, but Claudia also supports local farms for certain ingredients. A

Kitchen crew at Casa al Campo

dairy agriturismo that sits directly behind Casa al Campo produces excellent varieties of cow's-milk cheese, which Claudia pairs with her preserves for a delectable cheese plate. Stefano, having grown up in the area, knows everybody in the tight-knit small town beyond his farm and takes his pigs to the local butcher, who is known for his exceptional skills at producing salami and speck. With her own farm's products and trusted outside sources, Claudia cooks recipes that are traditional to the region but enhanced by modern techniques. Breads, desserts, pastas, preserves, pickled and marinated vegetables, and sauerkraut are all house-made. Everything done at Casa al Campo is done in a manner reflective of the family's collaboration to bring out the very best from their agriturismo and the land on which they live.

Potato, Leek, and Butternut Squash Soup

ZUPPA DI PORRI, ZUCCA, E PATATE

Cooking several of the ingredients in two different ways and then blending them together results in a final dish with highly concentrated flavors.

¼ cup (2 fl. oz. / 60 ml) extra-virgin olive oil, plus more for drizzling

3 leeks, cleaned and cut into slices

1 large yellow onion, cut into medium dice

1 large butternut squash, peeled and cut into ¼-inch pieces

3 Yukon Gold potatoes, peeled and cut into fine dice

2 carrots, peeled and cut into medium dice

1½ quarts (48 fl. oz. / 1.4 L) water

Kosher salt and freshly ground black pepper

1 tablespoon chopped rosemary

¼ cup grated Parmigiano Reggiano

In a 4-quart stockpot, heat 2 tablespoons of olive oil over medium heat. Sauté half of the leek slices along with the onion until tender but not browned, 5 to 7 minutes. Add half of the squash, half of the potatoes, and the carrots and sauté for about 5 minutes. Cover with the water and a generous pinch of salt and bring to a boil. Reduce heat to medium-low and gently simmer until the vegetables are extremely tender, 20 to 25 minutes.

Puree the contents of the pot with an immersion blender (or in a blender) until smooth, then pass through a fine mesh sieve.

In another large stockpot, heat 2 tablespoons of olive oil over medium-high heat. Add the remaining leek slices and sauté until tender, about 7 minutes. Add the remaining squash and potatoes and sauté another couple of minutes. Add the pureed broth to cover the potatoes and squash, and simmer gently until the potatoes and squash are tender but not falling apart, 12 to 15 minutes. Season to taste with salt and pepper. Add the fresh rosemary and cook another 3 to 5 minutes.

Serve the soup with a drizzle of extra-virgin olive oil and grated Parmigiano Reggiano.

SERVES 6

Chicken Breast with Porcini Mushroom Stuffing
PETTO DI POLLO AI PORCINI

A pureed dried porcini sauce makes an earthy filling for the white meat. Searing the chicken with its skin on adds fat and flavor to the often dry breast meat and makes a world of difference in the success of the dish.

Heat the oven to 450°F (230°C).

Soak the dried porcini mushrooms in warm water for 20 minutes, drain, and then chop into small pieces. Strain and reserve the soaking liquid.

Heat 2 tablespoons of canola oil in a 12-inch sauté pan over medium-high heat. Add the mushrooms and rosemary and a pinch of salt and pepper, and cook for 5 minutes. Add ½ cup of the reserved mushroom liquid and cook another 2 or 3 minutes. Remove the mushrooms from the heat and let cool completely. Place the mushrooms in the bowl of a food processor, along with the heavy cream and ¼ cup of reserved mushroom liquid, and puree until smooth.

Butterfly the chicken breast and season with salt and pepper. Spread a heaping tablespoon of filling over the breast and wrap and roll the chicken over the filling. Tie the chicken with kitchen string to secure the stuffing.

Heat 2 tablespoons canola oil in a 12-inch ovenproof sauté pan over medium-high heat. Sear the chicken breasts, skin side down, until deep golden brown, about 5 minutes. Turn the chicken over and place 1 tablespoon of butter on top of each breast. Put in the oven and cook 8 to 10 minutes, until the chicken is cooked through and registers 165°F (74°C) on a thermometer.

Remove the chicken from the oven and remove the kitchen string. Place chicken on a serving platter and drizzle with the pan juices.

SERVES 4

1 ounce (30 g) dried porcini
    mushrooms

1 cup (8 fl. oz. / 240 ml) warm water

¼ cup (2 fl. oz. / 60 ml) canola oil

4 ounces (115 g) cremini mushrooms,
    chopped

1 tablespoon chopped rosemary

Kosher salt and freshly ground black
    pepper

1 tablespoon (½ fl. oz. / 15 ml) heavy
    cream

4 chicken breasts with skin on
    (about 1½ pounds / 675 g)

4 tablespoons (2 oz. / 60 g) un-
    salted butter

Mascarpone, Potato, and Thyme Ravioli with Sautéed Mushrooms

RAVIOLI DI MASCARPONE, PATATE, E TIMO CON FUNGHI

The finished dish is definitely a showstopper and the presentation will impress any guests. The ravioli are first shaped into large rectangles and boiled. Once drained, they are formed into circles, stuffed with sautéed mushrooms, and topped with a silky velouté as a sauce. The flavors are unusual but work well together.

1 pound (450 g) russet potatoes

8 tablespoons (4 oz. / 115 g) butter

8 sprigs thyme plus 1 tablespoon chopped thyme

12 ounces (340 g) mascarpone cheese

2 tablespoons all-purpose flour

1 recipe basic pasta dough (see page x)

1 quart (32 fl. oz. / 960 ml) home-made chicken broth (see page xi) or canned low-sodium broth

1 cup grated Parmigiano Reggiano

Kosher salt and freshly ground black pepper

8 ounces (225 g) mixed wild mushrooms

2 ounces (60 g) slivered almonds

Put the potatoes in a 4-quart pan and cover with cold water. Place over medium-high heat and bring up to a boil. Lower the heat and simmer until the potatoes are tender when pierced with a a skewer, about 25 minutes. Drain the potatoes and let cool slightly, then peel and pass through a ricer.

In a small saucepan, melt 5 tablespoons of the butter over low heat with the thyme sprigs. Let steep for several minutes to infuse the flavors, then discard the thyme. In a medium bowl mix the potatoes with the mascarpone and the infused butter.

Make a roux: In a small nonstick skillet, melt 2 tablespoons of butter over medium heat, stir in flour, and cook until pale golden brown, 1 to 2 minutes. Remove from the heat and set aside to cool.

Meanwhile, make the ravioli: With a pasta machine, roll out the dough to the thinnest setting. Cut the dough into 6 to 8 5-inch-long rectangular pieces. Put the potato filling in a pastry bag and pipe a ½-inch-thick log of filling down the center of a piece of dough. Brush around the filling with water and fold the top portion of the dough over the filling to enclose. Make the remaining ravioli in the same manner.

Bring 6 quarts of salted water to a boil.

Bring the chicken broth to a boil, and gradually whisk in the cold roux, making sure there are no lumps. Simmer over medium heat to thicken and then stir in the Parmigiano Reggiano. Season to taste with salt and pepper.

In a large nonstick skillet, melt 1 tablespoon of butter over medium-high heat, add the mushrooms, and sauté until tender and a little bit browned, 5 to 7 minutes. Season with salt and pepper and chopped thyme.

Drop the ravioli into the boiling salted water and cook until tender, about 3 minutes. Remove the ravioli from the water with a slotted spoon and set on a flat dinner plate. When ravioli are cool enough to handle, shape each ravioli into a circle and place one ravioli in each individual shallow soup bowl. Spoon the sautéed mushrooms into the center of each ravioli and ladle the velouté around the ravioli. Garnish with thyme and slivered almonds.

SERVES 6–8

Potato ravioli

HUNTING IN THE DOLOMITES

The jagged peaks of the Dolomites, interspersed with dense pine forests, host wildlife that thrives in the rugged landscape. Deer and chamois are native to the region and play integral roles in the cuisine of Trentino–Alto Adige. Hunters must hike high into the peaks and be in good physical shape to pursue these mountain dwellers. Strict laws govern specific time periods when hunting is permitted and each town is allotted certain boundaries within which residents are allowed to hunt. These regulations ensure that the Dolomites will always be home to these indigenous animals and that they will remain an important element of the region's cuisine.

Wild mountain deer

Crème Brûlée with Blueberry Puree
CRÈME BRÛLÉE CON PUREA DI MIRTILLO

Claudia has a real talent for desserts and each night, at the end of the meal, guests are presented with her sweet masterpieces. Crème brûlée is not typical of Italy, but Claudia reinterprets the classic French custard with fresh blueberries that grow wild on her farm.

Heat the oven to 300°F (150°C).

In a small saucepan over medium-low heat, cook the blueberries with 1 tablespoon granulated sugar and 1 teaspoon lemon zest, until the blueberries break down and become juicy, about 5 minutes. Spoon 2 tablespoons of the blueberry mixture into the bottom of each of 6 shallow ramekins, and set aside.

In a 3-quart saucepan, combine the cream with the cinnamon stick, mint leaves, remaining lemon zest, and salt. Bring the cream to a boil over medium-low heat.

In a medium-size heatproof bowl, whisk the remaining granulated sugar with the egg yolks. Slowly pour the warmed cream into the eggs, whisking constantly. Strain the mixture through a fine mesh sieve into a large liquid measuring cup. Skim away any foam or bubbles and then pour the mixture into the ramekins.

Put the ramekins in a roasting pan and put in the oven. Pour hot water into the pan halfway up the sides of the ramekins and bake until the custard is firm around the edge but still jiggly in the center, about 30 minutes. Remove from the oven and let custards cool in the water bath, then refrigerate for at least 2 hours.

Heat the broiler to high. Place the ramekins on a sheet pan and sprinkle each custard with 2 tablespoons cane sugar. Place the ramekins as close to the heat as possible, and broil until the sugar has fully caramelized, about 1 minute. Remove from the oven, let cool slightly, and serve.

SERVES 6

1 pint (11 oz. / 315 g) blueberries

⅓ cup plus 3 tablespoons (105 g) granulated sugar

1 tablespoon lemon zest

2 cups (16 fl. oz. / 480 ml) heavy cream

1 cinnamon stick

3 mint leaves

4 large egg yolks

Pinch of table salt

12 tablespoons cane sugar

Walnut Tart

CROSTATA DI NOCE

This tart is not overtly sweet, and it can be served either for breakfast or as dessert. If serving at the end of a meal, pair it with either fresh whipped cream or a scoop of vanilla ice cream.

1 recipe sweet pastry crust (see page xi)

3 tablespoons (1½ oz. / 45 g) unsalted butter, at room temperature

½ cup (100 g) granulated sugar

2 large eggs plus 1 large egg yolk

1 tablespoon (½ fl. oz. / 15 ml) grappa

⅔ cup (5 fl. oz. / 150 ml) whole milk

1 tablespoon lemon zest

⅓ cup plus 1 tablespoon (50 g) all-purpose flour

¾ teaspoon (5 g) baking powder

½ teaspoon (4 g) baking soda

3 tablespoons (25 g) cornstarch

8 ounces (225 g) chopped walnuts

Heat the oven to 350°F (180°C).

Make the sweet pastry crust dough and refrigerate at least 1 hour. Remove from the refrigerator and roll out into a 14-inch circle, ⅛-inch thick. Butter a 9 × 13 × 2-inch tart pan and line with the dough. Prick the dough with the tines of a fork and then cover with foil. Line the foil with pie weights (or beans) and bake for 15 minutes, or until the crust has set. Remove from the oven, remove the foil and weights from the tart, and let cool on a wire rack.

Meanwhile, cream together the butter and the sugar. Add the eggs and egg yolk to the mixture and beat until well combined. Add the grappa, milk, and lemon zest.

In a small bowl, stir together the flour, baking powder, baking soda, and cornstarch. Add to the egg mixture. Mix in the walnut pieces.

Pour the mixture into the tart pan and bake for about 30 minutes, or until the mixture has set and slightly puffed up.

SERVES 6–8

CHAPTER 19
GLINZHOF

In an Italy where German is the mother tongue and pasta is practically considered a foreign import, the Jud family's agriturismo, Glinzhof, perches on a mountain, enveloped in even more mountains. A rugged farm in a region proudly torn between its Austro-Hungarian and Italian heritage, Glinzhof represents a vastly different cultural experience than that found at other agriturismi throughout Italy. Manfred Jud and his family restored their mountain house more than ten years ago, using only raw materials found on their property to create a mountain refuge. Today, Glinzhof prides itself on being a true working farm, self-sufficient in nearly everything. From the rearing of animals to the cultivation of vegetables to the wood-fired furnace fueled by fallen trees, Glinzhof is a model low-impact structure. Boasting some of Europe's best downhill skiing outside its front door as well as a classic Alto Adigean restaurant, this agriturismo is a perfect place to savor a small and very different slice of Italy.

With an Austrian chef and his country's border only 8 kilometers away, it's no wonder that many of Glinzhof's recipes have deep Austrian roots. Hans Peter takes 90 percent of his ingredients from Glinzhof's farm and his cooking transports diners to the charming postcard-like villages of his native land. Green cabbage salad heavily spiced with toasted cumin seeds, beef liver sautéed with apples and smoked bacon, and a giant sweet dessert pancake named *Kaiserschmarrn* are all classic examples of this distinct cuisine. While Alto Adige is known for the exceptional quality of its wine, Glinzhof also offers great local beer, made from icy-cold mountain waters. The pairing of it with Hans Peter's dishes further heightens the Alto Adigean cultural differences. Atypical of most agriturismi, Glinzhof's varied a la carte menu allows diners options for their meals and keeps Hans Peter on his toes in his one-man kitchen. In wintertime, the stoking of the stube, a large wood-fired stove and the centerpiece of all Alto Adigean dining rooms, brings guests inside to eat beside its radiant heat. Summer allows for al fresco dining on the large overhanging deck adorned with alpine flowers and unobstructed views of the jagged Dolomites. The view alone is worth the journey to the Jud family's mountain agriturismo, but it is the food that brings guests back time after time.

Green Cabbage Salad
INSALATA DI CAVOLO VERDE

Cabbage, cumin seeds, and vinegar create a different-tasting salad that is a great side with any meat dish.

2 tablespoons cumin seeds

1 teaspoon granulated sugar

2 tablespoons (1 fl. oz. / 30 ml) white wine vinegar

3 tablespoons (1½ fl. oz. / 45 ml) extra-virgin olive oil

Kosher salt and freshly ground black pepper

1 head green cabbage, shredded

In a small nonstick skillet, toast the cumin seeds until fragrant, 2 to 3 minutes.

In a small bowl, whisk together the sugar and white wine vinegar. Gradually whisk in the extra-virgin olive oil until emulsified. Season to taste with salt and pepper.

Place the cabbage in a large serving bowl with the toasted cumin seeds. Toss with the vinaigrette and let sit at room temperature for 30 minutes before serving.

SERVES 6

LA STUBE

The stube plays a vital role in wintertime living in Alto Adigean culture, both historically and in the present. Typical homes of the region house behemoth terra-cotta wood-fired stoves in their dining rooms, which continuously pump out heat throughout the long snow-filled months. Aside from generating warmth, the stube brings families together. Wooden benches commonly surround the hearth, creating the perfect place to play a game of cards, warm up with a glass of wine, or simply take a nap and forget about the bitter cold for a while.

Loaves of rye bread

Beet Dumplings with Poppy-Seed Butter

CANEDERLI DI BARBABIETOLA AL BURRO DI
SEMI DI PAPAVERO

Canederli, also known as Knodel in Alto Adige, share their heritage with the Austrians. They are made with various fillings but always include stale bread. The beets add a deep ruby color to the dumplings and add a sweetness that pairs well with the Gorgonzola and poppy-seed butter.

3 large beets (beetroot) (12 oz. / 340 g)

1 small yellow onion, cut into small dice

1 clove of garlic, peeled and minced

6 tablespoons (3 oz. / 85 g) unsalted butter

1 cup (200 g) stale white bread, cut into pieces

2 eggs

6 ounces (170 g) crumbled Gorgonzola

¼ cup (2 fl. oz. / 60 ml) whole milk

¼ cup chopped flat-leaf parsley

Kosher salt and freshly ground black pepper

1 tablespoon poppy seeds

Heat the oven to 400°F (200°C). Roast the beets in the oven, wrapped in foil and set on a sheet pan, until tender, 45 minutes to 1 hour. Let beets cool, then peel and pass through a ricer.

Sauté the onion and garlic in 1 tablespoon of butter over medium heat until tender, about 7 minutes. Add the bread and cook until the bread begins to soften, 3 to 5 minutes.

In a large bowl, combine the onion mixture with the beets, eggs, Gorgonzola, milk, and parsley. Season to taste with salt and pepper. Form the mixture into 6 to 8 large oval dumplings.

Bring a 6-quart pot of salted water to a boil. Drop the canederli into the water and cook at a gentle simmer until they begin to float to the top, 4 to 5 minutes. Remove from the water with a slotted spoon and place one canederli on each individual dish.

In a small saucepan, melt the remaining butter over medium-low heat until it begins to foam. Add the poppy seeds, cook 1 to 2 minutes, and then spoon over the beet dumplings.

SERVES 6–8

Beet canederli

Penne with Meat Sauce
PENNE AL RAGÙ BERGSTUBE

Glinzhof raises the cattle and pigs that provide the main ingredients for this dish, while wild mushrooms are foraged from the forested hills that encompass the land. This specialty was created for the restaurant so guests could enjoy the fruits of Glinzhof's labor.

¼ cup (2 fl. oz. / 60 ml) extra-virgin olive oil

1 medium yellow onion, cut into fine dice

8 ounces (225 g) ground pork

8 ounces (225 g) ground veal

Kosher salt and freshly ground black pepper

1 cup (8 fl. oz. / 240 ml) red wine

1 28-ounce (793 g) can whole plum tomatoes

8 ounces (225 g) wild mushrooms, trimmed and sliced

3 ounces (85 g) speck, thinly sliced and cut crosswise into ⅛-inch strips

½ teaspoon crushed red pepper flakes

1 pound (450 g) boxed penne pasta

¼ cup grated Parmigiano Reggiano

In a 7-quart heavy-bottomed casserole pan, heat 2 tablespoons of olive oil over medium heat and sauté the onion until tender, 7 to 10 minutes. Add the pork and the veal to the pan, season lightly with salt, and brown the meat, stirring occasionally to break it up. Add the red wine to the pan, and slowly reduce the wine until it is almost gone. Chop the tomatoes into small pieces and add them to the pan along with their juices.

In a separate medium-size nonstick sauté pan, heat another 2 tablespoons of olive oil over medium-high heat and add the mushrooms. Sauté until they release their water and begin to dry out, about 5 minutes. Add the speck and season with a little salt and pepper, continuing to cook another 3 to 4 minutes. Stir the mushrooms and speck into the ragu along with the red pepper flakes. Cook slowly over medium-low heat, stirring occasionally for about 2 hours. Adjust seasoning if needed.

Bring a large pot of salted water to a boil and cook the pasta, following the directions on the box, until al dente. Drain well and toss with the ragu. Serve with Parmigiano Reggiano.

SERVES 4–6

Calf's Liver with Apples and Speck
FEGATO TIROLESE

The smoky speck paired with sweet juicy apples uses two of Alto Adige's prime agricultural ingredients and cuts through the richness of the liver. Hans Peter serves this over a bed of white rice to further subdue the potent liver flavor and texture.

2 tablespoons (1 oz. / 30 g) unsalted butter

1½ pounds (675 g) calf's liver

Kosher salt and freshly ground black pepper

1 Golden Delicious apple, cored and sliced ¼ inch thick

2 ounces (60 g) speck, sliced thin

½ cup (4 fl. oz. / 120 ml) white wine

Melt butter in a 12-inch nonstick sauté pan over medium-high heat. Season the liver with salt and pepper and sear on one side until golden brown, about 3 minutes. Turn the liver over. Add the apple slices to the pan and cover the apples with the slices of speck. Cook another 2 minutes. Raise the heat to high, add the white wine, and cook another minute.

Serve the liver on individual plates, top with the apple and speck slices, and drizzle with the pan sauce.

SERVES 4

Sweet Pancake
KAISERSCHMARRN

This breakfast treat is a cross between a pancake and a sponge cake, with the flavor suggesting the former and the spongy texture the latter. The golden raisins add just a subtle hint of sweetness. Serve with a dusting of powdered sugar or a side of jam or applesauce to really enhance the flavor.

Heat the oven to 350°F (180°C).

Place the egg whites in a medium bowl. Use an electric mixer to beat the whites to stiff (but not dry) peaks.

In a large bowl, whisk together vigorously the sugar, flour, milk, and egg yolks. Stir a quarter of the egg whites into the bowl with the sugar mixture, and then gently fold the remaining egg whites into the mixture.

In a 10-inch nonstick skillet, melt 1 tablespoon of butter over medium-low heat. Pour in the batter and evenly distribute the raisins over the surface. Cook on top of the stove until the edges begin to set, and then finish cooking in the oven, 20 to 25 minutes, or until puffed up and firm to the touch.

Note: The top of the pancake will not turn golden brown.

SERVES 6

5 large eggs, separated

¼ cup (35 g) granulated sugar

¾ cup (100 g) all-purpose flour

⅓ cup (3 fl. oz. / 80 ml) whole milk

1 tablespoon (½ oz. / 15 g) unsalted butter

2 ounces (60 g) golden raisins (sultanas)

AUSTRIA

VENETO

▲▲ Mt. Coglians

▲▲ Mt. Cavallo

SLOVENIA

🏠 I Comelli

🏠 Casale Cjanor

🏠 Perusini

Udine ○

🏠 La Subida

Gorizi ○

Pordenone ○

VENETO

N

Grado ○

Golfo di Trieste

○ Trieste

0   15   30 KILOMETERS
0   15   30 MILES

MARE ADRIATIC

A region of conquests whose multiethnic culture arose from the crossroads of history traversing its land, today's Friuli–Venezia Giulia is a melting pot of influences. The Friuli north, with its landscape of mountains and rolling hills, shares borders with Austria and Slovenia, while coastal Venezia Giulia to the south connects to the Veneto and the Adriatic Sea. The entire region was once a part of the Austro-Hungarian empire, and prior to World War II, its eastern border extended deep into present-day Slovenia. The region's warring history and the accompanying gaining and forfeiting of territory have forged a unique cultural identity, with central European roots giving birth to a Friulian language that is more Slavic than Italian. Recently, a surge of regional pride has been directed at retaining that language, which is now taught in schools and written on road signs. To hear the language spoken is like being in another country altogether, and it is nearly impossible for any foreigner to decipher.

Friulian cuisine speaks of its tangled past, with many different cultures having left a mark on present-day eating. Heavy German influences are evident in jota, the popular bean and fermented cabbage soup, while thick and dense goulash claims Slavic origins. The seemingly non-Italian ingredients horseradish, paprika, and mustard all work their way into traditional fare, especially in the numerous pork dishes. They're best washed down with a crisp Moretti beer—recognizable by the mustached man enjoying the frothy lager on the label—which also hails from Friuli. The company was founded in 1859 by Luigi Moretti, who hoped to replicate the imported Austrian beer so highly appreciated by Friulians. The success of the brewery can be attributed to the beer-drinking origins of his region's populace, which can still be seen today in the many beer halls and grill restaurants all over the region.

Evidence of the Friulians' love for eating and drinking is apparent in the numerous wine bars, known as *osterie,* that proliferate through the region. Unlike in other popular wine destinations in Italy, where tourists often constitute the bulk of customers patronizing bars and restaurants, Friulians socialize with one another at all hours of the day. The region is best known for balanced, acidic whites with green apple characteristics, originating from the central hilly Colli Orientali. Quality has always been the primary consideration for Friulian wine, with vintners choosing not to produce in off years. Tocai and Ribolla Gialla best represent the drinkability of the region's whites and demonstrate why meeting for a glass or two has become such an integral part of everyday Friulian life.

Two types of cured ham are produced by prosciutto masters in Friuli. The most recognized hails from San Danielle, where pig legs are cured in salt and then left to hang in open warehouses for one year, absorbing fresh air from both the mountains and sea. Another prosciutto is produced in the mountain area known as Carnia. Up a winding road, in a tucked-away postcard-like setting, the wooden-house village of Sauris smokes prosciutto leg with beech wood and juniper berries. The result is a delicate ham that shares speck-like qualities with the sweet taste of prosciutto. The mountains of Friuli are also home to many farms where good-quality cheese is produced in the summer months, including the favorite Montasio. Whether eaten young and on its own or left to age and be grated, Montasio is a versatile and easy to digest cheese that is beginning to gain worldwide recognition.

The Friulian agriturismi and their restaurants present a large repertoire of regional specialties and ingredients, and the creativity and ingenuity emerging from their kitchens appeases the many international guests discovering the agriturismo vacation. Commonly referred to as "the next Tuscany," Friuli–Venezia Giulia is addictively charming to first-time travelers, who often find reason to return again and again.

Pruning I Comelli's vines

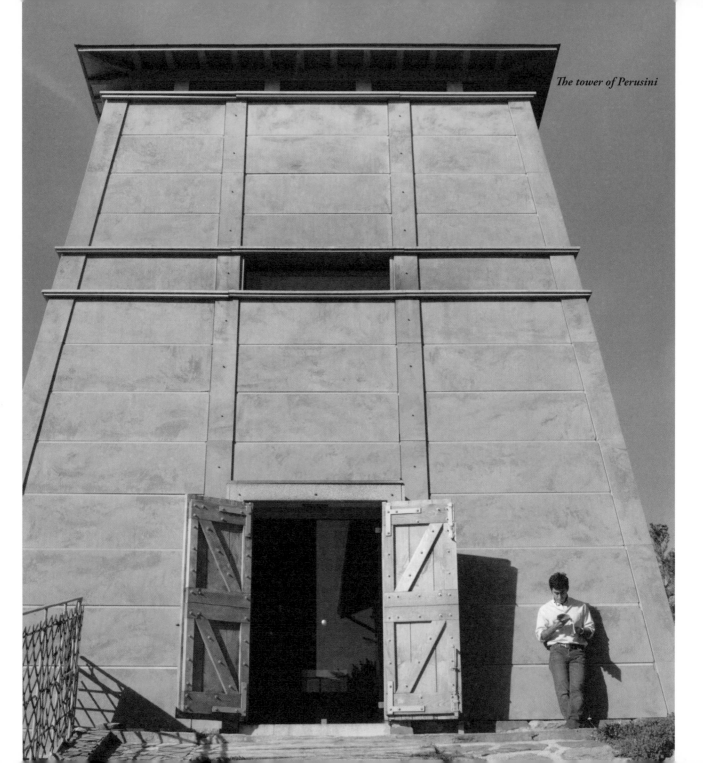

CHAPTER 20
❧ PERUSINI ❧

A visit to the Perusini vineyard and agriturismo represents a journey into winemaking history. With a storied past rich in nobility and castles, turmoil, and family feuds, the Perusini name represents a living history that reads like a romantic novel. The late Giacomo Perusini, grandfather of today's owner, Teresa Perusini, was credited with the rediscovery and replanting of Friuli's most coveted grape, the Picolit. After his untimely death during World War I, his wife, Giuseppina, continued his efforts, running the estate and bringing international recognition to her family's wine by promoting its sales abroad. Her two sons then inherited the property, each individually making significant advances in Friulian wine technology as well as in Perusini's production. Their eventual inability to work together would lead to a bitter quarrel resulting in the loss of three-quarters of the estate, including the family's castle.

Today, Teresa and her husband, Giacomo, manage the vineyard and are slowly re-establishing Perusini wines as a formidable player among Friuli's top producers. Several farmhouses, which are tucked into the surrounding hills, among the estate's vines, have been converted into apartments, complete with period furniture and splendid views, allowing guests an agriturismo vacation in the tranquil Friulian countryside. Also of recent construction is the Torre-Cantina, a three-story tower built by renowned Italian architect A.R. Burelli using typical Mediterranean materials. From the ceiling of the third floor, extending down into the tower's basement, hangs a replica of Foucault's pendulum, which gently swings among the estate's barrique (wood) barrels with the turning of the earth. Teresa had the inside of the tower painted by Polish artist Leon Tarasewicz, who matched the colors of the landscape, to parallel the north, south, east, and west views out of the tower's windows. The Torre-Cantina is an impressive structure, one that has been recognized not only for its architectural engineering, but also as the symbol of a new generation of Perusini wines.

Il Postiglione, the agriturismo's homey and comfortable trattoria, matches traditional Friulian fare with Perusini wines. It's good, simple food that doesn't mask or cover the flavor of the wines. In the heart of the Colli Orientali hills of Friuli, the restaurant is the kind of place where you can sit for a few hours, lingering over several glasses—or even bottles—of the estate's wines, and feel completely at ease. Teresa hopes that the newly planted olive trees will soon produce fruit to make oil for use in the restaurant as well.

Almost one hundred years ago, Teresa's grandmother, Giuseppina, wrote a cookbook, *Mangiare e Ber Friulani*. Still in print today, it's considered a classic on the region's specialties. Her thorough research into her countrymen's culinary ways focused on all segments of Friulian society and gives a lucid view into customary eating habits, which haven't changed much in today's vastly different Friuli.

Teresa explains the drying process of gra
for her Picolit wine.

Barley with Dried Porcini Mushrooms
ORZO AI PORCINI

At Perusini, they cook this dish in the same manner as risotto, and the results are phenomenal. The meatiness of the mushrooms matches well with the toothy nuttiness of the barley, and the cooking technique creates a creamy finish. Use fresh porcini, if available, in place of the dried mushrooms and cremini.

Soak the dried porcini in a small bowl with the warm water for about 20 minutes. Strain the mushrooms, using a fine mesh sieve, and reserve the liquid.

Meanwhile, in a 12-inch straight-sided sauté pan, cook the onion in 1 tablespoon butter and 1 tablespoon olive oil, over medium-high heat, until tender and translucent but not browned, 7 to 10 minutes. Add the barley, coat with the butter and oil, and toast for about 2 minutes. Add the white wine to the pan and reduce to almost dry.

Heat the chicken broth in a small saucepan, almost to a boil. Add the broth, one ladle at a time, to cover the barley, stirring constantly with a wooden spoon until the broth has been completely absorbed. Continue to cook in this manner, adding broth one ladle at a time, for about 15 minutes, stirring continuously. Cut the porcini and cremini mushrooms into slices and add to the pan. Cook for another 15 to 20 minutes in the same manner, adding the broth and the reserved mushroom broth one ladle at a time, until the barley is al dente. Season to taste with salt and a generous amount of pepper.

Stir in the remaining tablespoon of butter, the Parmigiano Reggiano, and the chopped parsley. Serve in individual shallow bowls.

SERVES 4

1 ounce (30 g) dried porcini mushrooms

1 cup (8 fl. oz. / 240 ml) warm water

1 medium yellow onion, cut into fine dice

2 tablespoons (1 oz. / 30 g) unsalted butter

1 tablespoon (½ fl. oz. / 15 ml) extra-virgin olive oil

1 cup (200 g) rinsed pearl barley

¾ cup (6 fl. oz. / 180 ml) white wine

1 quart (32 fl. oz. / 960 ml) homemade chicken broth (see page xi) or canned low-sodium broth

4 ounces (115 g) cremini mushrooms

Kosher salt and freshly ground black pepper

¼ cup grated Parmigiano Reggiano

¼ cup chopped flat-leaf parsley

Butternut squash gnocchi

Butternut Squash Gnocchi
GNOCCHI DI ZUCCA

The extremely wet dough of these bright orange gnocchi is easily managed with the help of a pastry bag and is cooked by piping drops of the mixture into simmering water. The smokiness of the mozzarella is an important addition to this classic Friulian recipe.

Heat the oven to 425°F (220°C).

Cut the squash in half and rub with olive oil. Place on a sheet pan with 1/2 cup of water and roast in the oven until tender, about 45 minutes. Remove from the oven and let cool completely.

In a large bowl, mash the squash with a fork and then mix in the egg, flour, nutmeg, salt, and Parmigiano Reggiano to form a loose dough. Cover with plastic wrap and place in the refrigerator for at least 30 minutes.

Bring 6 quarts of salted water to a boil. Spoon the dough into a pastry bag and pipe the gnocchi into the water, using a butter knife to cut the dough into individual ½-inch dumplings. Cook about 20 gnocchi at a time until they rise to the surface of the boiling water, 2 to 3 minutes. Using a spider or slotted spoon, transfer the cooked gnocchi into a bowl of ice water. Continue until all the gnocchi are cooked. Remove the gnocchi from the ice water and place on a kitchen towel to dry.

Melt the butter in a 12-inch sauté pan over medium-high heat. Add the sage leaves and the gnocchi to the pan and cook until the gnocchi are warmed through, 2 to 3 minutes. Season to taste with salt and pepper. Pour out into a large serving bowl and sprinkle with the shredded mozzarella.

SERVES 6–8

1½ pounds (675 g) butternut squash

1 tablespoon (½ fl. oz. / 15 ml) extra-virgin olive oil

½ cup (4 fl. oz. / 120 ml) water

1 egg

1¼ cups (150 g) all-purpose flour

¼ teaspoon freshly grated nutmeg

Kosher salt and freshly ground black pepper

½ cup grated Parmigiano Reggiano

5 tablespoons (2½ fl. oz. / 75 g) unsalted butter

2 tablespoons chopped sage

¼ cup shredded smoked mozzarella

PICOLIT

The jewel of Friulian viticulture only flourishes in the hills of the Colli Orientali. Known as Picolit, the sweet wine is made from small irregular white grapes that show a faint resemblance to a blossom. After undergoing a special drying process, the grapes are aged in both oak and acacia barrels. The wine's unique and intense floral aroma, its limited production, and the high demand for it by wine lovers around the world make it a pricey indulgence worthy of its classification as a "wine for meditation."

Perusini's pride and joy: Picolit

CHAPTER 21

LA SUBIDA

Teresa's favorite agriturismo restaurant lies a short distance away, on a road that skirts the Slovenian boundary, curving past the border checkpoint. An eerie militaristic structure guarded by serious-looking men holding semiautomatics is a silent reminder of the once-fierce—and not-too-far past—animosity between the two countries. The hostile environment forged a fierce division between Slovenia and Friuli, with little cultural influence permeating either side. With La Subida, Josko Sirk and his wife, Loredana, shattered this cultural divide, crumbling culinary barriers with what is now considered one of the best restaurants in all of Italy. Understanding the wealth of ingredients coming from small family farms and artisanal producers on both sides of the border, Josko fused together elements never seen before in Italian cooking. In a region known for its rustic and simple cuisine and a war-torn country where good food had been a scarce luxury, La Subida unites the two into a marriage of refinement, dignity, and sophistication. A delicate hand lends subtle heat to a phyllo dough bundle spiked with horseradish and filled with Montasio cheese and pear, while goat tenderloin with pumpkin seeds and coriander and a polenta and flour Slovenian pasta *(mlinci)* highlight a distinctly unique Italian dining experience. A journey to Italy's extreme northeast will open eyes and palates to a frontier of limitless boundaries, as put on display by the creations emerging from La Subida's kitchen.

Phyllo Bundles with Walnuts and Asiago
PACHETTI DI PASTA FILLO CON NOCE E ASIAGO

This dish exemplifies La Subida's ability to bring refinement to a few humble ingredients. The contrast of the flaky phyllo shell with the creamy, sweet, and tannic elements of the filling make for a bite-size bundle of good taste.

2 Bosc pears, peeled, cored and cut into fine dice

2 ounces (60 g) Asiago cheese, cut into fine dice

3½ ounces (100 g) finely chopped walnuts

1 tablespoon (½ fl. oz. / 15 ml) lemon juice

Kosher salt and freshly ground black pepper

1 1-pound (450 g) package phyllo dough

8 tablespoons (4 oz. / 115 g) unsalted butter, melted

2 cups (16 fl. oz. / 480 ml) canola oil

Heat the oven to 200°F (90°C).

In a large bowl, mix together the pear, cheese, walnuts, lemon juice, ½ teaspoon salt, and ¼ teaspoon pepper.

Place one sheet of phyllo onto a clean work surface. (Keep the remaining sheets covered with a damp towel.) Brush the sheet all over with melted butter, place another sheet on top to cover, brush with butter, and continue layering the phyllo sheets in this manner, ending with a fifth sheet, brushed with butter. Cut the phyllo dough into 3-inch squares, and place 1 tablespoon of pear filling on each square. Fold up the edges of the phyllo around the pear mixture, and pinch to make a purselike bundle.

In a deep saucepan, heat the canola oil to 375°F (190°C). Fry the phyllo bundles in the oil until they are golden brown, about 4 minutes. Drain on paper towels and keep warm in the oven while frying the remaining bundles. Serve warm.

YIELDS 32 PIECES

Lamb Tenderloin with Pumpkin Seeds and Cherry Tomatoes

FILETTO D'AGNELLO CON SEMI DI ZUCCA E POMODORINI

Lamb tenderloins are small in size, tender and delicate in flavor. Marinating the meat overnight really enhances the meat, but be sure to wipe the herb and spice mixture completely off the meat prior to cooking.

Rinse and pat dry the lamb tenderloins and trim away any silver skin. Rub the lamb with 1 tablespoon of olive oil, coat the tenderloins with the herbs, juniper berries, coriander, and garlic, and marinate overnight in the refrigerator.

Heat the oven to 400°F (200°C).

Toast the pumpkin seeds in the oven with salt to taste, until golden brown, about 5 to 7 minutes. Set aside to cool.

Remove the lamb from the marinade and wipe away the seasonings. Season the lamb with salt and pepper. Heat 1 tablespoon butter and 1 tablespoon olive oil in a large sauté pan over medium-high heat and sear lamb on all sides until nicely browned, 2 to 3 minutes per side. Remove from the pan and place on a carving board, loosely covered with foil. Add the cherry tomatoes and a pinch of salt to the pan and sauté just until they begin to soften, 2 to 3 minutes. Add the pumpkin seeds and sauté 1 more minute. Season to taste with salt and pepper.

Carve the lamb into slices and serve with the tomatoes and pumpkin seeds.

SERVES 4

1 pound (450 g) lamb tenderloin

2 tablespoons (1 fl. oz. / 30 ml) extra-virgin olive oil

2 tablespoons chopped thyme

2 tablespoons chopped rosemary

2 teaspoons lightly crushed juniper berries

1 tablespoon ground coriander

1 peeled and minced garlic clove

¼ cup (35 g) pumpkin seeds

Kosher salt and freshly ground black pepper

1 tablespoon (½ oz. / 15 g) unsalted butter

12 ounces (340 g) cherry tomatoes

Radicchio and apple salad

Radicchio with Horseradish, Apples, and Asiago Cheese

RADICCHIO CON RAFANO, MELE, E ASIAGO

The nose-tingling bite of fresh horseradish is much appreciated at the Friulian table. This warm salad highlights its ability to bring ingredients together, mellowing the chicory's bitterness and enhancing the natural sweetness of the apples. La Subida prefers the elongated, thinner radicchio di Treviso for a more elegantly plated dish, but feel free to use the more commonly found, round radicchio di Chioggia.

2 tablespoons (1 oz. / 30 g) unsalted butter

3 heads radicchio Treviso, cut into quarters

Kosher salt and freshly ground black pepper

3 tablespoons (25 g) grated fresh horseradish

2 Pink Lady apples, peeled, cored, and grated

½ cup shredded Asiago cheese

Heat a heavy sauté pan over medium heat. Melt the butter in the pan and add the radicchio. Cook on one side until golden brown, 2 to 3 minutes, then flip over, season with salt and pepper, and continue to cook, covered, until the radicchio is tender, 3 to 5 minutes.

In a small bowl, mix together the horseradish, apples, and cheese, and season with salt and pepper. Mound 2 tablespoons of the mixture on each individual plate. Place two wedges of radicchio over the apple mixture.

SERVES 6

Polenta Gnocchi with Rabbit and Porcini Mushrooms

GNOCCHI DI POLENTA CON SUGO DI CONIGLIO E PORCINI

In the polenta-eating world of northern Italy, these gnocchi take the grain to a higher level of sophistication. They are the perfect carrier for the rabbit ragu, absorbing and retaining the juices and flavors of the sauce.

1 recipe polenta (see page x)

1 cup (125 g) all-purpose flour, plus more for dusting

3 large eggs

1 ounce (30 g) dried porcini mush-rooms

1 cup (8 fl. oz. / 240 ml) warm water

¼ cup (2 fl. oz. / 60 ml) extra-virgin olive oil

1 rabbit, cut into 8 pieces (about 2 pounds / 900 g)

Kosher salt and freshly ground black pepper

1 yellow onion, cut into fine dice

2 stalks celery, cut into fine dice

1 carrot, peeled and cut into fine dice

1 cup (8 fl. oz. / 240 ml) white wine

2 cups (16 fl. oz. / 480 ml) home-made chicken broth (see page xi) or canned low-sodium broth

1 tablespoon chopped rosemary, plus more for garnish

½ tablespoon chopped marjoram

Pour the polenta out on a sheet pan to cool slightly, about 15 minutes. In a large bowl mix the polenta with the flour and eggs to form a soft dough. Cut the dough into 4 even pieces. Roll each piece out into a 1-inch-thick rope, and then cut each rope into ¼-inch gnocchi with a pastry cutter or knife. Place on a sheet pan lightly dusted with flour. Loosely cover and refrigerate until ready to cook.

Soak the dried porcini mushrooms in the warm water for 30 minutes, strain through a fine mesh sieve, and reserve liquid.

Meanwhile, in a heavy-bottomed casserole pan, heat 2 tablespoons of olive oil over medium-high heat. Season the rabbit pieces with salt and pepper and sear on all sides until golden brown, 3 to 4 minutes per side. Remove from the pan and set aside on a plate.

Add 1 tablespoon olive oil to the pan, then the onion, celery, and carrot, and cook until they become tender and slightly caramelized, about 12 minutes. Add the white wine to the pan, bring to a boil, and reduce by half. Add the reserved mushroom liquid and the chicken broth and bring to a boil. Place the rabbit, rosemary, marjoram, and bay leaf in the pan, cover, and reduce the heat to low. Simmer for about 45 minutes, then remove the breast pieces. Continue to simmer the rest of the meat, covered, another 20 minutes. Remove the legs from the pan and put them with the breasts.

When cool enough to handle, shred the meat, removing it from the bones. Strain the sauce through a fine mesh sieve, discard the vegetables, and skim the fat from the liquid and reserve.

Meanwhile, bring 6 quarts of salted water to a boil. Add the gnocchi and cook until they are tender and rise to the surface of the pot, 2 to 3 minutes. Drain well.

In a large sauté pan, heat 1 tablespoon of olive oil over medium-high heat. Add the porcini mushrooms and cook until they begin to brown, 3 to 5 minutes. Add the cherry tomatoes, season with salt and pepper, and sauté until tender, 3 to 4 minutes. Add the rabbit meat with ¼ cup of the reserved cooking liquid and heat through. Season to taste with salt and pepper. Add the gnocchi to the sauté pan and coat with the sauce, pour out into a large serving bowl, and garnish with chopped rosemary.

SERVES 6

1 bay leaf

12 ounces (340 g) cherry tomatoes, cut into quarters

Making pasta

Slovenian Toasted Pasta with Duck Sauce
MLINCI CON SUGA D'ANATRA

Mlinci *are rolled-out sheets of pasta that are toasted over a griddle, cut into irregular shapes, and boiled. The toasting of the dough imparts a toothy, nutty texture, allowing the sauce to adhere to its grooves.* Mlinci *have their roots in nearby Slovenia and reflect the duality of cuisines emerging from La Subida's kitchen.*

2½ cups (325 g) all-purpose flour

¾ cup (125 g) fine-ground cornmeal

4 eggs

2 duck breasts (about 2 pounds / 900 kg)

Kosher salt and freshly ground black pepper

1 medium yellow onion, cut into medium dice

5 tomatoes, peeled, seeded and cut into medium dice

1 zucchini (courgette), cut into medium dice

1 tablespoon chopped thyme

1 tablespoon chopped rosemary

2 tablespoons chopped flat-leaf parsley, plus more for garnish

½ cup (4 fl. oz. / 120 ml) homemade chicken broth (see page xi) or canned low-sodium broth

Make the pasta: On a clean work surface, mix the flour and cornmeal and then make a well. In the center, add the eggs, and gradually incorporate the flour and cornmeal into the eggs with a fork. Once a dough begins to form, knead the dough until it becomes smooth and elastic. Let rest, covered, about 20 minutes.

Divide the dough into 4 parts and roll out each part, using a pasta machine starting with the widest setting and ending with the second thinnest setting, into a long sheet. Cut each sheet into foot-long sections. Toast the raw sheets of dough on a griddle, 30 seconds per side, and then cut into rectangular slices, about 1 inch wide.

Score the skin of the duck breasts in a ½-inch crosshatch pattern, place skin side down in a heavy-bottomed skillet over medium-low heat, and slowly render the fat until the duck skin is rich golden brown and crisp, 20 to 25 minutes. Remove the duck from the pan and let cool completely. Cut the duck into ¼-inch cubes and season generously with salt and pepper. Reserve 2 tablespoons of the duck fat.

Prepare the sauce: Heat a 12-inch skillet over medium-high heat, add the reserved duck fat, the duck pieces, and salt and pepper and sauté until just cooked through, about 5 minutes. Remove the duck from the pan and set aside on a plate. Add the onion to the pan and sauté until tender and translucent, 5 to 7 minutes. Add the tomato, zucchini, herbs, and a pinch of salt and continue to cook until the vegetables release their liquid and soften,

5 to 7 minutes. Add the chicken broth, bring up to a boil, and reduce by half. Return the duck to the pan to warm through. Season to taste with salt and pepper.

Meanwhile, bring 6 quarts of salted water to a boil. Drop the pasta into the water and cook until tender, 3 to 4 minutes. Drain well and toss with the sauce. Pour out into a large serving bowl and garnish with some fresh parsley.

SERVES 6–8

Ducks hanging in the cooler

Casale Cjanor's flock of geese

CHAPTER 22
CASALE CJANOR

The thousands of geese and hundreds of ducks that live at Casale Cjanor spend their days cackling, swimming in watering holes, and sleeping beneath shady trees, living a tranquil life in a park-like setting before eventually making their way onto the farm's dinner table. Nestled in the flatlands at the heart of a bird sanctuary, the agriturismo run by three sisters and their parents has made its livelihood raising poultry in the San Danielle region of Friuli. Up until recently, chickens were also a mainstay of Casale Cjanor's farm, but with the potential threat of bird flu, the family decided to stop rearing the birds, preventing a possibly devastating affliction for their animals and the nature preserve. In an area most known for its superior production of prosciutto, the Missana family has received Slow Food accolades and recognition for its many goose specialties, whose place at the Friulian table has all but disappeared. Slow Food invited Casale Cjanor to participate in the Terra Madre exhibition, which brings food cultures from around the world together to raise awareness and preserve sustainable lifestyles.

Every fall, the slaughter brings the agriturismo to life with an all-out family effort. In a sterile room with a table piled high with naked carcasses of geese and ducks, the family gets to work, plucking, butchering, and preparing the birds for the kitchen. There is no waste involved and every part of the animal finds a place on the special annual all-goose-and-duck menu. The feast celebrates Casale Cjanor's year-long rearing of the flocks and includes a goose pâté, goose casserole, a surprisingly delicious duck stomach stew, and cured duck and goose prosciutto. In other months, Margherita, Casale Cjanor's ambitious chef, dishes out other specialties, all from farm products. From the pigs, she makes a pork loin roast packed with juniper, rosemary, and honey flavor and a specialty known as *pestat,* a condiment of lard, cooked vegetables, and herbs, which has all but disappeared from the Friulian kitchen. Casale Cjanor adds it to meats and potatoes for deep rich flavor. Margherita's past experience at a gelateria and love for desserts shows in her ability to combine unique ingredients, as evident in her saffron semifreddo. Her cherry panna cotta and chocolate ricotta tart also showcase her pastry skills. The gracious feminine hospitality of Casale Cjanor greets the many guests who fill the stone dining room nightly to experience a taste of old Friuli.

Sunchoke Soup with Chicken Liver–Filled Crackers

CREMA DI TOPINAMBUR

The liver-filled crackers complement the flavor of the silky sunchoke puree. The robust combination is better scaled down into small portions.

Soup

2 tablespoons (1 oz. / 30 g) unsalted butter

3 leeks, cleaned and cut into ¼-inch slices

1 pound (450 g) sunchokes (Jerusalem artichokes), scrubbed and cut into ¼-inch slices

Kosher salt and freshly ground black pepper

2 quarts (64 fl. oz. / 1.89 L) home-made chicken broth (see page xi) or canned low-sodium broth

1 bay leaf

1 sprig of thyme

½ cup (4 fl. oz. / 120 ml) heavy cream

Crackers

2 cups (250 g) all-purpose flour

¼ cup (25 g) cornstarch

¼ cup (25 g) cornmeal

1 egg plus 1 egg white

2 tablespoons (1 fl. oz. / 30 ml) whole milk

Prepare the soup: In a 4-quart saucepan, melt the butter over medium heat. Add the leeks and cook until tender and translucent, about 7 minutes. Add the sunchokes, season with salt, and cook 5 minutes. Add the broth, the bay leaf, and the thyme sprig and bring to a boil. Reduce the heat to medium-low and simmer until the sunchokes are tender, about 30 minutes. Season to taste with salt and pepper. Discard the bay leaf and thyme and with an immersion blender or in a blender puree the soup until smooth. Add the cream and gently warm before serving.

Make the crackers: Heat the oven to 375°F (190°C).

In the bowl of an electric mixer fitted with the paddle attachment, add the flour, cornstarch, cornmeal, 1 egg, milk, salt, and butter and mix on low speed until a dough forms. Turn the dough out onto a lightly floured surface and roll out to ¼ inch thick. Cut the dough into ½-inch squares and place on a parchment-lined baking sheet. Brush half of the squares with egg white and sprinkle with poppy seeds. Bake crackers in the oven until golden brown and set, 10 to 12 minutes. Remove to a wire rack and let cool completely.

Cook the chicken livers: Melt the butter in a 10-inch nonstick skillet over medium-high heat. Sauté the shallots until translucent, about 3 minutes. Add the chicken livers, along with the thyme, and season with salt and pepper. Cook 3 minutes or until golden brown. Turn the chicken livers over, add the Marsala, and continue to cook 3 minutes. Remove from heat and puree in a food processor until smooth. Adjust seasoning if necessary.

To serve, spread 1 teaspoon of chicken liver over a plain cracker, then top with a poppy-seed cracker, to make little sandwiches. Ladle the warm soup into shallow bowls, add 3 cracker sandwiches per bowl, and serve.

SERVES 4–6

½ tablespoon (5 g) salt

10 tablespoons (5 oz. / 150 g) unsalted butter

1 tablespoon poppy seeds

Chicken livers

2 tablespoons (1 oz. / 30 g) unsalted butter

1 shallot, cut into fine dice

½ pound (225 g) chicken livers

1 teaspoon chopped thyme

Salt and pepper, to taste

½ cup (4 fl. oz. / 120 ml) Marsala

Green Cabbage and Pear Salad
INSALATA DI CAVOLO VERDE E PERE

Poppy seeds are a common addition to Friulian recipes, and their subtle flavor adds depth while the tiny round seeds add a decorative touch to a dish. Here they do both, with specks of black dotting the cabbage, pear, and orange segments.

Working over a bowl to catch the juices, peel the orange and cut between the membranes to remove the sections. Place the orange segments in another bowl, reserving the juice.

Whisk together the reserved orange juice, the olive oil, and the white wine vinegar, a pinch of salt and pepper, and set aside.

In a large bowl, mix together the pear, the shredded cabbage, the celery, and the poppy seeds. Season with salt and pepper. Toss lightly with the orange vinaigrette. Mound a small portion of salad on individual plates and top with the orange segments.

SERVES 6

1 large navel orange

2 tablespoons (1 fl. oz. / 30 ml) extra-virgin olive oil

1 teaspoon white wine vinegar

Kosher salt and freshly ground black pepper

1 Bosc pear, cored and cut into thin slices

½ head green cabbage, shredded

2 stalks sliced celery

1 tablespoon poppy seeds

Crepes with Butternut Squash and Poppy Seeds

CRESPELLE ALLA ZUCCA E SEMI DI PAPAVERO

Béchamel sauce and ricotta cheese bind the butternut squash, making a rich filling for the crepes. Rolling these in plastic wrap and refrigerating them allows them to set before slicing. Margherita serves these in individual gratin dishes, bubbling with Parmigiano Reggiano and sprinkled with poppy seeds.

2 tablespoons (1 fl. oz. / 30 ml) extra-virgin olive oil

1 yellow onion, cut into fine dice

2 carrots, peeled and cut into fine dice

1 large butternut squash, peeled and cut into cubes

Kosher salt and freshly ground black pepper

8 ounces (225 g) ricotta cheese

1 recipe béchamel (see page x)

1 recipe crepes (see page ix)

½ cup grated Parmigiano Reggiano, plus more for garnish

2 tablespoons poppy seeds

In a large sauté pan, add 2 tablespoons olive oil and cook the onion over medium heat until it begins to soften, about 5 minutes. Add the carrots and continue to cook, until the vegetables begin to brown, about 7 minutes. Then add the butternut squash and ¼ cup of water and season with salt and pepper. Cover the pan and lower the heat to medium-low, cooking until the squash begins to soften, about 15 minutes. Remove the lid and allow some of the moisture to evaporate. Remove pan from the heat and set aside to cool.

Mash the squash mixture and combine it with the ricotta cheese. Mix in the béchamel. Adjust seasoning if necessary.

Lay each crepe flat on a piece of plastic wrap large enough to cover the rolled-up crepe. Spread 2 tablespoons of the squash mixture over each crepe and sprinkle with grated Parmigiano Reggiano. Roll the crepes lengthwise and then wrap in the plastic wrap. Place in the refrigerator until chilled through, at least 1 hour.

Heat the broiler on high. Remove crepes from the refrigerator and the plastic wrap. Cut the crepes into 1-inch slices and place filling-side up in a large baking dish. Sprinkle with the poppy seeds and Parmigiano Reggiano and cook until the cheese is melted and browned, 3 to 4 minutes.

SERVES 8

Rolled crepes wrapped in plastic

Herb-decorated pork loin before roasting

Pork Loin Roast with Juniper Berries and Honey

ARROSTO DI MAIALE CON BACCHE DI GINEPRO E MIELE

This simple recipe utilizes many staples from the northern Italian pantry. The syrupy honey sauce matches the juniper- and herb-encrusted pork loin well. Serve alongside a salad of bitter greens or sautéed green cabbage.

Heat the oven to 400°F (200°C).

Season the pork tenderloin with salt and pepper. Place in a large baking dish, rub with olive oil, and cover with the garlic, sage, rosemary, juniper berries, and bay leaves.

Place tenderloin in the oven and cook for 30 minutes. Turn the tenderloin over, add the white wine to the baking dish, and cook for another 20 minutes or until meat thermometer reads 150°F (65°C).

Remove the pan from the oven and put aside to rest. Strain the pan juices into a small saucepan. Add chicken broth and bring to a boil. Add the honey and some of the juniper berries and some of the garlic from the pork, and cook until the honey has dissolved, 2 to 3 minutes. Puree with an immersion blender. Continue to boil until reduced by half and syrupy. Season to taste with salt and pepper.

Carve the pork into thin slices, place on a serving platter, and drizzle with the sauce.

SERVES 4–6

1 2-pound (900 g) pork tenderloin

Kosher salt and freshly ground black pepper

1 tablespoon (½ fl. oz. / 15 ml) extra-virgin olive oil

2 cloves of garlic, peeled and sliced

1 tablespoon chopped sage

1 tablespoon chopped rosemary

1 tablespoon lightly crushed juniper berries

2 bay leaves

1 cup (8 fl. oz. / 240 ml) white wine

1 cup (8 fl. oz. / 240 ml) homemade chicken broth (see page xi) or canned low-sodium broth

2 teaspoons (⅓ fl. oz. / 9 ml) honey

Braised Duck
ANATRA IN CASSERUOLA

At Casale Cjanor, this recipe is made with either duck or goose and is always on the fall menu after the annual slaughter. Simmering the duck first renders most of the fat, making it leaner and more palatable. Be sure to flambé the brandy to burn off the alcohol before adding the red wine.

1 whole duck (about 5 pounds / 2.5 kg)

Kosher salt and freshly ground black pepper

2 tablespoons (1 fl. oz. / 30 ml) extra-virgin olive oil

1 yellow onion, cut into fine dice

1 clove of garlic, peeled and minced

2 ounces (60 g) pancetta, cut into fine dice

½ cup (4 fl. oz. / 120 ml) brandy

1 cup (8 fl. oz. / 240 ml) red wine

1 tablespoon chopped thyme

3 bay leaves

3 cups (24 fl. oz. / 720 ml) home-made chicken broth (see page xi) or canned low-sodium broth

Prick the duck all over with the tines of a fork to pierce the skin. Place in an 8-quart stockpot and add enough water to cover and 1 tablespoon of salt. Place the pot over medium-high heat and bring to a boil. Reduce heat to medium-low and simmer the duck for 30 minutes to render the fat. Drain the duck and set aside to cool. Once cooled, cut the duck into 8 pieces and season with salt and pepper.

In a heavy casserole pan, add 2 tablespoons of olive oil over medium-high heat and sear the duck pieces until browned on all sides, 5 to 7 minutes per side. Remove the duck from the pan and set aside.

Add the onion, garlic, and pancetta to the pan and brown over medium-high heat, 5 to 7 minutes. Add the brandy to the pan and flambé either with a match or by catching the flame from a gas stove. Add the red wine to the pan and reduce by half.

Return the duck to the pan along with the thyme and bay leaves. Cover with the chicken broth and bring to a boil. Reduce the heat to low, cover pan, and simmer the duck for 30 minutes, and remove the breast and set aside. Continue to cook the legs 30 minutes more until fork-tender.

Remove the duck legs from the pan and place on a large serving platter with the breasts. Strain the sauce through a fine mesh sieve into a small saucepan over medium-high heat. Reduce the sauce by half and season to taste with salt and pepper. Drizzle the duck with the sauce and serve.

SERVES 4

Braised duck

Cherry panna cotta

Panna Cotta with Cherry Marmalade
PANNA COTTA ALLA MARMELATTA DI CILIEGIE

A traditional Italian custard translating as "cooked cream," panna cotta can be prepared simply with vanilla or dressed up with other flavors. At Casale Cjanor, Margherita uses the farm's own cherry marmalade in the panna cotta base. This recipe works with any fruit marmalade.

In a 4-quart saucepan over medium heat, combine the sugar, lemon zest, and lemon juice and cook until the sugar dissolves, 1 to 2 minutes. Add the cherries to the pan and cook until the cherries are tender and begin to break down, about 15 minutes. Remove from the heat, let cool completely, and then gently puree in a blender or food processor.

Pour the milk into a 2-quart saucepan. Sprinkle the gelatin evenly over the surface. Let stand for about 10 minutes. Warm the milk over low heat, add the sugar and salt, and stir until the sugar is completely dissolved.

In a large bowl, combine the heavy cream, the vanilla, and the cherry marmalade. Whisk in the warm milk until combined. Pour into 8 individual ramekins, cover with plastic wrap, and place in the refrigerator until set, at least 4 hours.

To serve, unmold the panna cotta by running a butter knife between the custard and the ramekin. Invert each panna cotta onto an individual plate and carefully remove the ramekin.

SERVES 8

Cherry marmalade

3 tablespoons (42.5 g) granulated sugar

1 teaspoon lemon zest

1 tablespoon (½ fl. oz. / 15 ml) lemon juice

12 ounces (340 g) pitted cherries

Panna cotta

1 cup (8 fl. oz. / 240 ml) milk

2 tablespoons (15 g) powdered gelatin

½ cup (85 g) granulated sugar

Pinch of table salt

3 cups (24 fl. oz. / 720 ml) heavy cream

1 teaspoon vanilla extract

Vanilla Saffron Semifreddo
SEMIFREDDO ALLA VANIGLIA E ZAFFERANO

Semifreddo translates as "half cold" and is a partially frozen custard. Margherita's inclusion of saffron, a spice often reserved for savory dishes, lends a unique element to the quick-melting dessert.

10 large egg yolks

¾ cup (150 g) plus ⅛ cup (25 g) granulated sugar

Pinch of saffron threads

1 vanilla bean, split in half

2 cups (16 fl. oz. / 480 ml) heavy cream

1 tablespoon (1/2 fl. oz. / 15 ml) dry Marsala

In the pan of a double boiler, combine the egg yolks, ¾ cup sugar, the saffron, and the vanilla bean, scraping the pulp into the pan. Place over barely simmering water and whisk constantly, until thickened and doubled in volume and the temperature reaches 175°F (80°C), about 4 minutes. Remove pan from the heat and immediately submerge in an ice water bath, stirring constantly to bring down the temperature. Discard the vanilla bean.

Meanwhile, beat the cream until soft peaks form. Gradually add ⅛ cup of sugar in a steady stream, continuing to whip until stiff peaks form.

In the bowl of an electric mixer fitted with the paddle attachment, whip the egg yolk mixture with the Marsala until it becomes very thick and pale in color, 3 to 5 minutes.

Using a spatula, add a quarter of the whipped cream to the egg mixture and stir together gently to lighten the base. Fold the remaining whipped cream into the egg mixture and then spoon the custard into 8 individual ramekins. Cover with plastic wrap, and freeze until firm, at least 8 hours.

To serve, run a butter knife around the edge of the ramekin, invert the semifreddo onto individual plates, and serve.

SERVES 8

Saffron semifreddo

Chocolate and Ricotta Tart
CROSTATA DI RICOTTA E CIOCCOLATO

This is one of the most sinfully luxurious desserts. The combination of cocoa and ricotta creates a rich and creamy sensation that tastes like pure chocolate.

1 recipe savory pie crust (see page xi)

³/₄ cup (150 g) granulated sugar

7 tablespoons (3½ oz. / 100 g) unsalted butter, at room temperature

3 egg yolks

21 ounces (600 g) ricotta

½ cup (60 g) Dutch-process cocoa powder

1 tablespoon (½ fl. oz. / 15 ml) dark rum

⅓ cup plus 1 tablespoon (3½ fl. oz. / 100 ml) heavy cream

Heat the oven to 350°F (180°C).

Lightly flour a work surface and roll out the dough into a 13-inch round and ¼ inch thick. Butter a 12-inch tart pan with a removable bottom, and gently place the dough inside the pan, taking care to push the crust into the indentations in the side. Prick the dough with the tines of a fork and cover with foil. Place pie weights or dried beans in the center of the crust and bake until the crust is set, about 15 minutes. Place on a wire rack to cool and remove the foil and weights.

In the bowl of an electric mixer fitted with the paddle attachment (or using an electric beater), cream together the sugar and the butter until light and fluffy. Add the egg yolks, ricotta, and cocoa powder, mixing until thoroughly combined. Stir in the rum and heavy cream.

Pour the mixture into the tart crust and bake for about 40 minutes, or until the filling has set. Remove from the oven and let cool on a wire rack. Remove the outer rim from the tart pan and chill tart in the refrigerator until ready to serve.

SERVES 12

CHAPTER 23
❧ I COMELLI ❧

The Comellis are a strong male-dominated family unit, whose core and success stem from the nurturing tough love of mother Livia. Together with her husband, Alessandro, she has raised three fine sons, Paolo, Francesco, and Enrico, who today help run the agriturismo and continue the family tradition of making excellent wine. At a young age, Paolo, the eldest, was sent to South Africa to study new-age winemaking techniques he now applies in the Comelli cantina. Eight types of wine are produced here, but the Ramandolo, a sweet, intense golden-yellow wine from air-dried grapes, is the liquid gold of which they are most proud. In a region full of wine lovers who appreciate the time-honored tradition of sharing a glass or two of Friulian nectar with friends, Alessandro graciously invites guests of the agriturismo to join him in sampling his family's wine. The clinking of glasses and jovial banter are a nightly occurrence at the I Comelli bar, testimony to the good-hearted nature that permeates the farmhouse.

I Comelli is centrally located in the small town of Nemis. With a population of only 3,500, Nemis boasts more than forty eating and drinking establishments, celebrating the Friulian appreciation for the pleasures of good food and wine. The loyal patronage of the Comelli family agriturismo has been there since opening night, drawn by Livia's down-home cooking. Nutrition and balance unite in her preparation of traditional recipes,

I Comelli's urban farmhouse

and she looks to eliminate unnecessary calories and fat. In today's nonagrarian world, where the majority of work is done sitting in front of a computer, Livia realizes the impracticalities of heavy cooking, once necessary to sustain farmers working all day in the fields. Olive oil, a nonnative ingredient in the area, replaces butter in her kitchen and makes a somewhat lighter béchamel sauce for her crepe lasagna. Not all dishes work with health-conscious substitutions, however, and her fricco, a fried potato pancake with copious amounts of Montasio cheese, shines with oily butter and dairy decadence. The cuisine is an equilibrium of moderation, whose acceptance by I Comelli's dedicated patrons validates Livia's more modern approach to the region's cuisine.

Sweet and Sour Vegetables

VERDURE IN AGRODOLCE

Almost every farm in Italy has its own way of preserving the summer's bounty. At I Comelli, Livia boils vegetables in a vinegar and sugar solution that slightly pickles them and imparts an addictive sweet and sour taste.

2 quarts (64 fl. oz. / 1.89 L) water

1 quart (32 fl. oz. / 960 ml) white wine vinegar

3 tablespoons (30 g) kosher salt

¾ cup (190 g) granulated sugar

1 head cauliflower, broken into florets

4 large carrots, peeled and cut on the bias, ¼ inch thick

1 yellow bell pepper, cut into ¼-inch strips

1 red bell pepper, cut into ¼-inch strips

1 orange bell pepper, cut into ¼-inch strips

1 zucchini (courgette), cut into ¼-inch rounds

In a 6-quart stockpot, combine the water, white wine vinegar, salt, and sugar.

Bring contents of the pot to a slow boil over medium heat. Add the cauliflower and return to a boil. Add the carrots and return to a boil, then add the peppers and zucchini. Once the pot returns to a boil, remove from heat and let the vegetables cool in the liquid.

Put the vegetables in mason jars and cover with the cooking liquid. Cover tightly and keep refrigerated up to 1 week. Serve as an appetizer.

SERVES 6

Peppers cooling in vinegar

Bean and Barley Soup
MINESTRE D'ORZO E FAGIOLI

Barley, cabbage, and potatoes represent the hardy cold-weather crops of Friuli. Here they come together in a half-pureed soup that is texturally pleasing, full bodied, and packed with nutrients.

Heat a heavy stockpot over medium-high heat, add 2 tablespoons oil, and sauté the onion, celery, carrots, cabbage, and rosemary until tender but not browned, 10 to 12 minutes. Season lightly with salt and pepper.

Add the beans and potato to the pot. Cover with the vegetable broth, bring to a boil, and reduce the heat to low, cooking slowly for about 2 hours. Puree half of the bean soup, either in a blender or by passing through a food mill. Return the soup to the pot and season to taste with salt and pepper. Keep warm.

Meanwhile, bring 2 cups of water to a boil with a pinch of salt and add the barley. Reduce the heat to medium-low and simmer until the barley is tender, about 45 minutes. Drain the barley and then add to the pot with the pureed soup.

Ladle the soup into individual soup bowls, drizzle with a little olive oil, and serve with grated cheese.

SERVES 6

2 tablespoons (1 fl. oz. / 30 ml) olive oil, plus more for drizzling

1 white onion, cut into medium dice

2 stalks celery, cut into medium dice

2 carrots, peeled and cut into medium dice

6 ounces (170 g) savoy cabbage, shredded

2 tablespoons chopped rosemary

Kosher salt and freshly ground black pepper

8 ounces (225 g) cranberry beans, soaked overnight in cold water and drained

1 Yukon Gold potato, peeled and cut into medium dice

1 quart (32. fl. oz. / 960 ml) homemade vegetable broth (see page xii) or canned low-sodium broth

$1/2$ cup (100 g) rinsed pearl barley

$1/4$ cup grated Parmigiano Reggiano

Potato and Asiago Cheese Pancake

FRICO

Prepared either with potatoes and onions or only cheese, frico is a traditional specialty of Friuli that showcases the simplicity of a cuisine with bucolic roots. When made with potatoes and onions, the dish becomes a substantial meal. The crispy outer crust and soft, chewy interior create a pleasing texture that tastes just as good warm, at room temperature, and even cold.

2 tablespoons (2 oz. / 30 g)
   unsalted butter

3 peeled and grated Yukon Gold
   potatoes

1 grated white onion

Kosher salt and freshly ground black
   pepper

4 ounces (115 g) shredded
   Montasio cheese (or substitute
   Asiago cheese)

3 ounces (85 g) grated Parmigiano
   Reggiano

Heat the broiler to high.

Melt the butter in a heavy 12-inch nonstick pan over medium heat. Add the potatoes and the onions and cook, stirring often, until they begin to soften, 10 to 12 minutes. Season with salt and pepper. Stir the cheeses into the potato and onion mixture and cook until the cheeses begin to melt. With a wooden spoon, spread the mixture evenly in the pan and cook until the bottom turns deep golden brown and begins to set, 12 to 15 minutes.

Place the pan underneath the broiler and broil until the top of the potato pancake is also a deep golden brown, another 12 to 15 minutes. Remove from the oven and invert the frico onto a large flat serving plate.

Cut into wedges and serve hot, as a side or as a main course.

SERVES 6

Frico

234

Friulian Mountain Cheese Farms

Malaghe are small isolated mountain farms where cows spend their summers, grazing in the alpine meadows. In Friuli, many different cheese varieties are produced from sweet cow's milk, but Montasio is the cheese most recognized in the area, and it is used in many regional specialties, including the frico. Throughout the entire summer, farmers live in the mountains tending to their cattle and making cheese. The malaghe are only accessible by foot and visitors must trek up to them to purchase the freshly made wheels of cheese. After the last days of warmth come to an end, the farmer leads the cattle back down to the stables where they spend the winter.

Leek Crepe Lasagna
CRESPELLE DI PORRI

2 tablespoons (1 oz. / 30 g) unsalted butter

1 tablespoon (½ fl. oz. / 15 ml) extra-virgin olive oil

3 bunches leeks, cleaned and cut into ½-inch slices

1 recipe béchamel (see page x)

½ cup grated Parmigiano Reggiano

1 cup shredded Asiago cheese

1 recipe crepes (see page ix)

Once considered a peasant dish, crespelle are now eaten in great abundance in Friuli and appear on the menus of the region's most upscale restaurants. I Comelli slow-cooks leeks to bring out their natural sweetness and uses a béchamel sauce to add body to a dish whose end result seems much more complex than the few ingredients used in the actual preparation.

Heat the oven to 375°F (190°C).

In a 12-inch skillet, melt the butter together with the olive oil over medium heat. Sauté the leeks until extremely tender, but not browned, 15 to 20 minutes. Add the béchamel, 3 tablespoons Parmigiano Reggiano, and the shredded Asiago cheese to the pan. Cook until the cheese has melted, about 3 minutes.

Spread one ladle of the leek mixture out evenly to just to cover the bottom of a 12 × 8½-inch baking dish. Arrange the crepes to cover all the leek mixture. Spread a thin layer of the leek mixture on the crepes and repeat the process until all the crepes have been used. There should be about 3 layers. Top with a thin layer of leek sauce and sprinkle with the remaining Parmigiano Reggiano. Cover the pan with foil and bake in the oven for 30 minutes. Remove the foil and continue to bake until the top is bubbly and browned, another 10 to 12 minutes. Remove from the oven and let cool slightly prior to serving.

SERVES 6

Almond Cake
TORTA DI MANDORLE

Baked in a Bundt pan, this spongy cake resonates with nutty flavor from almond meal flour.

Heat the oven to 350°F (180°C). Butter a Bundt pan.

Place the egg whites in a medium bowl with a pinch of sugar. Use an electric mixer to beat egg whites to stiff (but not dry) peaks.

In another bowl, beat together the egg yolks and the remaining sugar until thickened and pale yellow. Add lemon zest, almond meal, and a pinch of salt and stir well to combine. Fold the egg whites into the egg yolk mixture. Pour into the prepared Bundt pan.

Bake for 35 minutes, or until a toothpick inserted into the center comes out clean. Remove from the oven and place on a wire rack to cool. Once completely cooled, invert the cake onto a cake dish and sprinkle with confectioners' sugar.

SERVES 10–12

8 eggs, separated

1 cup (200 g) granulated sugar

1 tablespoon lemon zest

2½ cups (250 g) almond meal flour

Table salt

Confectioners' sugar (icing sugar),
  for dusting

TAJUT

Traditionally, Friulian wine has had low levels of alcohol, due to the petite size of the grapes grown in a northern climate. To add balance and more alcohol, grapes of a higher sugar content, grown in southern Puglia, were squashed alongside the native fruit. This addition to their winemaking became known as the tajut in Friuliano, meaning "to cut." Today, grapes from the south are no longer needed in Friulian winemaking, but the word *tajut* has evolved to mean the act of meeting with friends and drinking several glasses of wine together. The tajut occurs at any time of the day, and local wine bars are constantly filled with customers enthusiastically supporting the imbibing tradition.

Cornmeal Cookies with Raisins and Pine Nuts

BISCOTTI AI PIGNOLI E UVETTE

Plump raisins, intoxicatingly sweet from their soak in grappa, and crunchy cornmeal give these cookies their distinct kick. At I Comelli these always greet guests taking a glass of wine at the agriturismo's bar.

Heat the oven to 350°F (180°C).

In the bowl of a stand mixer fitted with the paddle attachment, mix together all of the ingredients, except for the pine nuts and raisins, until a dough begins to come together. Gently mix in the raisins and pine nuts. Cover the bowl with plastic wrap and chill in the refrigerator for 20 minutes.

Remove dough from the fridge. Spoon 1 scant tablespoon of dough, roll it into a ball, place on a sheet pan lined with parchment paper, and gently press down on it to flatten. Continue with the remaining dough. Bake in the oven until lightly golden and set, 15 to 20 minutes. Place on a wire rack to cool.

YIELDS 2 DOZEN

12 tablespoons (5½ oz. / 160 g) unsalted butter, room temperature

1 cup (200 g) granulated sugar

1 large egg yolk

1 cup (125 g) all-purpose flour

¾ cup (125 g) fine-ground cornmeal

1 teaspoon (5 g) baking powder

1 teaspoon (5 g) baking soda

Table salt

½ teaspoon vanilla extract

1 tablespoon (½ fl. oz. / 15 ml) rum

1 tablespoon (½ fl. oz. / 15 ml) white wine

1 tablespoon lemon zest

¼ cup (40 g) pine nuts

¼ cup (40 g) raisins, soaked in ½ tablespoon (½ fl. oz. / 15 ml) grappa

15   30 KILOMETERS
15   30 MILES

N

TRENTINO-
ALTO ADIGE

FRIULI-
VENEZIA GIULIA

*Cortina
d'Ampezzo*

Belluno

Rechsteiner

*Lago di
Garda*

Treviso

Vicenza

LOMBARDIA

Le Vescovane

Verona

Corte Verze

Venezia

Chioggia

MARE
ADRIATIC

Serenading gondoliers and architecturally awe-inspiring San Marco square, as well as Venice's marvelous construction and history, have overshadowed the towns and countryside of the less traversed interior of the Veneto. The region's ever-changing landscape is dramatic, from the canals of picturesque Treviso, inland to the vine-covered rolling hills of the Soave region, and farther up toward the mountains of alpine-chic Cortina d'Ampezzo. Fish dominates on the tables of the coast and ports are filled with the boats of men who make their livings from the sea. Farther into the hinterland, where the majority of the agriturismi are situated, a heartier, more agricultural cuisine exists, with slow-cooked meats and poultry replacing the delicacies of the Adriatic. Dining at these farm restaurants is a broadly fulfilling gastronomic experience, offering greater insight into the depths of the Veneto's culinary heritage.

In the central hills of the Veneto and along the shores of Lake Garda, olive trees flourish. Their oil is the region's primary cooking medium. The Veneto's abundance of interesting produce is a vegetarian utopia of good eating. Numerous varieties of radicchio are cultivated and they are prepared in myriad ways. The slightly bitter flavor of chicory gives it great versatility in the kitchen, and it can be eaten raw as a salad, grilled, braised, or as a base for lasagnas and vegetable napoleons. White asparagus, which gets its pale hue from being covered during its growth, and tender spiked baby artichokes set a high standard for garden produce. Risotto serves as the perfect carrier for these local ingredients and its preparations parallel the seasons. A common first course, rice is the preferred starch of the Veneto. Risi e bisi pairs the creamy grain with fresh spring peas, and in restaurants by the sea, seafood risotto is a mainstay. The peasant-inspired pasta e fagioli hails from this region, and its simple roots bring out the quality of the locally grown beans. Bigoli, thick wheat spaghetti, represents one of the only native pasta dishes, usually paired with sardines on the coast and duck ragu inland. Poultry, both domesticated and wild, is eaten in great abundance, and specialties include small birds cooked on a spit and served with polenta, farm-raised quail, and locally hunted pheasant. Pork appears in a variety of different cured preparations and throughout the fall, small family farms keep busy making their own salami and fresh and dried sausages. Once the animals are butchered, it is an all-out collaborative effort to prepare and grind the meat, which must be immediately encased in intestines and tied closed. This nonstop work continues unabated until all of the swine are slaughtered and their salamis left to age in cool, dry basements. A favorite second course is a mixed platter of boiled meats, referred to as bollito misto. Beef tongue and cotechino, a soft fresh sausage, are piled high next to chicken and other beef cuts, all which showcase the many condiments of the Veneto. Mostarda, a spicy fruit jelly, and pearà, thick peppery bone marrow gravy, are the two most common accompaniments. While many foreigners may never explore beyond the bridges and waterways of Venice, they're guaranteed to have indulged in the region's most famous culinary creation—tiramisu—during their travels.

Easy-drinking whites, big reds, and light effervescent wines all are produced in the Veneto. In a country where co-ops are often considered inferior to independent wineries, the Veneto is challenging this antiquated mentality. The Rocca Sveva co-op in Soave is a huge collaboration of local farmers who all share the same vision for making quality wine. Their dedication has earned them awards from Italy's premier wine publication, *Gambero Rosso*. A port-like wine called Recioto comes from the pressing of dried grapes, which produces minute quantities of an intensely rich after-dinner wine. Amarone, a by-product of Recioto that sees longer maturation in oak barrels, is the region's most sought-after red. And as the world catches on to the white bubbly Prosecco, Venetians have taken the dry fizzy taste to another level by adding Aperol, a locally made bitter, creating the Aperol spritz. At cafes throughout the Veneto, the trendy aperitif has made a splash with its sweet, bitter taste.

Olive grove

Freshly tilled fields

CHAPTER 24
RECHSTEINER

With a name that doesn't exactly evoke an Italian wine estate in the Veneto, Rechsteiner has attained great success from its German lineage. The winery and agriturismo appeals to a German audience that often drives the scenic mountain route down to the flatlands of the Veneto for a weekend getaway in sunny Italy. Purchased in 1881 by Friedrich Rechsteiner, the estate today is managed by his great-great-grandson. The property extends over 280 hectares, 45 of which are vineyards. Today, the Rechsteiners' family mansion, Villa Bonamico, houses the cantina, the wine office, and farm equipment for the vineyard. The impressive facility is capable of producing 400,000 bottles of wine annually, much of which is exported to Germany. A large vegetable garden, enveloped by endless rows of vines, provides fresh produce for the agriturismo, five kilometers down the street.

What was once a farmhouse for the men who worked Villa Bonamico's land in exchange for crops has been restored into the winery's agriturismo and restaurant. Where fifty-two people once shared only one bathroom, there are now seven apartments and an additional twelve guest rooms, all with private bath. Vines surround the house, and large fenced-in areas house geese, ducks, chickens, and turkeys. These are all used effectively in Chef Stefano's kitchen, where the a la carte menu changes weekly. An experienced chef, whose résumé boasts stints in restaurants throughout all of Western Europe, Stefano brings agriturismo cooking to another level. His small, well-thought-out menus reflect the seasons and each dish is matched with one of Rechsteiner's wines. In addition, guests can book special meals cooked over a wood fire in the original kitchen fireplace. An interesting specialty Stefano has created requires slow-roasting the neck of a pig wrapped in hay and covered in a salt crust. He swears it is the most tender piece of meat you will ever eat, so perhaps this alone merits the journey to the plains of the Veneto.

Flan with Ricotta and Chestnuts
SFORMATO DI RICOTTA E CASTAGNE

This savory flan, flavored with chestnuts and a hint of porcini mushroom, is best served at room temperature to bring out the flavor composition.

3 tablespoons (1½ fl. oz. / 45 ml) extra-virgin olive oil

1 leek, cleaned and sliced ¼ inch thick

1 tablespoon chopped rosemary

5 ounces (142 g) boiled chestnuts, finely chopped

Kosher salt and freshly ground black pepper

½ ounce (115 g) dried porcini mushrooms, reconstituted in warm water and minced

1 peeled and minced garlic clove

2 tablespoons minced flat-leaf parsley

1 pound (450 g) ricotta

3 eggs

1½ tablespoons (¾ fl. oz. / 25 ml) heavy cream

¼ cup grated Parmigiano Reggiano

Heat the oven to 350°F (180°C).

In a 10-inch sauté pan, heat 2 tablespoons olive oil over medium heat. Add the leeks and rosemary and cook until tender, about 7 minutes. Add the chestnuts and a pinch of salt and continue to sauté until the chestnuts begin to break apart, about 10 minutes. Transfer to a bowl and let cool.

Wipe the skillet clean and heat 1 tablespoon olive oil over medium-high heat. Cook the porcini mushrooms with the garlic and parsley until the garlic begins to slightly brown, 3 to 5 minutes. Season with salt and pepper to taste, remove from heat, and let cool.

In a large bowl, stir together the ricotta cheese with the eggs, heavy cream, and Parmigiano Reggiano. Salt and pepper to taste. Stir in the chestnut mixture and then fold in the porcini mushrooms.

Ladle the mixture into 6 individual buttered ramekins. Bake in a water bath in the oven until set and golden brown, about 20 minutes.

Remove from the oven and let cool in the water. Unmold the ramekins onto individual plates and serve at room temperature.

SERVES 6

Lasagna with Radicchio Treviso and Asiago Cheese

LASAGNETTA AL RADICCHIO E ASIAGO

This dish takes an Italian classic and showcases the Veneto's favorite vegetable, radicchio. The creaminess of the béchamel, the sharpness of the Asiago, and the sweetness of the leeks soften the bitterness of the radicchio. For a more refined presentation, the lasagna can also be baked in individual crocks.

Heat the oven to 375°F (190°C).

In a 12-inch skillet over medium heat, cook the leeks in the olive oil until tender, about 7 minutes. Add the radicchio to the pan and continue to cook until the radicchio wilts and becomes very tender, about 15 minutes. Season with salt and pepper. Transfer the leeks and radicchio to a large bowl and stir in the béchamel until thoroughly combined.

Bring 6 quarts of salted water to a boil. Drop the pasta into the water and cook, following the instructions on the box, until al dente. Drain the pasta well.

Spread a ladleful of the radicchio mixture out evenly in a medium-size baking dish (12 × 8½ inches), to just cover the bottom. Arrange lasagna noodles to cover the sauce. Spread a thin layer of the radicchio mixture on top and sprinkle with the shredded Asiago cheese. Repeat this process until all the pasta noodles have been used; there should be about 3 layers. Cover the top noodles with a thin layer of radicchio sauce and sprinkle with the remaining cheese. Cover the pan with foil and bake for 30 minutes. Remove the foil and continue to bake until the top of the lasagna is bubbly and browned, another 10 to 12 minutes. Remove from the oven and let cool slightly before serving.

SERVES 6–8

2 leeks, cleaned and cut into
  ¼-inch slices
2 tablespoons (1 fl. oz. / 30 ml)
  extra-virgin olive oil
3 heads shredded radicchio Treviso
Kosher salt and freshly ground black
  pepper
1 recipe béchamel (see page x)
1 pound boxed lasagna
4 ounces (115 g) shredded Asiago
  cheese

Veal Cheeks Braised in Red Wine
GUANCIALE DI VITELLO

Veal cheeks are tender noisettes of meat taken from the calves' jowls. After hours of slow-cooking, they break down and become exceedingly delicate. The juniper berries, cloves, and cinnamon Stefano adds to the red wine braising liquid penetrate the meat with their strong aromatic essence.

2 tablespoons (1 fl. oz. / 30 ml) extra-virgin olive oil

2½ pounds (1.13 kg) veal cheeks

Kosher salt and freshly ground black pepper

1 yellow onion, cut into fine dice

1 stalk celery, cut into fine dice

1 carrot, peeled and cut into fine dice

3 whole cloves

1 cinnamon stick

1 tablespoon lightly crushed juniper berries

2 bay leaves

1 bottle (750 ml) red wine

2 tablespoons (1 oz. / 30 g) unsalted butter

2 tablespoons (20 g) all-purpose flour

In a heavy casserole pan, heat the olive oil over medium-high heat. Add the veal cheeks to the pan, season with salt and pepper, and brown on all sides, about 4 minutes. Remove from the pan and set aside. Add the onion, celery, and carrot to the pan and sauté until tender, about 7 minutes.

Tie the cloves, cinnamon stick, juniper berries, and bay leaves in cheesecloth and add to the pan. Add the veal cheeks back to the pan and pour in the wine to cover. Bring the contents of the pan to a boil, then reduce the heat to low, cover, and simmer slowly for about 3½ hours or until the veal is fork-tender.

Make a roux: In a small nonstick pan, melt the butter over medium heat, stir in the flour, and cook until nutty brown, about 3 minutes. Remove from heat and let cool completely.

With a slotted spoon, carefully remove the veal cheeks from the sauce and set aside to cool. Strain the sauce into a small saucepan, discarding the vegetables and cheesecloth. Place the saucepan over medium-high heat and bring the sauce to a boil. Whisk in the roux and simmer until the sauce is thick enough to coat the back of a spoon. Season to taste with salt and pepper.

Serve the veal cheeks on a platter, drizzled with the sauce.

SERVES 6

CHAPTER 25
❧ LE VESCOVANE ❧

The area known as the Colli Berici is dense with chestnut and oak forests, where wild boar and pheasants live deep in the woods. Its proximity to Venice made it a favorite among Venetian nobility, who built hunting manors in the hills. Le Vescovane shares this history as a former Venetian nobleman's weekend escape. A larger, less intimate agriturismo experience, Le Vescovane's productive farm provides an abundant bounty for the many reunions and celebratory events hosted here. A wedding on the expansive grass veranda overlooking vines and olive trees will satisfy any romantic dream of tying the knot at an Italian vineyard. The trails that meander throughout the property and into the woods allow for good short day hikes as well as the opportunity to view a landscape unchanged since the Renaissance.

The pigs, chickens, turkeys, goats, and substantial vegetable garden of Le Vescovane all support a kitchen whose elegant presentations bring farm cuisine to a higher level. Amedeo Sandri, Le Vescovane's long-time chef, molds his staff into his creative mindset, and the farm has become a destination for young cooks looking to begin their careers. Amedeo's cookbooks have proven his expertise on his region's cuisine and his vast knowledge has brought the farm's cooking admiration from Slow Food. With an entire farm's bounty at his disposal, Amedeo is able to recreate classic dishes with

artful presentations that lend a modern flair. Bigoli, Venetian whole-wheat pasta, pairs nicely with a duck ragu, the fatty meat cutting through the strong flour. Phyllo dough filled with caramelized leeks, local Asiago cheese, and crispy pancetta is baked and topped with a saffron potato chip, uniting local ingredients into a morsel of good taste. A sage panna cotta infuses the classic Italian dessert with the floral herb, showcasing Amedeo's ability to marry two polar opposites. Wild game is a constant on Le Vescovane's menu, bringing to the table the roots of the agriturismo while appeasing the spirit of the estate's founding father.

Leek Tart with Pancetta and Phyllo Dough

SFORMATO DI PORRI E PANCETTA IN CESTINO DI PASTA FILLO

Crispy caramelized pancetta and creamy leeks baked in a buttery phyllo cup make this appetizer one of Vescovane's house favorites. Brushing the pancetta with butter and sugar before baking ensures a sweet, crisp crust that looks as good as it tastes.

16 tablespoons (8 oz. / 230 g) unsalted butter

4 ounces (115 g) pancetta, cut into thin slices

1 tablespoon (10 g) cane sugar

4 leeks, cleaned and cut into slices

5 tablespoons (50 g) all-purpose flour

3 cups (24 fl. oz. / 720 ml) whole milk

3½ ounces (100 g) shredded Asiago cheese

3½ ounces (100 g) grated Parmigiano Reggiano

Kosher salt and freshly ground black pepper

¼ teaspoon freshly grated nutmeg

1 1-pound (450 g) package phyllo dough

Heat the oven to 375°F (190°C).

Melt 2 tablespoons of butter in a 1-quart saucepan. Place the pancetta on a baking sheet, brush with the melted butter, and sprinkle with the cane sugar. Bake until the pancetta is crispy and caramelized, 12 to 15 minutes. Remove from the oven and place pancetta slices on a plate lined with a paper towel to drain the fat.

In a 3-quart pan, melt 5 tablespoons of butter over medium heat. Add the leeks and cook for 15 minutes, until leeks are tender and translucent but not browned. Add the flour to the pan, stir well to combine, and cook another 2 to 3 minutes. Pour the milk into the pan, and whisk to remove any lumps from the flour. Cook at a gentle simmer until the mixture begins to thicken slightly, about 5 minutes.

Stir the Asiago cheese and the Parmigiano Reggiano into the leek mixture. Cook until the cheese has melted and the consistency is creamy and thickened. Season with salt and pepper and nutmeg.

Prepare the phyllo dough: Melt the remaining butter in a 1-quart saucepan over medium-low heat. Place 1 sheet of phyllo on a clean work surface. (Keep the remaining sheets covered with a damp towel.) Brush the sheet all over with melted butter, cover with another sheet, and brush with butter. Continue layering the phyllo sheets in this manner, ending with a fifth sheet, brushed with butter. With a round cookie cutter or a glass cut the phyllo into 4-inch circles. Carefully push the circles into the cups of a buttered 12-cup muffin pan, pressing them firmly against bottom and sides.

Cut the pancetta into pieces, and add 1 tablespoon to each muffin cup. Pour the leek mixture over the pancetta. Bake in the oven for 15 minutes, or until the custard has set and the phyllo dough is golden brown.

Let the custard cool slightly before removing from the muffin pan. Serve warm.

YIELDS 1 DOZEN

Bigoli Pasta with Duck Ragu
BIGOLI ALL'ANATRA

This thick, dense pasta was traditionally made with a special machine called a bigolaro, which forced the dough through holes to give the pasta its unique thick shape. A modern-day meat grinder produces similar results when making the fresh thick pasta at home. Traditionally bigoli are made with whole-wheat flour, but it can be made with white flour as well. Milk is always included as a key ingredient in the dough.

Ragu

1 5-pound (2.27 kg) whole duck

Kosher salt and freshly ground black pepper

3 bay leaves

3 sprigs thyme

3 sprigs rosemary

10 sage leaves

2 tablespoons (1 fl. oz. / 30 ml) extra-virgin olive oil

1 medium onion, cut into fine dice

1 stalk celery, cut into fine dice

1 carrot, cut into fine dice

1 pound (450 g) ground duck breast, including skin

½ cup (4 fl. oz. / 120 ml) Marsala Fine

1 cup (8 fl. oz. / 240 ml) white wine

1 28-ounce (793 g) can whole plum tomatoes, chopped

1 tablespoon chopped flat-leaf parsley plus 1 sprig

1 teaspoon ground cinnamon

Heat the oven to 450°F (230°C).

Wash and pat dry the duck. Season the duck inside and outside with salt and pepper. Place bay leaves, 2 sprigs thyme, 2 sprigs rosemary, and sage in the cavity of the duck. Tie up the legs, and place duck in a roasting pan. Prick the duck all over (top and bottom) with a fork, and then roast in the oven, turning every 30 minutes, until the meat is cooked through, about 1½ hours. Remove from the oven and let cool. Shred the meat from the carcass, cutting it into small pieces and discarding the skin.

Meanwhile, in a heavy casserole pan, heat the olive oil over medium heat. Add the onion, celery, and carrot and sauté until tender, about 7 minutes. Add the ground duck to the pan and continue to cook over medium heat until browned, 5 to 7 minutes. Pour the Marsala into the pan and cook until reduced to dry.

Add the shredded duck meat to the pan with the ground duck. Add the white wine, the chopped tomatoes and their juices, and a cheesecloth containing the remaining thyme, bay leaf, and 1 sprig of parsley. Cook until the wine has reduced by half. Season with salt and pepper and the cinnamon.

Make the pasta: On a clean work surface, form a well in the flour. Add the eggs to the center of the well and beat lightly with a fork. Add the butter and milk to the eggs, along with a pinch of salt. Gradually pull the flour into the egg mixture with the fork and mix until dough starts to form. Knead the dough until it is smooth and elastic and not at all sticky. Cover the dough with a bowl or kitchen towel and let rest at least 30 minutes.

Divide the dough into 8 small pieces. Knead each piece of dough with a little extra flour, then, using a meat grinder (electric or manual) with the plate with the smallest holes, put dough through the grinder, set at the lowest setting, one piece at a time. As the pasta comes out, cut each strand with scissors or a sharp knife at 6-inch intervals. Place pasta on a sheet pan lightly dusted with flour. Put the remaining pieces of dough through the grinder in the same manner.

Bring 6 quarts of salted water to a boil. Drop the bigoli into the water and cook until tender, 5 to 7 minutes. Meanwhile reheat the duck ragu. Drain the pasta and toss immediately with the warm duck ragu. Garnish with the chopped parsley and serve immediately.

SERVES 6

Pasta

5 3/4 cups (600 g) whole-wheat flour

4 eggs, at room temperature

3 tablespoons (1 1/2 oz. / 45 g) unsalted butter, melted

1/2 cup (4 fl. oz. / 120 ml) whole milk, warmed

Making bigoli: whole-wheat pasta

Plated bigoli with duck ragu

Stuffed Quail with a Red Wine Sauce
QUAGLIA FARCITA ALL'ESTENSE CON SALSA AL VINO

These little birds populate the forests surrounding the farm and are a favorite at Le Vescovane. Quail are often roasted on a spit over a fire, but the agriturismo prefers to roast them with a meat filling. Tying them ensures even roasting and traps in heat to cook the stuffing.

½ cup (62 g) bread crumbs

2 tablespoons (1 fl. oz. / 30 ml) whole milk

4 ounces (115 g) ground beef

4 ounces (115 g) ground pork

1 tablespoon chopped thyme, plus 1 sprig thyme

1 tablespoon chopped rosemary,

1 tablespoon chopped flat-leaf parsley

1 tablespoon chopped sage

½ cup grated Parmigiano Reggiano

1 egg

Kosher salt and freshly ground black pepper

6 semiboneless quail (about 4 oz. each / 115 g each)

2 tablespoons (1 fl. oz. / 30 ml) extra-virgin olive oil

1 small yellow onion, cut into fine dice

1 stalk celery, cut into fine dice

1 carrot, peeled and cut into fine dice

½ cup (4 fl. oz. / 120 ml) port

1 bay leaf

¼ cup (2 fl. oz. / 60 ml) homemade chicken broth (see page xi) or canned low-sodium broth

Heat the oven to 375°F (190°C).

In a small bowl, dampen the bread crumbs with the milk. In a large bowl, mix together the ground meats, the chopped herbs, and the cheese. Add the eggs and the bread crumbs, season with salt and pepper, and mix well to combine.

Rinse each quail and pat dry. Season both the inside and the outside of the quail with salt and pepper. Stuff the cavity of each quail with the filling and then tie up the legs with kitchen string.

In a heavy ovenproof sauté pan, heat the olive oil over medium-high heat. Sear the quail on all sides, until golden brown, about 4 minutes per side. Remove quail from the pan and set aside on a plate. Add the onion, celery, and carrot to the pan and sauté until tender, about 7 minutes. Place the quail on top of the vegetables and roast in the oven until cooked through, 20 to 25 minutes.

Remove the quail from the oven. Place on a cutting board and allow to rest, removing the kitchen string.

Meanwhile, prepare the sauce: Place the pan back on the stove over medium-high heat. Add the port, the sprig of thyme, and the bay leaf. Bring to a boil and reduce by half. Add the chicken broth and continue to boil, reducing until syrupy. Season with salt and pepper and strain the sauce, discarding the vegetables.

Serve the quail on individual plates, drizzled with the sauce.

SERVES 6

CHAPTER 26
CORTE VERZE

The Verzes opened the doors of their agriturismo to the public in 2005 and have not stopped working since. The transition from farm to agriturismo came naturally for the family, as they have been living off this land for generations. With a solid family unit tending to different aspects of the farm, Corte Verze has the ability to focus on many diverse types of agriculture. Situated among the rolling hills outside of Verona, in the winemaking territory of Soave, Valpolicella, and Amarone, Corte Verze's main crop is grapes, which are sent to a co-op recognized as one of the best in Italy. The mild climate of the region allows olives to flourish, and olive trees have been planted in steep, rocky areas where vines cannot successfully grow. Cherry trees are abundant throughout the property as well. Sheep, chickens, geese, ducks, turkeys, and wild hare range freely among the vines and olive groves, and veal and pigs are reared in a separate farmhouse down the road. Work at the farm follows the seasons, and all that is produced goes toward the restaurant and agriturismo. Whether harvesting fruits, vegetables, olives, or grapes; making jams and marmalades; butchering animals; preparing salami; or seeding the fields, work continues unabated throughout the year.

The philosophy behind the reconstruction of Corte Verze was to only use raw materials endemic to the area. Local artists painted each room with a different theme and all rooms have cherry furniture constructed from regional trees. A spa and wellness center on the ground floor offers guests a different kind of agriturismo experience, with incredible views out over the farm's vines. Since the opening of Corte Verze's restaurant, outsiders have flocked here in droves to indulge in the genuine cuisine in a sophisticated but not stuffy dining room. Dishes in abundance pile up on every table, reminiscent of a Renaissance feast. The Verze mother prepares nearly everything over an eighty-year-old wood-fired stove, in a rustic kitchen with a large fireplace as the only source of heat. Entering is like taking a step back in time and her meals replicate this sentiment: unadulterated honest flavors from another period. She has no secrets, she proclaims, just the natural ingredients from her farm and cooking how she always has, like a true Italian mama.

Risotto with Butternut Squash and Radicchio

RISOTTO ALLA ZUCCA E RADICCHIO

Risotto takes well to many different flavor combinations, acting as a creamy canvas to showcase other ingredients. Here the chewy grain turns bittersweet with radicchio and butternut squash.

2 tablespoons (1 fl. oz. / 30 ml) extra-virgin olive oil

1 large yellow onion, cut into fine dice

½ butternut squash, peeled and cut into ½-inch cubes

1 tablespoon chopped sage

1 head radicchio, shredded

2 cups Arborio rice

1 cup (8 fl. oz. / 240 ml) white wine

1 quart (32 fl. oz. / 960 ml) home-made chicken broth (see page xi) or canned low-sodium broth

Kosher salt and freshly ground black pepper

1 tablespoon (½ oz. / 15 g) unsalted butter

½ cup grated Parmigiano Reggiano

1 tablespoon chopped flat-leaf parsley

In a 12-inch straight-sided sauté pan, heat the olive oil over medium-high heat. Add the onion, butternut squash, sage, and a pinch of salt and cook until the onion becomes tender, about 7 minutes. Add the radicchio to the pan and continue to cook until it begins to wilt, 10 to 12 minutes.

Add the rice to the pan and toast, 2 to 3 minutes. Pour in the white wine and let reduce to almost dry.

Heat the chicken broth in a 4-quart pan over medium-high heat until it comes to a boil. Reduce heat and keep warm. Ladle enough broth over the rice to cover, and stir continuously until the broth begins to be absorbed and dips below the rice line. Add another ladleful of broth to cover, and continue cooking in this manner, stirring continuously, until the rice is al dente, 15 to 20 minutes.

Season to taste with salt and pepper. Finish with the butter, Parmigiano Reggiano, and parsley. Spoon into individual shallow bowls and serve immediately.

SERVES 6

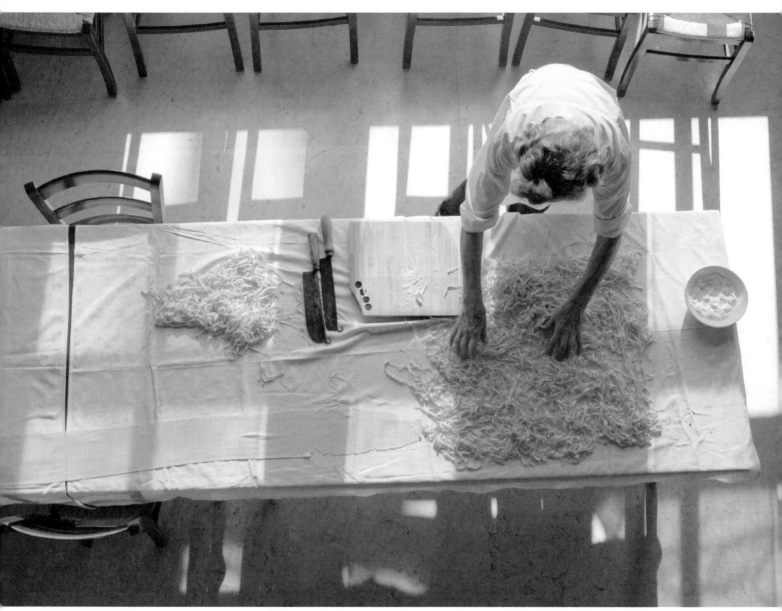

Making fresh pasta

Turkey Breast with Orange and Pomegranate

PETTO DI TACCHINO ALL'ARANCIA E MELEGRANA

Introduced to Italy from the United States, turkey plays a minor role in the Italian diet. Searing the breast with the skin on ensures a moist interior, which gets especially tender when roasted in sweet orange juice. A pomegranate juice reduction lends a hint of tartness and tames some of the sweetness.

1 2½-pound (1.14 kg) turkey breast, boned, skin on

Kosher salt and freshly ground black pepper

6 tablespoons (3½ fl. oz. / 90 ml) orange juice

2 tablespoons (1 fl. oz. / 30 ml) extra-virgin olive oil

1 tablespoon chopped rosemary

1 tablespoon chopped sage

2 tablespoons (1 oz. / 30 g) unsalted butter, cut into small pieces

1 cup (8 fl. oz. / 240 ml) water

¾ cup (6 fl. oz. / 180 ml) pomegranate juice

¼ cup pomegranate seeds

Heat the oven to 425°F (220°C).

Season the turkey breast on both sides with salt and pepper. Brush all over with 2 tablespoons orange juice and olive oil, and coat the flesh side with the chopped rosemary and sage. Tie the breast up like a roast.

In a heavy ovenproof 12-inch sauté pan, melt the butter over medium-high heat. Sear the turkey breast skin side down until deep golden brown, 3 to 4 minutes. Flip the breast over and add the remaining 4 tablespoons of the orange juice and 1 cup of water to the pan. Place in the oven and bake, basting occasionally, for 30 minutes, or until the meat registers 165°F (74°C) on a meat thermometer. Remove from the oven and place the turkey on a cutting board. Let rest loosely covered with foil, about 10 minutes.

Place the pan back over medium-high heat. Add the pomegranate juice to the pan, bring to a boil, and reduce by half. Carve the turkey into thin slices and place on a large serving platter. Drizzle with the pan sauce and garnish with the pomegranate seeds.

SERVES 6

Lamb Stew
BOCCONCINO D'AGNELLO

The Verzes' flock of sheep lives beneath the farm's overhanging vines, together with turkeys, chickens, and guinea hens. When slaughtered, they are hung from the vines to bleed, which also makes it easy to remove their wool coats. Redolent of good honest flavors, this simple stew is a marriage of floral rosemary and gamy lamb, with slight acidic overtones from cooking in white wine.

In a heavy casserole pan over medium-high heat, heat 1 tablespoon of olive oil with 1 tablespoon of butter. Add the lamb, sprinkle with lemon juice, and season with salt and pepper. Brown on all sides, 3 to 4 minutes per side.

Add the herbs and the garlic to the pan and cook for several minutes more. Pour in the white wine and allow it to reduce until almost dry, 2 to 4 minutes. Add the water to the pan and bring to a boil. Cover, reduce the heat to medium-low, and simmer gently for 1½ to 2 hours, until fork-tender.

Meanwhile make a roux: In a small nonstick pan, melt 2 tablespoons butter over medium heat. Stir in flour and cook until pale golden brown, about 2 minutes. Set aside to cool.

Remove the lamb from the pan and place on a large serving platter. Strain the cooking liquid through a fine mesh sieve into a 3- or 4-quart saucepan, discarding the solids. Place saucepan over medium-high heat and reduce liquid by half. Then whisk in the roux and simmer until the sauce has thickened. Spoon the sauce over the lamb and garnish with chopped rosemary.

SERVES 6

1 tablespoon (½ fl. oz. / 15 ml)
  extra-virgin olive oil

3 tablespoons (1½ oz. / 45 g)
  unsalted butter

3 pounds (1.36 kg) lamb neck stew
  meat, on the bone

¼ cup lemon juice (2 fl. oz. / 60 ml)

Kosher salt and freshly ground black
  pepper

2 tablespoons chopped sage

2 tablespoons chopped rosemary,
  plus more for garnish

2 bay leaves

2–3 cloves of garlic, peeled and
  sliced

1 cup (8 fl. oz. / 240 ml) white wine

3 cups (24 fl. oz. / 720 ml) water

2 tablespoons (22 g) all-purpose
  flour

Cutting up pork for salami and sausage

Mixing in salt and spices

Stuffing meat into casing

Tying up the sausage and salami

Ready for hanging

Testa Sal

This local Veronese phrase translates as "to test for salt." Traditionally, when making salami, a handful of the pork, fat, and spice mixture would be used to make risotto to determine if the seasonings were correct. Today at Corte Verze, they continue this tradition by making risotto during the fall months when they prepare salami from their freshly butchered pigs, to ensure the seasoning is just right. The intense saltiness and spice of the dish calls for a carafe or two of the quaffable house white wine.

Stewed Cabbage
VERZA STUFFATA

Slowly cooking cabbage softens its sulfurous flavor, making it sweet and tender—especially when paired with crisp golden apples. This dish makes a perfect side to Corte Verze's turkey breast with pomegranate.

3 tablespoons (1½ fl. oz. / 45 ml) extra-virgin olive oil

1 medium yellow onion, cut into fine dice

1 Golden Delicious apple, peeled, cored and cut into fine dice

Kosher salt and freshly ground black pepper

1 head savoy cabbage, shredded

2 tablespoons (1 fl. oz. / 30 ml) red wine vinegar

1 tablespoon honey

3 large tomatoes, peeled, seeded, and cut into fine dice

In a heavy-bottomed casserole pan, heat the olive oil over medium heat. Add the onion and cook until tender and translucent, about 7 minutes. Stir the apple into the onion mixture with a pinch of salt, and sauté another 2 to 3 minutes. Add the cabbage to the pan and stir to combine with the apples and onion.

Add the red wine vinegar, honey, and tomatoes to the pan. Stir to combine, reduce the heat to low, and cover. Cook for 30 minutes, stirring occasionally, or until the cabbage is tender. Season to taste with salt and pepper. Serve warm.

SERVES 6

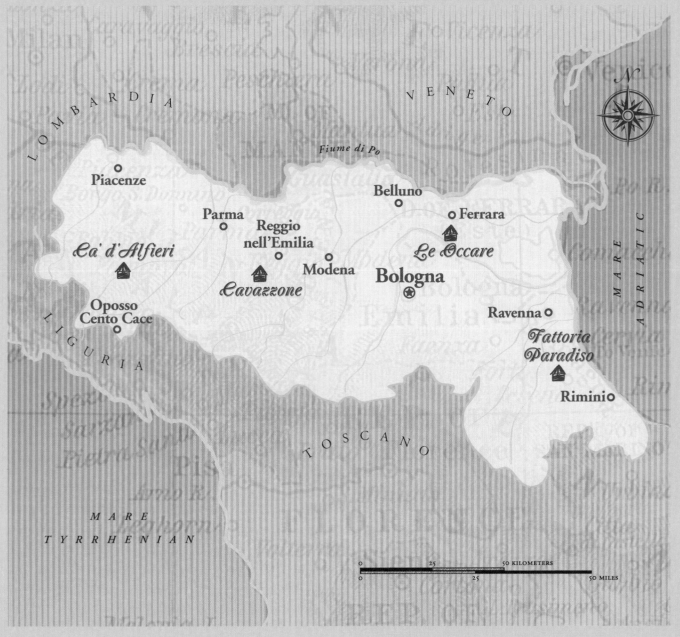

N

LOMBARDIA

VENETO

Fiume di Po

Piacenze

Parma

Reggio
nell'Emilia

Ca' d'Alfieri

Cavazzone

Modena

Belluno

Ferrara

Le Occare

Bologna

LIGURIA

Oposso
Cento Cace

Ravenna

Fattoria
Paradiso

Rimini

MARE
ADRIATIC

TOSCANO

MARE
TYRRHENIAN

0   25   50 KILOMETERS
0   25   50 MILES

A region whose wealth stems from the innumerable bounties of the land, Emilia-Romagna is all about food and good eating. Home to Barilla, the largest pasta manufacturer in the world, as well as smaller-scale artisanal producers of balsamic vinegar, prosciutto di Parma, and Parmigiano Reggiano, the region exports its culinary riches around the globe. These top-notch ingredients have been fundamental in the creation of a beloved cuisine, appreciated throughout the country. Divided in two, with Emilia to the west and Romagna to the east, each territory has its individual differences, but these nuances are trivial in the broader picture of the region as a major contributor to Italy's acceptance as the world's favorite cuisine.

The quintessential Emilia-Romagnan meal epitomizes a decadent food culture. Pork products abound, encompassing much more than the world-traveling prosciutto di Parma. Culatello, a prosciutto-type ham derived from the rump, and mortadella, the world's first bologna, barely scratch the surface of the region's love for cured salty delicacies. Cotechino, a young fresh sausage often boiled and paired with lentils, and zampone, a stuffed pig's foot eaten on New Year's, exemplify the meat that justly dominates second courses. In the land of pork maestros who stuff, grind, and leave to dry nearly every part of the common pig, there exists a different swine for immediate consumption. Baby suckling pig and black free-range pigs provide succulent, juicy meat for cooking. Reared on rural farms, they constitute a greatly heralded second course, common on the tables of the region's agriturismi.

While not possessing an especially strong winemak-ing tradition, Emilia-Romagna boasts balsamic vinegar that transforms grapes once destined for mediocre wine into something sublime. While much of what one finds on supermarket shelves around the world is a mass-produced caramelized by-product of the real thing, incredible top-quality vinegars quietly age in wooden barrels around the towns of Modena and Reggio Emilia. The most coveted and expensive can be more than one hundred years old. Their thick syrup is appreciated like a fine wine, with true connoisseurs preferring to sip the substance rather than mingle its flavor with food.

Parmigiano Reggiano is perhaps the region's greatest culinary achievement. Strict laws dating from 1955 mandate that the cheese be made from the milk of free-range organic dairy cows who live within a limited zone. These state policies protect Parmigiano Reggiano's status from the many imitators who attempt to pass their cheeses off as the real thing. The consortium of Parmigiano makers is a tight-knit group and their time-consuming and labor-intensive product is traded on the world market. Their monopoly on the cheese extends much deeper than mere economics, showcasing the innate passion Emilia-Romagnans have for the quality and consistency of their superior agricultural goods.

While one may encounter wafer-thin prosciutto di Parma in Tokyo or fifty-year-old balsamic vinegar in Chicago, Emilia-Romagna's fresh egg pasta is best experienced at the source. Across the region exist hundreds of pasta varieties, each with its own unique shape, size, or filling, and each with a significant history. A tortellini recipe may have hundreds of variations from family to family.

The meats used can vary from mortadella to prosciutto, ground beef to pork, and they may be served floating in broth or lightly tossed with a sauce. The iconic little old Italian lady hand-rolling her dough with a rolling pin still exists in private homes throughout the region. Agriturismi provide ample opportunities to experience this dying art, pasta crafted by masterful hands whose wrinkled lines speak of tradition and culture. These elderly pasta makers provide something that no machine or technology will ever challenge: the heart and soul of Italian cuisine.

Parma cheese cow

*Christina with a basket of
fresh-cut cardoons*

Chapter 27
Le Occare

In the plains surrounding the renaissance city of Ferrara and near the national park of the Po delta, down a gravel road surrounded by woods, is the vine-engulfed home and agriturismo of husband and wife Gianni and Christina. The farmhouse, owned by Gianni's family for generations, historically produced tobacco and hemp. The surrounding fields were lush and full with their large green plants, and once harvested, the leaves were left to dry in Le Occare's barns. When Christina and Gianni first moved here, they had a vision for restructuring their land to see what else could grow from its fertile soil. With the help of scientists from the University of Bologna who believed the environment ripe for the growth of truffles, pine, poplar, and walnut saplings were planted, in hopes of one day becoming a small forest where the knotty delicacy could conceivably flourish. Today, the experiment has come full circle, and Christina and Gianni spend the fall months truffle hunting with their five dogs in the new-growth forest. A meticulous vegetable garden, lush with the oversized leaves of cardoons, and a small field of corn and wheat provide an ample bounty for the farm's minute three-table restaurant.

Le Occare exudes a familiar atmosphere of elevated country living, furnished with period pieces passed down from Gianni's family. A product of Christina's critical eye for detail, the hand-woven rugs and antiques of the agri-turismo's three bedrooms are reminiscent of a nobleman's estate. The same can be said for the restaurant, where white linens, polished silverware, and soft classical music are pure elegance without pretension, paralleling Christina's style of cooking. Typical Ferrarese dishes that have been handed down for generations, with strict adherence to tradition, embody all meals at Le Occare. Preferring the feel of the dough in her hands and beneath her rolling pin, Christina hand rolls and cuts all of her fresh pasta. Her commitment to these time-honored methods and ideals warrants much appreciation. No dish represents this dedication more than her recreation of a Renaissance classic called pasticcio. A sweet pastry crust envelops a squab ragu, penne, béchamel, and truffle mixture that is sealed and baked. The resulting intoxicating flavors are reminders of two centuries worth of decadence and opulence in Emilia-Romagna's history and culture. As their region is not especially known for its wine, Gianni and Christina take weekend journeys throughout all of Italy, visiting vineyards and gathering bottles for their eclectic high-end wine list. They also have an apartment in Paris, and the occasional French label has been known to make an appearance at their tables. Christina's perfectionist ways bring to life classic cuisine from times past, and Le Occare's refined setting provides the perfect complement to the region's culinary heritage.

Stuffed Cheese Pillows in Broth
PASTA IMBOTTITA

3½ ounces (100 g) ricotta

3½ ounces (100 g) stracchino cheese (or substitute quark)

2 ounces (60 g) Parmigiano Reggiano, grated, plus more for garnish

Pinch of freshly grated nutmeg

1 tablespoon lemon zest

1 large egg

Kosher salt and freshly ground black pepper

1 recipe basic pasta dough (see page viii)

1 quart (32 fl. oz. / 960 ml) home-made chicken broth (see page xi) or canned low-sodium broth

This recipe is one of Christina's family recipes, passed down through the generations. Gianni, Christina's husband, jokes that whenever they go to her mom's for dinner this is his request. It is understandable why: These tiny pillow-shaped ravioli are served bobbing in the broth they are cooked in and each bite explodes with a mixture of lemon-scented cheese and an essence of nutmeg.

In a large bowl, mix together the ricotta, stracchino, Parmigiano Reggiano, nutmeg, lemon zest, and egg until thoroughly combined.

On a clean work surface lightly dusted with flour, roll out the pasta dough into a 18-inch circle ⅛ inch thick. Spread a thin layer of the cheese filling over the bottom half of the dough. Fold the top half of the dough over the filling to form a half moon. With a handheld pasta cutter, cut the dough into long vertical strips, ½ inch wide. Then cut horizontally every ¼ inch to make small rectangles. Alternatively, use a pasta machine and roll the dough out to the thinnest setting. Spread the cheese mixture thinly over the bottom half of the dough. Fold the top over to cover the filling, and, using a pastry cutter, cut the dough into ½-inch by ¼-inch rectangles.

Place the stuffed pillows on a lightly floured sheet pan. Place in the freezer at least 1 hour prior to cooking.

In a 6-quart pot, bring the chicken broth up to a boil. Add 2 tablespoons salt. Drop the pasta into the broth and gently simmer until tender. Ladle the soup into shallow bowls and serve with pepper and grated Parmigiano Reggiano.

SERVES 6

Cheese-stuffed pasta imbottita

Maccheroni Pie
PASTICCIO

A Renaissance dish through and through, this pasta evokes the lavish tables of a duke's court. Pasticcio is a macaroni pie enveloped in a sweet pastry crust and layered with béchamel, truffles, pasta, and a squab and chicken liver ragu. A good resource for squab and truffles is D'Artagnan (www.dartagnan.com).

2 tablespoons (1 fl. oz. / 30 ml) extra-virgin olive oil

1 small yellow onion, cut into fine dice

8 ounces (225 g) ground beef

1 1-pound (450 g) squab, boned, skin removed, and cut into ¼-inch pieces

2 ounces (60 g) chicken livers, minced

10 ounces (283 g) boxed penne mezzani

4 tablespoons (2 oz. / 60 g) unsalted butter

1 recipe sweet pastry crust (see page xi)

1 recipe béchamel (see page x)

½ cup grated Parmigiano Reggiano

1 ounce (30 g) thinly shaved black truffle (optional)

Make the ragu: In a 3-quart saucepan, heat the olive oil over medium heat. Add the onion and cook until it becomes tender, 5 to 7 minutes. Add the ground beef, squab, and chicken livers to the pan and stir to combine. Cover, reduce the heat to medium-low, and cook for 20 to 30 minutes, stirring occasionally.

Meanwhile, bring 4 quarts of salted water to a boil. Drop in the pasta and cook for about 8 minutes. Drain and toss with 2 tablespoons of butter.

Heat the oven to 375°F (190°C).

Divide the pastry dough into two pieces, one slightly larger than the other. Roll out the larger half on a lightly floured surface until ¼ inch thick. Line a deep casserole dish with the dough, overhanging the edge of the dish by ½ inch.

Pour a large ladleful of béchamel into the casserole dish, and sprinkle generously with Parmigiano Reggiano. Add half of the shaved truffle and then add half of the pasta. Sprinkle with more Parmigiano Reggiano and dot with 1 tablespoon of butter, cut into small pieces. Add all of the ragu to the casserole pan and sprinkle generously with more grated Parmigiano Reggiano. Add another layer of truffle over the meat, then add the rest of the pasta and 1 tablespoon of butter, cut into small pieces. Pour the remaining béchamel on top.

Roll out the smaller piece of the dough and place on top to close the pie. Crimp together the edges and bake in the oven for 1 hour, or until the crust is firm to the touch and golden brown. Remove from the oven and let cool on a wire rack for at least 30 minutes before serving. Serve cut into slices.

SERVES 6

TARTUFO BIANCHETTO

Although not as famous as its cousins from Alba and France, the Bianchetto truffle has a mild flavor and has gained notoriety as an Emilia-Romagnan delicacy. Special truffle dogs bred only in the region sniff out the truffles, which grow beneath the ground and need to be removed carefully with a spade. The truffle hunter must be quick, however, because the dogs are also great lovers of the knotty fungus and will gobble up the pricey treats if not carefully watched.

Le Occare's truffle hunter

Unearthed truffle

Cornish Hen with Hazelnuts
FARAONA ALLE NOCCIOLE

The Italian concept of making a few quality ingredients into something sublime is on full display here. This buttery hazelnut sauce is all that is needed to dress up the simple Cornish hen.

2 Cornish game hens (about 2 pounds each / 900 g each), breastbones and backbones removed, cut in half

Kosher salt and freshly ground black pepper

1 tablespoon (½ oz. / 15 g) unsalted butter

1 tablespoon (½ fl. oz. / 15 ml) extra-virgin olive oil

1 sliced scallion

¼ cup (2 fl. oz. / 60 ml) homemade chicken broth (see page xi) or canned low-sodium broth

2 ounces (60 g) roasted, peeled, and coarsely chopped hazelnuts

1 tablespoon chopped rosemary

Heat the oven to 450°F (230°C).

Season the Cornish hens all over with salt and pepper. In a 3-quart oven-proof sauté pan, melt the butter with the olive oil over medium-high heat. Add the Cornish hens and sear skin side down until deep golden brown, 3 to 4 minutes. Turn the hens over, add the scallion, and cook for 2 minutes. Add the broth and the hazelnuts. Place the pan in the oven and roast until the birds are cooked through, 25 to 30 minutes, or until an instant-read thermometer registers 165°F (74°C).

Remove the pan from the oven and place half a bird on each individual plate. Drizzle with the pan juices and garnish with the rosemary.

SERVES 4

Rolled Beef with Mortadella
UCCELLINI SCAPPATI

The name of this common northern Italian dish translates as "the little birds that escaped." In Christina's version, thin slices of beef are topped with mortadella and rolled into small bundles. They are simmered briefly in a tomato-based sauce, and the result is a quick and easy flavorful dish. Be sure to simmer the rolled meat only briefly, as flank steak can become exceedingly tough when overcooked.

2 pounds (900 g) flank steak, cut into thin slices

Kosher salt and freshly ground black pepper

4 ounces (115 g) mortadella, cut into ½-inch cubes

2 tablespoons (1 fl. oz. / 30 ml) extra-virgin olive oil

1 yellow onion, cut into medium dice

1 28-ounce (793 g) can crushed tomatoes

Lay a slice of the flank steak on a flat surface. Season with salt and pepper. Place a slice of mortadella on top of the flank steak. Roll the meat up and secure it with a toothpick. Continue with the remaining meat and mortadella.

In a 2-quart sauté pan, heat the olive oil over medium heat, add the onion, and sauté until tender and translucent, about 7 minutes. Add the meat to the pan and brown on both sides, about 6 minutes total. Season with salt and pepper and add the crushed tomatoes. Bring the contents of the pan up to a simmer and cook for 10 minutes. Serve on a large platter.

SERVES 4

Chocolate Cake

TORTA DI CIOCOLATTO

This recipe makes a dense fudgelike chocolate cake that should only be served to real chocolate lovers. It is simple to whip up and makes a great dessert for entertaining, leaving an impression on guests long after the last morsel has been licked from the lips.

10½ ounces (300 g) bittersweet (70%) chocolate, cut into small even pieces

2 tablespoons (1 oz. / 30 g) unsalted butter

1 cup (200 g) granulated sugar

3 eggs, separated

2 tablespoons (20 g) all-purpose flour

Heat the oven to 350°F (180°C). Butter and flour a 9-inch springform pan.

Place the chocolate and the butter in the top of a double boiler, over barely simmering water. Stir to melt, then let cool.

Add the sugar, egg yolks, and flour to the chocolate and stir to combine, mixing well.

Place the egg whites in a medium bowl. Use an electric mixer to beat egg whites to stiff (but not dry) peaks.

Using a spatula, add a quarter of the egg whites to the chocolate mixture. Stir together gently to lighten the base. Fold the remaining egg whites into the chocolate. Pour batter into prepared pan and bake until the top begins to brown and a toothpick inserted in the center comes out nearly clean, with some moist crumbs attached, 25 to 30 minutes.

Remove from the oven and place on a wire rack to cool. Once cooled completely, remove cake from the springform pan and place on a large serving plate or cake stand.

SERVES 10–12

Jam Tart
CROSTATA DI MARMELLATA

Jam tarts are probably the most popular breakfast treat at the agriturismo table. Every farm we visited served this simple tart, showcasing house-made marmalades for the filling. Pick your favorite jam, jelly, or marmalade to create your own version of this much adored breakfast favorite.

1 recipe sweet pastry crust (see page xi)

1 13-ounce (370 g) jar fig marmalade or jam, jelly, or marmalade of your choice

Heat the oven to 350°F (180°F). Butter and flour a 9-inch springform pan.

Roll out half of the dough on a lightly floured surface into a 10-inch round ¼ inch thick and place in the prepared pan. Spread the fig marmalade over the pastry crust, making sure it is spread evenly.

Roll out the second half of the dough to a 10-inch round, ¼ inch thick, on a lightly floured surface. Cut it into ¼-inch-thick strips. Lay 4 of the strips diagonally across the marmalade, and then another 4 strips across in the opposite direction.

Bake for about 30 minutes, or until the tart is golden brown all over. Remove from the oven and place on a wire rack to cool completely. Remove the tart from the springform pan and place on a large serving dish or cake stand.

SERVES 10–12

Cavazzone agriturismo

CHAPTER 28
CAVAZZONE

The Cavazzone property has been a working farm since the 1800s, when Baron Franchetti, a Venetian nobleman, purchased the property to plant a vineyard and to use the grounds for hunting. Current owner Giovanni Sidoli's great-grandfather bought the farm in the early 1900s and replaced the vines with herds of dairy cattle for Parmigiano Reggiano production. He soon discovered the climate suitable for the aging of balsamic vinegar, and he converted one of the rooms of the farmhouse into a tomb-like cave, dark and still, lined with wooden casks. While much has changed since the opening of the agriturismo, the fundamental activities of the farm remain the same. The Sidoli family comes from a lineage of avid hunters, and weekends are spent on horseback and with their dogs, combing the surrounding forests for wild boar, hare, and pheasant. Whatever luck is had in the wild gets passed to the kitchen, which offers a game-rich cuisine. Although suckling pigs are now reared where cows once grazed, balsamic vinegar remains Cavazzone's principal product and the farm's original barrels are still used in the aging process. With the opening of the agriturismo, Cavazzone has evolved into a farm where tourism and agriculture come together, continuing the changing cycles of the estate for a new generation.

Beneath the red-brick vaulted ceilings of the original barn and stable, Cavazzone's farm restaurant reflects typical Emilian cuisine. The rustic room is evocative of a hunting manor, exuding masculinity through its hunt-themed artwork and dark wooden tables. The farm's own suckling pig represents the house specialty: a Goliath portion of moist, succulent oven-roasted pork with crispy, crackly skin. Game meat constitutes the bulk of the second courses. A wild boar loin doused in a vin brûlé reduction with figs, dates, and prunes removes any trace of gamy flavor. The meat also makes a hearty ragu with homemade pasta that calls for a robust red to match. Giovanni Sidoli's own separate vineyard provides nearly all of Cavazzone's wines, which are beginning to gain recognition in the United States. His reasonably priced high-quality Lambrusco wins respect for the sparkling red so often disdained in foreign markets. With a successful and growing agriturismo and a vineyard following suit, Giovanni harbors a greater vision for his family's agriturismo, including a gym, a bar and lounge with billiard tables, and a spa. Although these amenities will represent new nonagrarian activities, agriculture and hunting will continue to serve as the backbone of Cavazzone's future.

Onion Soup
ZUPPA DI CIPOLLA

At Cavazzone this dish is more like a gratin than a soup. You can adjust the amount of broth based on your preference. The addition of juniper and cinnamon adds an interesting twist to the sweet onions.

1 tablespoon (½ fl. oz. / 15 ml) extra-virgin olive oil

3 ounces (85 g) prosciutto, cut crosswise into thin strips

3 tablespoons (1½ oz. / 45 g) unsalted butter

1 teaspoon cinnamon

2 bay leaves

2 whole cloves

½ tablespoon lightly crushed juniper berries

Kosher salt and freshly ground black pepper

5 red onions cut into thin slices

1½ quarts (54 fl. oz. / 1.6 L) homemade chicken broth (see page xi) or canned low-sodium broth

4 ounces (115 g) shaved Parmigiano Reggiano

Heat the oven to 425°F (220°C).

In a 12-inch straight-sided sauté pan over medium-high heat, add the olive oil and the prosciutto and cook until crispy, 2 to 3 minutes. Remove prosciutto from the pan and set aside on a plate lined with paper towel to drain.

Add the butter to the pan, along with the cinnamon, bay leaves, cloves, juniper berries, and a pinch of salt. Sauté until the spices become fragrant, about 1 minute. Add the onions and a pinch of salt to the pan and stir well to combine. Cover the pan and reduce the heat to medium-low. Cook for 40 minutes, stirring occasionally, until the onions are meltingly tender. Remove the lid, raise the heat to medium high, and continue cooking until the onions are a deep brown, 10 to 15 minutes more. Pour in the chicken broth and bring the mixture to a boil, reduce heat to medium-low, and let simmer about 5 to 10 minutes. Adjust seasoning with salt and pepper.

Spoon the onion mixture into 6 individual crocks, top each with 1 tablespoon of the crispy prosciutto, and divide the shaved Parmigiano Reggiano evenly among the crocks. Bake in the oven until the cheese is bubbly and browned, 5 to 10 minutes.

SERVES 6

Balsamic Vinegar of Reggio Emilia

To the foreigner, balsamic vinegar is most often associated with Modena, whose dark, sweet, syrup like vinegar has become famous worldwide. To citizens of Reggio, however, there could be no greater insult than to compare their balsamic vinegar to that of Modena. Produced in minute quantities, aging between twelve and one hundred years in various types of wooden barrels, Reggio's balsamic vinegar is to be savored in droplike measures. The dense, concentrated flavor retains the essence and aroma of history and tradition and justly commands a high price.

Aging balsamic vinegar

Artichoke and Mascarpone Cheese Flan
SFORMATO DI CARCIOFI E MASCARPONE

An artichoke puree lightened with whipped egg whites gets spooned into the bottom of individual ramekins and topped with a creamy mascarpone mousse. As they bake, the flans rise to resemble soufflés. The additions of Parmigiano Reggiano crisps and crunchy pancetta bring an enhanced salty bite to the silky flan.

1 tablespoon (1 oz. / 15 g) unsalted butter

2 tablespoons (20 g) bread crumbs

3 ounces (85 g) thinly sliced pancetta

3 cups (24 fl. oz. / 720 ml) homemade chicken broth or canned-low sodium

6 quartered artichoke hearts (675 g), outer leaves removed and trimmed

6 egg whites

1 tablespoon chopped thyme

1 tablespoon lemon zest

Kosher salt and freshly ground black pepper

8 ounces (225 g) mascarpone cheese

⅓ cup (3 fl. oz. / 80 ml) heavy cream

1 cup grated Parmigiano Reggiano

Heat the oven to 400°F (200°C). Butter 6 individual ramekins and coat with bread crumbs.

Place the pancetta slices on a sheet pan and bake in the oven until crispy, 15 to 20 minutes. Remove from the oven and drain on paper towels.

Bring the chicken broth to a boil, add 2 tablespoons of salt, and add the artichoke hearts. Simmer over medium heat until tender, 20 to 25 minutes. Remove artichoke hearts from the pan, and reserve ½ cup (120 ml) of the broth.

Place egg whites in a medium bowl. Use an electric mixer to beat egg whites to stiff (but not dry) peaks, about 4 minutes.

In the bowl of a food processor, puree the artichoke hearts with the thyme, lemon zest, and reserved broth. Season to taste with salt and pepper. With a spatula, carefully fold in half of the egg whites. Spoon the artichoke mixture into the individual ramekins to fill halfway.

In another large bowl, mix together the mascarpone cheese, heavy cream, and ¼ cup grated Parmigiano Reggiano. Fold in the remaining egg whites, and spoon the cheese mixture on top of the artichoke mixture in the ramekins.

Put the ramekins on a sheet pan and place in the center of the oven. Lower the heat to 350°F (180°C) and bake until the flans are golden brown on top but still slightly wobbly in the center, 15 to 20 minutes. Remove from the oven and place on a wire rack to let cool slightly.

Meanwhile, make the cheese crisps: Heat a 4-inch nonstick skillet over medium-high heat. Sprinkle 2 tablespoons grated Parmigiano Reggiano evenly over the surface of the pan. Cook until the crisp is set and golden brown, 2 to 3 minutes. Flip over and cook 1 minute more. Remove from the pan and place on a sheet pan lined with parchment paper. Continue cooking cheese crisps in the same manner. You should have 6 crisps.

Invert the flans onto individual plates and top each with a slice of crispy pancetta and a cheese crisp.

SERVES 6

Emilia-Romagna country road

Wild Boar with Vin Brûlé

CINGHIALE AL VIN BRÛLÉ

This dish is emblematic of Cavazzone's origins as a hunting lodge and showcases the wild game that thrives in the surrounding hills. The Chef, Giusseppe adds an assortment of dried fruit to his sweet wine reduction, which grows plump and juicy in the sugary liquid, making an impressive garnish over the sliced wild boar loin. The sauce cuts through the gamy elements of the meat and brings out its succulent pork flavors. As this dish demonstrates, wild boar is rich and satisfying and well worth the effort to seek out; a great resource for it in the United States is Broken Arrow Ranch (www.brokenarrowranch.com).

1 pound (450 g) wild boar loin, trimmed of all fat

Kosher salt and freshly ground black pepper

1 tablespoon chopped rosemary

2 teaspoons lightly crushed juniper berries

½ cup (4 fl. oz. / 120 ml) Marsala

1 cup (8 fl. oz. / 240 ml) red wine

1 cup (8 fl. oz. / 240 ml) white wine

1 tablespoon orange zest

6 tablespoons (3½ fl. oz. / 90 ml) orange juice

1 cinnamon stick

3 whole cloves

1 stalk celery, cut into small dice

3 tablespoons (45 g) granulated sugar

2 ounces (60 g) dried figs

2 ounces (60 g) dates

2 ounces (60 g) dried pitted prunes

Season the wild boar loin generously with salt, pepper, rosemary, and juniper berries. Place in a bowl, cover with plastic wrap, and let marinate for several hours in the refrigerator. One hour before cooking, remove the wild boar from the refrigerator and let come up to room temperature.

Make the vin brûlé: In a medium-size saucepan, combine the Marsala, red wine, and white wine along with the orange zest, orange juice, cinnamon stick, cloves, celery, and sugar. Bring the contents of the pan to a boil over medium-high heat. Reduce the heat to medium-low and simmer gently for about 40 minutes.

Heat the grill to medium-high heat, and grill the wild boar on all sides until it is cooked, about 4 to 5 minutes per side.

Meanwhile, strain the sauce into a clean saucepan. Add the figs, dates, and prunes and cook over medium heat until the figs and prunes soften, about 10 minutes.

Slice the wild boar, and serve with the fig sauce.

SERVES 4

Wild boar loin with figs

Almond brittle

Almond Brittle

CROCCANTE DI MANDORLE

Caramelized sugar and toasted almonds mixed together make a crunchy, chewy snack.

1 cup (150 g) almond slivers
½ cup (100 g) granulated sugar

Heat the oven to 375°F (190°C). Place the almonds on a sheet pan and toast in the oven until golden brown, 5 to 7 minutes. Remove from the oven and let cool.

In a 10-inch nonstick skillet, melt the sugar over medium heat without stirring. Once the sugar begins to caramelize, add the almond slivers. Lower the heat to medium-low and stir the sugar and almonds together, making sure that the almonds are fully coated with the caramel.

Pour the almond mixture out onto a piece of parchment paper. With a spatula, spread the mixture out, and with a meat mallet, lightly push down on the mixture to flatten. With a sharp knife, cut the brittle into squares while it is still warm, and place on a plate.

SERVES 6

Fattoria Paradiso's private wine cellar

CHAPTER 29
❧ FATTORIA PARADISO ❧

The Mario Pezzi name epitomizes serious winemaking tradition. A vineyard of great merit and historical importance, Fattoria Paradiso was a founding father in delivering great Italian wine to the world market. In the 1950s, when his region's wines were very little known, Mario Pezzi was a pioneer in bringing exposure and recognition to the wines of Emilia-Romagna. His passionate love for his profession and profound understanding of his land and the native grapes he grew brought him monumental accomplishments. With his fame came many special guests to the Emilia-Romagnan hills to pay their respects, including a pope, a U.S. president, a Nobel prize winner, an astronaut, political figures, actors, and artists. The awards and accolades that adorn the walls of the offices of Fattoria Paradiso speak volumes of the honors given to Mario Pezzi. A tour of the cantina ends with a viewing of his incredible private wine collection, whose thousands of bottles span the globe and represent years of his dedication to his craft. Today, his daughter Graziella carries on the family's name, and with the opening of the vineyard's agriturismo and restaurant, she has begun a new chapter for the future of Fattoria Paradiso's wines and the estate itself.

Overlooking the classic Italian hill town of Bertinoro and tucked into the estate's vines, Fattoria Paradiso offers wine lovers ample opportunity to drink up Italian vineyard life. The formal restaurant presents classic Romagnan cuisine, influenced by the late food historian Pellegrino Artusi, who came from nearby. Each morning, in strict Emilia-Romagnan fashion, fresh egg pasta is rolled out with wooden rolling pins by two elderly women. In rapid succession they roll, shape, and form the dough with a precision and mastery only attained through years of experience. From there, three cooks divvy up the remaining kitchen duties and serve an a la carte menu demonstrating the dishes that have made Emilia-Romagna a destination for Italian food lovers. The many varieties of pasta are the obvious house specialty. Passatelli is pasta dough passed through the large holes of a ricer, the snakelike shapes of which are then cooked in simmering chicken broth. A local fresh cheese, squaquerone, gets paired with a must jelly made from Fattoria Paradiso's own balsamic vinegar and is great when eaten with a piadina, a typical regional flatbread. Not to be overlooked are, of course, Fattoria Paradiso's celebrated wines. A glass or two paired with the robust flavors emerging from the kitchen offers a clear insight into the visionary mindset of Mario Pezzi and his exquisite wines.

Mixed Green Salad with Caramelized Prosciutto and Pancetta in Balsamic Vinegar

INSALATA DI MISTICANZA CON BRUCIATINI AL BALSAMICO

A combination of bitter lettuces, crispy pancetta and prosciutto, and sweet balsamic vinegar makes for a unique salad. The final addition of butter makes a silky dressing that should be spooned over the salad while still warm.

1 head radicchio

1 head Belgian endive

1 head arugula

1 tablespoon chopped thyme,

1 tablespoon chopped chives,

1 tablespoon chopped flat-leaf parsley

2 tablespoons (1 fl. oz. / 30 ml) extra-virgin olive oil

Kosher salt and freshly ground black pepper

3 tablespoons (1½ oz. / 45 g) unsalted butter

¼ pound (115 g) pancetta, cut into thin strips

¼ pound (115 g) prosciutto di Parma, cut crosswise into this strips

¼ cup (2 fl. oz. / 60 ml) balsamic vinegar

Wash and pat dry all of the lettuces. Cut into bite-size pieces and toss in a salad bowl to mix, along with the herbs and extra-virgin olive oil. Season with salt and pepper to taste.

In a heavy sauté pan, melt 1 tablespoon of butter over medium heat. Cook the pancetta and the prosciutto until just beginning to crisp, 2 to 3 minutes. Remove from the pan and drain on paper towels. Degrease the pan, then return the pancetta and prosciutto to the pan. Cook another 2 minutes, until crispy. Add the balsamic vinegar to the pan, let it reduce by half, and then add the remaining butter and whisk in to incorporate.

Spoon the pancetta-prosciutto mixture over the lettuces and serve warm.

SERVES 6

Cheese-filled "Hats" with Wild Mushroom Sauce

CAPPELLETTI CON FUNGHI DI BOSCO

A classic regional stuffed pasta, cappelletti are shaped like the three-pointed hats from which they take their name. Cappelletti can be made with a meat or cheese filling and can be served in broth or with a sauce. At Fattoria Paradiso, they use a local soft cow's milk cheese called squaquerone, which is difficult to find outside of Emilia-Romagna; stracchino, crescenza, and telame cheese are all available in the U.S. and make fine substitutes.

In a large bowl, mix together the ricotta, basket cheese, Parmigiano Reggiano, pecorino cheese, egg, nutmeg, and salt and pepper to taste.

Divide the pasta dough into 6 pieces. Using a pasta machine, roll each piece out, starting with the widest setting and ending with the thinnest. Cut the pasta sheets into 2-inch squares. Place 1 teaspoon of filling in the center of each square. Fold the square into triangles and press firmly to secure the filling. Bring the two bottom points of each triangle together to form the "little hats." Place the cappelletti on a lightly floured sheet pan and continue filling the rest of the pasta.

Make the sauce: Sauté the shallot in 2 tablespoons of olive oil over medium heat until tender, about 5 minutes. Add the mushrooms and cook until the mushrooms release their liquid, 5 to 7 minutes. Season with salt and pepper to taste, then add the white wine and let reduce by half.

Bring 6 quarts of salted water to a boil. Drop the cappelletti into the water and cook until they start to float to the top, 2 to 3 minutes. Drain the pasta and toss in the sauté pan with the mushrooms. Sprinkle with chopped parsley. Serve in individual shallow bowls.

SERVES 8

½ pound (225 g) ricotta

¼ pound (115 g) squaquerone cheese

1 cup grated Parmigiano Reggiano

½ cup grated pecorino cheese

1 egg

Pinch of freshly grated nutmeg

Kosher salt and freshly ground black pepper

1 recipe basic pasta dough (see page viii)

1 shallot, cut into fine dice

2 tablespoons (1 fl. oz. / 30 ml) extra-virgin olive oil

1 pound (450 g) sliced mixed wild mushrooms

½ cup (4 fl. oz. / 120 ml) white wine

½ cup chopped flat-leaf parsley

Bread Noodles in Broth
PASATELLI

1¼ cups (155 g) bread crumbs

1¼ cups grated Parmigiano Reggiano, plus more for garnish

1 tablespoon (10 g) flour

1 teaspoon freshly grated nutmeg

Kosher salt and pepper

3 eggs

1 quart (32 fl. oz. / 960 ml) homemade chicken broth (see page xi) or canned low-sodium broth

This recipe makes an appearance in one of the oldest cookbooks in Italy, by Pellegrino Artusi, who resided nearby. His book is treated as a bible in the Fattoria Paradiso kitchen. The chef has adapted this recipe for the modern cook, but the basic premise of savory bread noodles in a rich broth remains intact.

In a large bowl, mix together the bread crumbs and grated Parmigiano Reggiano. Add the flour, the nutmeg, and a pinch each of salt and pepper, and stir to combine.

Add the eggs to the bread crumb mixture and stir until a dough begins to form. Remove the dough from the bowl and knead until the dough is smooth. Cover with a kitchen towel and let rest for at least 20 minutes.

Bring the chicken broth up to a gentle simmer. Place the dough in a ricer and press the dough into the chicken broth. Cook until the pasatelli double in size. Ladle the soup into shallow bowls and garnish with pepper and Parmigiano Reggiano.

SERVES 4

PELLEGRINO ARTUSI

The nearby small town of Forlimpopoli is recognized in the culinary world as the birthplace of perhaps Italy's most recognized food historian, Pellegrino Artusi. Artusi's fundamental cookbook, *La Scienza in Cucina e l'Arte di Mangiare Bene* (The Science of Cooking and the Art of Eating Well), explored Italian cuisine not as a singular unified tradition, but as an extremely varied and diverse food culture, differing from region to region. His was the first book to represent all of Italy's regional cuisines in one manuscript. Over one hundred years later, not much has changed in today's Italian provincial cuisine, and Artusi's research remains the authority for authentic regional recipes.

Squeezing pasatelli into simmering chicken broth at Fattoria Paradiso

Wild boar ragu with fresh tagliatelle

Wild Boar Ragu
RAGÙ DI CINGHIALE

Ground wild boar meat soaked overnight in a red wine marinade makes a rich ragu that demands fresh pasta to absorb its strong flavor. The meat can simmer for hours, and the flavor only improves the longer it cooks. Be sure to add water as the liquid evaporates from the sauce. A great resource for wild boar in the United States is Broken Arrow Ranch (www.brokenarrowranch.com).

Marinate the wild boar overnight with 1½ cups red wine, half of the onion, half of the celery, half of the carrot, the garlic, the juniper berries, and the cloves.

The next day, strain the wild boar, reserving the wine and vegetables, but discarding the garlic, juniper berries, and cloves.

In a heavy casserole pan over medium-high heat, add the olive oil along with the remaining onion, celery, and carrot. Sauté until tender, about 7 minutes. Add the wild boar, along with the vegetables from the marinade, and cook about 10 minutes. Season with salt and pepper to taste.

Add the red wine from the marinade, along with the remaining 1½ cups red wine, and let reduce by half. Add the crushed tomatoes, the bay leaf, and the rosemary. Reduce heat to medium-low and let simmer for 2 to 2½ hours. Discard the bay leaf.

Bring 6 quarts of salted water to a boil. Drop the pasta into the boiling water, and cook until al dente, 1 to 2 minutes. Drain the pasta and toss with the ragu. Serve immediately.

SERVES 4–6

2 pounds (900 g) ground wild boar

3 cups (24 fl. oz. / 720 ml) red wine

2 onions, cut into fine dice

2 stalks celery, cut into fine dice

2 carrots, peeled and cut into fine dice

1 clove of garlic, peeled and minced

1 tablespoon lightly crushed juniper berries

5 whole cloves

3 tablespoons (2 fl. oz. / 60 ml) olive oil

Kosher salt and freshly ground black pepper

1 28-ounce (793 g) can crushed tomatoes

1 bay leaf

1 sprig rosemary

1 recipe basic pasta dough (see page viii), cut into tagliatelle

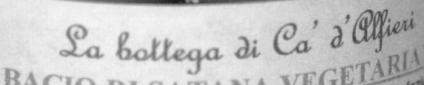

La bottega di Ca' d'Alfieri

BACIO DI SATANA VEGETARIANO

Ingredienti:
Peperoncini piccanti (40%), Melanzane (20%),
Olio extravergine di oliva, Capperi (2,6%), Aceto di vino,
Sale, Prezzemolo, Aglio, Origano

Prodotto e confezionato da
Az. Agricola Ca' D'Alfieri
Loc. Predario, 29 - Parma (PR)
Tel. e fax 0525771114

270 g e

peso sgocciolato **180 g** e

info@cadalfieri.it

da consumarsi preferibilmente entro il: Settembre 2009

Lotto N° 0078/07

Conservare in luogo fresco ed asciutto

Dopo l'apertura conservare

Jarred stuffed hot peppers

CHAPTER 30
CA' D'ALFIERI

The mundane pepper and the ordinary pig are ubiquitous on farms throughout Italy, yet they have earned Ca' d'Alfieri a unique agricultural niche. These are not, however, your typical red and yellow peppers, nor your everyday common swine. Maurizio and Louisa have established a working farm and agriturismo whose numerous varieties of exotic peppers and herd of free-range black Parma pigs have forged a loyal following. Once scoffed at by locals who believed peppers to be a vegetable of the south and who thought their piquant flavor unwelcome on the northern table, they have since quelled any doubts. Habañero, jalapeño, and serrano peppers are a few of the intense capsicums grown for Ca' d'Alfieri jellies and spreads, which hit all levels of the heat index. In the forest below the farm live the prized and unusual black pigs. Native to nearby Parma, their jet-black coats, floppy ears, and lean torsos make them a much different looking species from their pink and blubbery cousins. Maurizio and Louisa's agricultural efforts have both helped reintroduce a near-extinct regional delicacy to the public and proved the possibility of growing nonnative produce in the not-so-fertile hills of Emilia-Romagna.

While pigs and peppers play a significant role in Ca' d'Alfieri's gardens and kitchen, Maurizio and Louisa also grow numerous other organic crops. In addition to their jarred spicy jams, the couple bottle their own pickled vegetables to sell in their small store in the historic center of nearby Bardi. They have found a considerable liking for their products in Germany, which has kept them busy trying to ship orders to satisfy the high demand. Back on the farm, a seat in Ca' d'Alfieri's intimate stone dining room becomes a coveted commodity when the agriturismo hosts special eight-course dinners focusing on one ingredient from the land. The black pig naturally stars at one of these meals, proving the exceptional quality and versatility of the meat. Beginning with traditional cured salamis and hams, the meal builds to a climax of inventive dishes, like a walnut pork ragu sandwiched between cheesy polenta, a chestnut-flour crepe with pork and prunes, and a strongly flavored spreadable pâté. These events reveal a pork with a taste and texture that is a far cry from the commonly overcooked other white meat. Summer months bring alfresco dining to the farm, where a wood-fired grill and a brick oven provide great summer eating. Smoky varieties of local meats and dense, chewy chestnut bread are warm weather specialties. Ca' d'Alfieri has broken the mold of tradition with its progressive approach towards farming and agriculture and has slowly brought change to an old-fashioned mentality.

Chestnut Flour Crepe with Pork Ragu
CRESPELLE DI CASTAGNA CON SUGO DI MAIALE

Chestnut flour gives these crepes their decisively unique taste. The prunes and chestnuts mixed with the pork ragu add a layer of sweetness to the dish that works well with the subdued cinnamon taste. These interesting combinations make for a savory dish worthy of serving to guests.

Crepe

⅔ cup (100 g) all-purpose flour

⅓ cup (35 g) chestnut flour

Pinch of table salt

1 cup (8 fl. oz. / 240 ml) milk

3 large eggs

Butter, melted, for brushing

Filling

2 tablespoons (1 fl. oz. / 30 ml) extra-virgin olive oil

1 peeled clove of garlic

1 yellow onion, cut into fine dice

1 pound (450 g) ground pork

1 cup (8 fl. oz. / 240 ml) white wine

1 cup (8 fl. oz. / 240 ml) homemade chicken broth (see page xi) or canned low-sodium broth

1 tablespoon chopped sage

1 tablespoon chopped thyme

1 teaspoon chopped marjoram

1 bay leaf

1 cinnamon stick

5 whole cloves

Combine all the ingredients for the crepes in a blender and puree until smooth. Heat a 8-inch nonstick skillet over medium-high heat, brush the pan with a little melted butter, and ladle enough batter into the skillet to coat the bottom of the pan. Make the coating as thin as possible. Cook the crepe until it begins to dry out and set, about 1 minute. Using a spatula, flip the crepe over and cook another 30 seconds to 1 minute. Remove crepe from pan and lay flat on a dish. Continue cooking the crepes in this manner until the batter is all used. Set the crepes aside while you make the filling.

Heat 2 tablespoons of olive oil in a 12-inch straight-sided sauté pan over medium-high heat. Add the garlic to the pan, and sauté until golden brown. Discard the garlic clove. Add the onion to the pan and cook until tender, about 7 minutes. Add the ground pork and brown well, about 12 minutes. Add the white wine, chicken broth, herbs, cinnamon stick, and cloves to the pan and bring to a boil. Reduce the heat to medium-low and simmer for about 1 hour. Season with salt and pepper to taste and remove pan from the heat.

Discard the bay leaf, cinnamon stick, and cloves from the pork ragu. Stir in the chestnuts and the prunes, and adjust seasoning if necessary.

Lay a crepe out on a flat surface. Spread 1 heaping tablespoon of ricotta evenly over the crepe, top with 2 tablespoons of the pork ragu, and then sprinkle with the Parmigiano Reggiano. Roll the crepe up lengthwise. Continue filling the crepes in the same manner. Wrap each crepe in plastic wrap. Refrigerate crepes at least 4 hours and up to 24 hours.

Heat the oven to 375°F (190°C).

Butter the bottom of a 9 × 13-inch gratin dish and sprinkle ½ cup of Parmigiano Reggiano evenly over the bottom. Cut the crepes into ½-inch slices and place filling-side up in a single layer in the gratin dish. Brush the crepes with melted butter, then sprinkle evenly with Parmigiano Reggiano and fennel seeds. Bake in the oven for 25 to 30 minutes, or until the cheese has melted and become crispy. Remove from oven and let cool slightly before serving.

SERVES 8

Kosher salt and freshly ground black pepper

8 ounces (225 g) boiled chestnuts, roughly chopped

3½ ounces (100 g) pitted prunes, roughly chopped

1 pound (450 g) ricotta

2 cups grated Parmigiano Reggiano

3 tablespoons (1½ oz. / 45 g) unsalted butter, melted

2 tablespoons fennel seeds

SUINO NERO DI PARMA

Native to Parma, these black, floppy-eared pigs were nearly extinct until recently, when an effort by the University of Parma to restore their breeding thwarted their demise. Today, farms like Ca' d'Alfieri successfully raise the animals naturally, allowing them to live freely in dense forests where they forage for acorns and chestnuts. The free-range animals are leaner and more muscular, and the time for rearing them is significantly longer, but the final product justifies these peculiarities with a far superior and tastier meat.

Polenta Molds with Ground Pork and Walnuts

POLENTINA CON RAGÙ DI MAIALE E NOCI

A molded polenta is the perfect base for absorbing the juices of the pork ragu. Louisa adds walnuts to the long-simmering sauce to bring a slightly bitter, appealing crunch to the dish, which she serves on Ca' d'Alfieri's all-pork menu celebrating the farm's black free-range pigs.

3 tablespoons (1½ fl. oz. / 45 ml) extra-virgin olive oil

1 yellow onion, cut into fine dice

1 stalk celery, cut into fine dice

1 carrot, peeled and cut into fine dice

2 pounds (900 g) ground pork

2 cups (16 fl. oz. / 480 ml) red wine

1 28-ounce (793 g) can crushed tomatoes

2 bay leaves

2 sprigs rosemary

Kosher salt and freshly ground black pepper

4 tablespoons (2 oz. / 60 g) unsalted butter

1 sprig marjoram

4 sage leaves

¾ cup grated Parmigiano Reggiano

1 recipe polenta (see page x)

¼ cup (25 g) chopped walnuts

Heat the oven to 350°F (180°C). In a heavy-bottomed casserole pan, heat olive oil over medium-high heat. Sauté the onion, celery, and carrot until tender, about 7 minutes. Add the ground pork and brown well, about 12 minutes. Pour the red wine into the pan and cook slowly over medium-low heat until reduced by half. Add the crushed tomatoes, along with 1 bay leaf and 1 sprig of rosemary. Gently simmer for 2 hours. Season to taste with salt and pepper.

Melt butter in a 1-quart saucepan over medium heat. Add the remaining bay leaf, 1 sprig of rosemary, marjoram, and sage leaves, and cook until fragrant 1 to 2 minutes.

Brush 6 individual ramekins with the herbed butter, coat each with 1 tablespoon of grated Parmigiano Reggiano, and then fill the ramekins with the polenta. Brush the top of the polenta with the herbed butter and sprinkle with another tablespoon of Parmigiano Reggiano. Bake in the oven until the cheese has melted, about 5 to 10 minutes.

To serve, invert the polenta onto individual dishes and gently remove the ramekins. Spoon the ragu over the molds and garnish with the chopped walnuts.

SERVES 6

Pork Tenderloin with Pine Nuts and Pancetta

FILETTO DI MAIALE CON PIGNOLI E PANCETTA

Pork in milk is a traditional cooking method used in northern Italy, and it produces a succulent and juicy piece of meat and a sweet, robust sauce. Once the pork is removed, be sure to whisk the sauce vigorously to bring it together while it simmers, as the milk will have slightly curdled.

In a large skillet, heat the olive oil and butter over medium-high heat. Sauté the garlic and the sage leaves until fragrant and golden, 2 minutes. Remove from the pan and discard. Season the pork all over with salt and pepper. Add the pork tenderloin to the skillet and brown on all sides until deeply golden, 12 minutes total. Remove from the pan and set aside.

Add the pancetta to the skillet and cook until the pancetta is crispy, 5 to 7 minutes. Add the milk and broth and bring to a boil. Return the pork tenderloin to the pan. Reduce heat to medium-low and cover pan. Cook 10 minutes, or until the pork is done. Remove the pork from the pan, add the pine nuts, and cook another 2 or 3 minutes, allowing the sauce to thicken and whisking to break up any clumps. Season with salt and pepper to taste.

Cut the pork into medallions and serve with the sauce.

SERVES 4

1 tablespoon (½ fl. oz. / 15 ml) extra-virgin olive oil

1 tablespoon (1 oz. / 15 g) unsalted butter

1 peeled clove of garlic

20 sage leaves

Kosher salt and freshly ground black pepper

1 pork tenderloin (about 1-1¼ pounds / 450–500 g)

2 ounces (60 g) pancetta, cut into fine dice

1 cup (8 fl. oz. / 240 ml) whole milk

¼ cup (2 fl. oz. / 60 ml) homemade chicken broth (see page xi) or canned low-sodium broth

¼ cup (30 g) pine nuts

Chestnut Bread
PANE DI CASTAGNE

Chestnut flour, made only from the grinding of the dried nut, is gluten free. This bread has a smooth crumb and irresistibly sweet earthy flavor, making the uncommon flour worth seeking out.

1¼-ounce (7 g) package dry active yeast

3 cups (24 fl. oz. / 720 ml) water

2 tablespoons honey

¼ cup (2 fl. oz. / 60 ml) extra-virgin olive oil

5½ cups (700 g) all-purpose flour

2 cups (250 g) chestnut flour

2 tablespoons (20 g) salt

½ cup (4 fl. oz. / 120 ml) ice water

Bloom the yeast in ½ cup of tepid water, for about 5 minutes. Mix the honey and olive oil with the remaining 2½ cups water.

In the bowl of an electric mixer fitted with the dough hook, combine the flours and salt. Mix on low speed to combine. Gradually add the yeast water and the honey water and mix on medium speed for 12 minutes. Turn the dough out onto a lightly floured surface and knead the dough until smooth and elastic. Place the dough into a lightly oiled bowl, cover with a kitchen towel, and place in a warm spot. Let rise until doubled in volume, about 2 hours.

Turn the dough out onto a lightly floured surface and divide in half. Place each half in a lightly oiled 8½ × 4½-inch loaf pan, and let rise until doubled in volume, about 1 hour.

Heat the oven to 475°F (240°C). As the oven heats, place a sheet pan on the lowest oven rack and a pizza stone on the next rack, set on the second shelf from the bottom.

Once the oven is heated, quickly place the loaf pans on the hot stone. Toss the ice water into the sheet pan below the stone and quickly close the door. Bake for 20 minutes, then lower the heat to 400°F (200°C) and bake another 20 minutes, or until the bread is a deep golden brown and a skewer inserted into the middle comes out clean.

Remove the bread from the oven and place on a wire rack to cool. Invert the bread onto the rack and continue to cool at least 1 hour before slicing.

YIELDS 2 LOAVES

FARM CONTACTS

If calling from the U.S., dial −011 39 before each telephone number. From the U.K., dial 0039.

LIGURIA
La Giara
Via Federici, 15
Beverino (SP) 19020
0187883129
www.agriturismolagiara.it

Giandriale
Loc. Giandriale, 5
Tavarone di Maissana (SP) 19010
0187840156
www.giandriale.it

Terre Bianche
Loc. Arcagna
Dolceaqua (Imperia) 18035
018421426
www.terrebianche.com

PIEMONTE
Tra Sole e Vigne
Loc. Manzoni, 33
Monforte d'Alba (CN) 12065
017378110
www.trasolevigne.it

La Traversina
Stazzano (AL) 15060
014361377
www.latraversina.com

Ca' Villa
Via Stefano 19
Gabiano (AL) 15020
0142945126
www.ca-villa.it

La Quercia Rossa
Strada Grazzano 23
Moncalvo (AT) 14036
0141917535
www.querciarossa.com

La Miniera
Via delle Miniere 9
Valcava
Calea di Lessolo (TO) 10010
0125561963
www.laminiera.it

La Capuccina
Via Novara 19
Cureggio
0322839930
www.lacapuccina.it

VALLE D'AOSTA
Les Ecureuils
Fraz. Homene' Dessus, 8
0165903831
Saint Pierre (AO) 11010
www.lesecureuils.it

Maison Rosset
Via Risorgimento, 39
Nus (AO) 11020
0165767176
www.maisonrosset.it

Plan de la Tour
Frazione Epinel, 8
Cogne (AO)
3498389945
www.plandelatour.it

LOMBARDIA
Cascina Caremma
Strada per il Ticino
Besate (MI) 20080
029050020
www.caremma.com

La Ribunta'
Caiolo (SO)
Fraz. San Bernardo 23010
0342561297
www.agriturismoribunta.it

Casa Clelia
Via Corna 1/3
Sotto il Monte (BG) 24039
35799133
www.casaclelia.com

Macesina
Via Borghetto 22
Bedizole (BS)
0306871737
www.macesina.it

TRENTINO–ALTO ADIGE
Baite di Pra
Loc. Pra
Val di Borzago, Trentino
3480025707
www.baitedipra.it

Casa al Campo
Loc. Pescicoltura
Giustino, Trentino 38086
0465500290
www.casalcampo.com

Glinzhof
Innichberg 5
Innichen/ S. Candido
Sudtirolo 39038
0474913448
www.glinzhof.com

FRIULI–VENEZIA GIULIA
Perusini
Gramogliano
Corno di Rosazzo (UD)
0432675018
www.perusini.com

La Subida
Loc. Monte, 22
Cormons (GO) 34071
048160531
www.lasubida.it

Casale Cjanor
Via Casali Lini 9
Fagagna (UD) 33034
0432801810
www.casalecjanor.com

I Comelli
Largo Armando Diaz 8
Nimis (UD) 33045
0432790685
www.icomelli.com

VENETO
Rechsteiner
Via Monte Grappa
S. Nicolo di Ponte di Piave,
Treviso
0422752074
www.rechsteiner.it

Le Vescovane
Via San Rocco, 19
Longare (VI) 36023
0444273570
www.levescovane.com

Corte Verze
Via Cambran 5
Cazzabo di Tramigna, Verona
37030
368243877
www.corteverze.it

EMILIA-ROMAGNA
Le Occare
Via Quartiere 156
Runco (FE) 44010
0532329100
www.leoccare.com

Cavazzone
Via Cavazzone 4
Viamo (RE) 42030
0522858100
www.cavazzone.it

Fattoria Paradiso
Via Palmeggiana 285
Bertinoro (FC) 47032
0543445044
www.fattoriaparadiso.it

Ca' d'Alfieri
Loc. Predario, 29
Bardi (PR)
3478927775
www.cadalfieri.it

Metric Conversion Tables

Approximate U.S. Metric Equivalents

LIQUID INGREDIENTS

U.S. MEASURES	METRIC	U.S. MEASURES	METRIC
¼ TSP.	1.23 ML	2 TBSP.	29.57 ML
½ TSP.	2.36 ML	3 TBSP.	44.36 ML
¾ TSP.	3.70 ML	¼ CUP	59.15 ML
1 TSP.	4.93 ML	½ CUP	118.30 ML
1¼ TSP.	6.16 ML	1 CUP	236.59 ML
1½ TSP.	7.39 ML	2 CUPS OR 1 PT.	473.18 ML
1¾ TSP.	8.63 ML	3 CUPS	709.77 ML
2 TSP.	9.86 ML	4 CUPS OR 1 QT.	946.36 ML
1 TBSP.	14.79 ML	4 QTS. OR 1 GAL.	3.79 L

DRY INGREDIENTS

U.S. MEASURES		METRIC	U.S. MEASURES	METRIC
17⅗ OZ.	1 LIVRE	500 G	2 OZ.	60 (56.6) G
16 OZ.	1 LB.	454 G	1¾ OZ.	50 G
8⅞ OZ.		250 G	1 OZ.	30 (28.3) G
5¼ OZ.		150 G	⅞ OZ.	25 G
4½ OZ.		125 G	¾ OZ.	21 (21.3) G
4 OZ.		115 (113.2) G	½ OZ.	15 (14.2) G
3½ OZ.		100 G	¼ OZ.	7 (7.1) G
3 OZ.		85 (84.9) G	⅛ OZ.	3½ (3.5) G
2⅘ OZ.		80 G	1/16 OZ.	2 (1.8) G

INDEX

About the Authors

Matthew Scialabba and Melissa Pellegrino, a husband-and-wife cooking and writing team, met while both living in Italy. Their shared passion for Italian food and culture led them to embark on many culinary journeys throughout the country. These experiences include apprenticing at a Roman bakery, studying winemaking at a Ligurian vineyard, graduating from a professional culinary school in Florence, and working and cooking together at several Italian agriturismi. For more information about the authors and this project, please visit their Web site: www.theitalianfarmerstable.com. They live in Guilford, Connecticut.